The Quotable
ROBERT E. LEE

BOOKS BY LOCHLAINN SEABROOK

Everything You Were Taught About the Civil War is Wrong, Ask a Southerner! - Correcting the Errors of Yankee "History"
A Rebel Born: A Defense of Nathan Bedford Forrest - Confederate General, American Legend (winner of the 2011 Jefferson Davis Historical Gold Medal)
Nathan Bedford Forrest: Southern Hero, American Patriot - Honoring a Confederate Icon and the Old South
The Quotable Nathan Bedford Forrest: Selections From the Writings and Speeches of the Confederacy's Most Brilliant Cavalryman
Give 'Em Hell Boys! The Complete Military Correspondence of Nathan Bedford Forrest
The Quotable Jefferson Davis: Selections From the Writings and Speeches of the Confederacy's First President
The Quotable Robert E. Lee: Selections From the Writings and Speeches of the South's Most Beloved Civil War General
The Old Rebel: Robert E. Lee As He Was Seen By His Contemporaries
Abraham Lincoln: The Southern View - Demythologizing America's Sixteenth President
Lincolnology: The Real Abraham Lincoln Revealed in His Own Words - A Study of Lincoln's Suppressed, Misinterpreted, and Forgotten Speeches and Writings
The Unquotable Abraham Lincoln: The President's Quotes They Don't Want You To Know!
Encyclopedia of the Battle of Franklin - A Comprehensive Guide to the Conflict that Changed the Civil War
Carnton Plantation Ghost Stories: True Tales of the Unexplained from Tennessee's Most Haunted Civil War House!
The McGavocks of Carnton Plantation: A Southern History - Celebrating One of Dixie's Most Noble Confederate Families and Their Tennessee Home
The Caudills: An Etymological, Ethnological, and Genealogical Study - Exploring the Name and National Origins of a European-American Family
The Blakeneys: An Etymological, Ethnological, and Genealogical Study - Uncovering the Mysterious Origins of the Blakeney Family and Name
Britannia Rules: Goddess-Worship in Ancient Anglo-Celtic Society - An Academic Look at the United Kingdom's Matricentric Spiritual Past
UFOs and Aliens: The Complete Guidebook
Christmas Before Christianity: How the Birthday of the "Sun" Became the Birthday of the "Son"
The Book of Kelle: An Introduction to Goddess-Worship and the Great Celtic Mother-Goddess Kelle, Original Blessed Lady of Ireland
The Goddess Dictionary of Words and Phrases: Introducing a New Core Vocabulary for the Women's Spirituality Movement
Aphrodite's Trade: The Hidden History of Prostitution Unveiled

Thought Provoking Books For Smart People
www.SeaRavenPress.com

The Quotable
ROBERT E. LEE

*Selections From the Writings & Speeches
of the South's Most Beloved Civil War General*

Collected and Edited, with an Introduction and Notes, by

LOCHLAINN SEABROOK

WINNER OF THE JEFFERSON DAVIS HISTORICAL GOLD MEDAL

SEA RAVEN PRESS, FRANKLIN, TENNESSEE

THE QUOTABLE ROBERT E. LEE

Published by
Sea Raven Press, P.O. Box 1054, Franklin, Tennessee 37065-1054 USA
www.searavenpress.com • searavenpress@nii.net

Copyright © 2011 Lochlainn Seabrook
in accordance with U.S. and international copyright laws and regulations, as stated and protected under the Berne Union for the Protection of Literary and Artistic Property (Berne Convention), and the Universal Copyright Convention (the UCC). All rights reserved under the Pan-American and International Copyright Conventions.

First Sea Raven Press edition: November 2011
ISBN: 978-0-9838185-3-3
Library of Congress Catalog Number: 2011939780

This work is the copyrighted intellectual property of Lochlainn Seabrook and has been registered with the Copyright Office at the Library of Congress in Washington, D.C., USA. No part of this work (including text, covers, drawings, photos, illustrations, maps, images, diagrams, etc.), in whole or in part, may be used, reproduced, stored in a retrieval system, or transmitted, in any form or by any means now known or hereafter invented, without written permission from the publisher. The sale, duplication, hire, lending, copying, digitalization, or reproduction of this material, in any manner or form whatsoever, is also prohibited, and is a violation of federal, civil, and digital copyright law, which provides severe civil and criminal penalties for any violations.

The Quotable Robert E. Lee: Selections From the Writings & Speeches of the South's Most Beloved Civil War General / collected and edited, with an introduction and notes, by Lochlainn Seabrook. Includes bibliographical references.

Front and back cover design, book design and layout, by Lochlainn Seabrook
Typography: Sea Raven Press Book Design
Front cover sketch of Robert E. Lee © Chris Rommel
Sketch of the author on "Meet the Author" page © Tracy Latham
All images are from 19th-Century public domain sources, unless otherwise indicated

The views on the American "Civil War" documented in this book *are* those of the publisher.

The paper used in this book is acid-free and lignin-free. It has been certified by the Sustainable Forestry Initiative and the Forest Stewardship Council and meets all ANSI standards for archival quality paper.

PRINTED & MANUFACTURED IN OCCUPIED TENNESSEE, FORMER CONFEDERATE STATES OF AMERICA

DEDICATION

To the Lee family, to whom I am related.

EPIGRAPH

"A Union that can only be maintained by swords and bayonets, and in which strife and civil war are to take the place of brotherly love and kindness, has no charm for me."

CONTENTS

Notes to the Reader - 8
Introduction, by Lochlainn Seabrook - 9
Historical Time Line - 11

1 CHARACTER - 17
2 PERSONAL LETTERS - 31
3 NATURE - 81
4 RELIGION - 83
5 THE UNION & SECESSION - 95
6 THE CAUSE & PURPOSE OF THE WAR - 101
7 SLAVERY - 105
8 ABOLITION - 109
9 CONFEDERATE OFFICERSHIP - 115
10 THE SOUTHERN PEOPLE - 133
11 THE NORTHERN PEOPLE - 135
12 LINCOLN'S WAR ON THE SOUTH - 137
13 UNION WAR CRIMES - 177
14 LINCOLN'S WAR ON THE NORTH - 185
15 POSTBELLUM - 189
16 IN DEFENSE OF THE SOUTH - 215

Appendix A - Lee's Plan to Emancipate & Enlist Southern Slaves - 225
Appendix B - Robert E. Lee's Descendants - 227
Appendix C - Interesting & Unusual Facts About the Lee Family - 230
Notes - 233
Bibliography - 243
Meet the Author - 247
Meet the Cover Artist - 249

NOTES TO THE READER

🖐 In an effort to retain the true character and meaning of Robert E. Lee's words, they have been printed here exactly as they appear in the original manuscripts, including typographical and grammatical peculiarities inherent to 19th-Century Southern writing and speaking. Lee's quotes are marked with a traditional Victorian "hand" pointer. My chapter introductions are in normal font, my explanatory comments appear in italics above Lee's quotes, and my clarifications are in brackets within his quotes.

🖐 In any study of the "Civil War" it is vitally important to keep in mind that the two major political parties were then the opposite of what they are today. The Democrats of the 19th Century were conservatives, akin to the Republican Party of today, while the Republicans of the 19th Century were liberals, akin to the Democratic Party of today. Thus the Confederacy's Democratic president, Jefferson Davis, was a conservative (with libertarian leanings); the Union's Republican president, Abraham Lincoln, was a liberal (with socialistic leanings).

🖐 I have included a Lee family tree and a "historical time line" of Lee's life (a biographical encapsulation), both which will provide context to Lee's quotes, as well as proving helpful to readers in making sense of the many and varied members, occupations, movements, and homes of the Lee family throughout the 1800s as described in this book.

🖐 For those interested in the truth about the War for Southern Independence, see my books:

Everything You Were Taught About the Civil War is Wrong, Ask a Southerner! - Correcting the Errors of Yankee "History"
The Old Rebel: Robert E. Lee As He Was Seen By His Contemporaries
A Rebel Born: A Defense of Nathan Bedford Forrest - Confederate General, American Legend
Abraham Lincoln: The Southern View - Demythologizing America's Sixteenth President
Lincolnology: The Real Abraham Lincoln Revealed in His Own Words - A Study of Lincoln's Suppressed, Misinterpreted, & Forgotten Speeches & Writings
The Quotable Jefferson Davis: Selections From the Writings & Speeches of the Confederacy's First President
The Unquotable Abraham Lincoln: The President's Quotes They Don't Want You to Know!
Nathan Bedford Forrest: Southern Hero, American Patriot - Honoring a Confederate Icon & the Old South
The McGavocks of Carnton Plantation: A Southern History - Celebrating One of Dixie's Most Noble Confederate Families & Their Tennessee Home
Carnton Plantation Ghost Stories: True Tales of the Unexplained from Tennessee's Most Haunted Civil War House!

INTRODUCTION

Who is your favorite Civil War general? If you love Lincoln or are from the North, the odds are that you will pick Ulysses S. Grant, the well-known Yankee military hero.

Here in the South, however, we have never understood his appeal. While it is true that he behaved nobly at Appomattox during Lee's so-called "surrender," this seems to have been an exception to his normal behavior.

For example, the cigar-chomping, hard drinking Grant is known to have kept his family's slaves until he was forced to free them under the ratification of the Thirteenth Amendment (in December 1865), eight months *after* Lincoln's death

Southern hero Confederate General Robert E. Lee.

and almost three years *after* the president issued his illegal and fraudulent Final Emancipation Proclamation.[1] The Yankee general—still widely known across the South as "the Butcher"—was also directly responsible for the destruction of millions of dollars of Southern property as well as the deaths of tens of thousands of Southern men, women, and children (many of them, of course, non-combatants); he committed countless war crimes by repeatedly violating both the U.S. Constitution and the Geneva Conventions;[2] and, after the War—as president of the U.S.—he led the country through two of the most lawless, un-Christian, and corrupt administrations on record.[3]

This may be the kind of man the North enjoys apotheosizing and whose image they like to see engraved on their money, but we in the South find very little, if anything, about Grant the military man that is attractive or deserving of praise.

For us as Southerners there can only be one "greatest" Civil War hero, and that individual is the non-smoking, non-drinking paragon of Christian virtue, Robert E. Lee—the reasons for which are clearly laid out in his own words in this very book.

If one were to ask a Southerner how Grant stacks up in comparison to Lee, the Southern answer would be, not very well!

Northern hero Union General Ulysses S. Grant.

Lee and his family were discussing abolition decades before the "Civil War," and he emancipated his wife's family's slaves four months *before* Lincoln issued the Emancipation Proclamation. While Lee did indeed destroy millions of dollars of U.S. property, unlike Grant this was done in *defense* of his country (the Confederate States of America), and non-combatants and civilian property were strictly off limits. Lee committed no war crimes, respected the rights of the Northern people and their soldiers, complied with the Geneva Conventions, and obeyed the Confederate Constitution.

General Lee at Appomattox

And finally, quite unlike Grant, after the War, when the ever modest Lee was pushed to run for both governor of Virginia and later president of the United States, he unhesitatingly turned down both jobs, preferring to earn an honest living and be at home with his family. Needless to say, he would have never wanted his picture on the fifty-dollar bill or any other currency, Union or Confederate. It is for such reasons that Southern journalist Edward A. Pollard said in 1867 that one day Lee "will be declared to have been much greater in defeat than Grant . . . in victory."[4]

After reading through these pages, and after objectively comparing Grant's life with Lee's, I am in no doubt that many former skeptics will come to agree with Pollard. For in Dixie's opinion, in his gentle, dignified, empathetic, generous, loyal, courageous, simple, uncontrived, respectful, and self-sacrificing ways, no Civil War officer ever came closer to embodying the true American—or the Christian ideal—than the incomparable Southern gentleman and beloved Confederate General, Robert Edward Lee. This book is my memorial to him.

God bless the "Great Virginian," and God bless the South.

Lochlainn Seabrook
Franklin, Williamson County, Tennessee, USA
November 2011

HISTORICAL TIME LINE

- From Birth to Death -

1807 - Robert Edward Lee, the author's cousin, is born on January 19, at the family's manor house, Stratford Hall, in Stratford, Westmoreland County, Virginia. (Lee shares his January 19th birthday with two other Southerners of note, Dolly Parton and Paula Deen.)

1811 - Lee's father, General Henry "Light Horse Harry" Lee, moves his family to Alexandria, Virginia.

1818 - On March 25 Lee's father dies. Lee is eleven years old.

1825 - At age eighteen Lee enters West Point Military Academy as a cadet, where he trains as a military engineer, specializing in engineering science.

1829 - On July 4 Lee graduates from West Point, second in his class.

1829 - On July 26 Lee's mother dies.

1829 - Lee is appointed second lieutenant of Topographical Engineers in the U.S. army.

1831 - On June 30, at Arlington, Virginia, Lee marries his cousin (and the author's cousin), Mary Ann Randolph Custis, the great-granddaughter of Martha (Dandridge) Washington, the wife of U.S. President George Washington. (Robert and Mary bear seven children between 1832 and 1846.)

1832 - On September 16 Lee's first son is born: George Washington Custis Lee (known by his middle name, "Custis").

1834-1837 - Lee works as assistant to the chief engineer of the U.S. army.

1835 - On July 12 Lee's first daughter is born: Mary Custis Lee (nicknamed "Life").

1835 - Lee is appointed assistant astronomer "on the commission for marking out the boundary line between Ohio and Michigan."

1836 - On September 21 Lee is promoted to the rank of first lieutenant in the U.S. army.

1837 - On May 31 Lee's second son is born: William Henry Fitzhugh Lee (nicknamed "Rooney," but called "Fitzhugh" by his family).

1837 - In June Lee is placed in charge of "improving" the Mississippi River at St. Louis, Missouri.

1838 - In July Lee is promoted to captain of the engineer corps.

1839 - On June 18 Lee's second daughter is born: Anne Carter Lee (nicknamed "Annie").

1841 - This year Lee's third daughter is born: Eleanor Agnes Lee (nicknamed "Wigs," but usually called by her middle name "Agnes").

1842 - Lee is stationed at Fort Hamilton in New York Harbor, in charge of defenses.

1843 - On October 27 Lee's third son is born: Robert Edward Lee, Jr., nicknamed "Rob."

1844 - Lee is appointed a member of the board of visitors at West Point.

1845 - Lee becomes a member of the U.S. Board of Engineers.

1846 - Lee's fourth daughter, and last child, is born: Mildred Childe Lee (nicknamed "Precious Life").

1846-1848 - Lee fights with distinction in the Mexican-American War and is brevetted major for gallantry at the Battle of Cerro Gordo, April 18, 1847; he is wounded at the assault on Chapultepec, September 13, 1847, and receives the brevet promotion of lieutenant-colonel.

1849-1852 - Lee constructs fortifications at Baltimore, Maryland.

1852-1855 - September 1, 1852, Lee begins serving as superintendent of West Point.

1855 - Lee is appointed lieutenant colonel of the Second Cavalry, and his family moves to Arlington, Virginia.

1856 - Lee is sent to Jefferson Barracks, Missouri, then on to western Texas to reduce Indian attacks and protect the U.S. border from Mexican bandits.

1857 - Lee is stationed with the Second Cavalry at San Antonio, Texas. Among those serving in this regiment are numerous future Civil War officers of note, including John Bell Hood, Albert S. Johnston, Fitzhugh Lee, Earl Van Dorn, George H. Thomas, William J. Hardee, Innis N. Palmer, George Stoneman, and Edmund Kirby Smith.

1857 - In Autumn Lee returns home to Arlington House for a year.

1859 - On October 17 Lee is selected by the U.S. secretary of war to suppress the infamous "John Brown Raid" at Harper's Ferry. Lee adroitly commands a battalion of marines, successfully capturing the psychopathic Yankee and releasing his hostages unharmed.

1859 - In late Fall, after the Harper's Ferry incident, Lee again returns home to Arlington House.

1860 - Lee is assigned to the command of the department of Texas.

1861 - March 1 Lee returns to his family at Arlington House.

1861 - On March 16 Lee receives his last promotion in the U.S. army: Colonel in the First Cavalry (he held this position for only a few weeks).

1861 - On April 17, just a week after Lincoln made his intentions clear (to subjugate the South) at the Battle of Fort Sumter, Lee, a political conservative, sides with Virginia at her secession from the Union—this after being offered the position of general-in-chief of U.S. armies by Lincoln himself.

THE QUOTABLE ROBERT E. LEE 13

1861 - On April 20 Lee officially resigns from the U.S. army.
1861 - On April 23 Lee is promoted to major general and appointed commander-in-chief of Virginia's military and naval forces by Governor John Letcher.
1861 - On May 7 Lee is made commander of all forces from other States tendering their services to Virginia.
1861 - On May 10 Lee is made commander of Confederate States forces.
1861 - On May 14 Lee is appointed brigadier general.
1861 - On May 24 Lee's beloved Arlington House is occupied by Yankee troops and turned into Union headquarters. His wife and children are driven from the home and it is then pillaged of its contents, including rare family heirlooms belonging to George Washington.
1861 - By June 14 Lee is general of the Confederate States army.
1861 - By August 3 Lee is commanding forces in the Army of the North-west.
1861 - On November 5 Lee is assigned to the command of the department of Florida, South Carolina, and Georgia.
1862 - On March 13 Lee begins his new position as "military advisor" to President Jefferson Davis at Richmond, Virginia. As part of his new position he is charged with conducting the military operations of all the armies of the Confederacy.
1862 - On June 1 Lee assumes command of the Army and Department of Northern Virginia, a position he retains until the close of the war.
1863 - Lee contracts a "severe sore throat" during the many difficult operations this year, producing complications, such as rheumatism and a heart condition, that help lead to his premature death seven years later.
1863 - On January 11 Lincoln "purchases" Lee's stolen home, Arlington House, for two-thirds its original value and gives it to the U.S. War Department. The transaction is made permanent when Lee's former front yard is turned into a Union burial ground. This became the site for the later development of Arlington National Cemetery.
1863 - Now virtually homeless, during the Fall Lee's wife Mary rents a small house for their family on Clay Street in Richmond, Virginia.
1865 - On January 31 Lee is made general-in-chief of the Confederate States armies.
1865 - On February 6 Lee is made commander-in-chief of all Confederate States armies (sadly, too late to change the outcome of the War).
1865 - On April 9 Lee meets with Yank General Ulysses S. Grant at Appomattox to negotiate the terms of the Confederacy's "surrender." Lincoln's War ends and Lee returns home a hero.
1865 - In the Spring of this year Lee is denied amnesty and instead is indicted for the crime of "treason" against the U.S. government. (Grant intervenes

and Lee is spared going to trial—though he remains a U.S. "prisoner on parole" for the remainder of his life.)

1865 - Lee returns "home" after the War only to find that his family estate, Arlington House, is still occupied by the Yanks, and their second family estate, the beautiful White House (on the Pamunkey River), has been burned to the ground by vengeful Union troops.

1865 - In June Lee rents a "quiet country home" in Powhatan County, Virginia, on the James River.

1865 - June 13 Lee applies for a "pardon" from the U.S. government. It is rejected.

1865 - On August 4, against his own wishes, Lee is elected president of Washington College (now Washington and Lee University), at Lexington, Virginia, and moves his family there.

1865 - Sometime during the latter half of the year, Lee becomes a member of the vestry of Grace Episcopal Church in Lexington, Virginia.

1866 - In February "criminal" Lee is called to Washington, D.C. to sit before the Reconstruction Committee of Congress, a hostile board of Yankees that tries to catch him in a lie or espousing anti-North views. He detests the entire charade, but speaks diplomatically, and evasively, to the Northern congressmen and is "allowed" to return home.

1867 - On February 4 Lee declines an invitation to become a candidate for governor of Virginia.

1868 - Sometime this year or perhaps in 1869, Lee is made president of the Valley Railroad Company.

1868 - Sometime this year Lee attends the Episcopal Council at Lynchburg, Virginia, as a delegate of the Grace Episcopal Church.

1869 - Lee is once again elected church delegate, and in June goes to the Episcopal Council at Fredericksburg, Virginia, to represent his church.

1869 - In October Lee is diagnosed with "inflammation of the heart."

1870 - In early Spring, at the suggestion of friends, Lee spends six restful weeks in Georgia and Florida. During the Summer he travels to the Virginia Hot Springs for more recuperation.

1870 - On October 12, at 9:00 AM, at age sixty-three, Lee casts off his physical body and passes into the Next Life. Modern doctors and historians say he died from "heart disease," but we in the South know better. Lee's death was brought on by a combination of chill damp weather, exhaustion and general weakness resulting from Lincoln's War, and, most importantly, a broken heart over the Confederacy's loss.

The Quotable
ROBERT E. LEE

1

CHARACTER

While many authors understandably focus on his astounding military career, I believe that understanding the character of Lee the man, the everyday civilian, is just as important, if not more so. In this chapter, in an attempt to get closer to the real Robert E. Lee, we will examine—using his own words—the traits that made him who he was on and off the battlefield.

General Lee at the Battle of Fredericksburg. The author descends from Lee's fourth great-grandparents, Richard Eltonhead and Ann Sutton of Lancashire, England.

☞ "Honesty in its widest sense is always admirable. The trite saying that 'Honesty is the best policy' has met with the just criticism that honesty is not policy. This seems to be true. The real honest man is honest from conviction of what is right, not from policy."[5]

☞ "Those who oppose our purposes are not always to be regarded as our enemies. We usually think and act from our immediate surroundings."[6]

☞ "The better rule is to judge our adversaries from their standpoint, not from ours."[7]

☞ "Obedience to lawful authority is the foundation of manly character."[8]

☞ "If you want to be missed by your friends—be useful."[9]

☞ "God disposes. This ought to satisfy us."[10]

☞ "Drive all your work with judgment and energy . . ."[11]

☞ "My experience through life has convinced me that, while moderation and temperance in all things are commendable and beneficial, abstinence from spirituous liquor is the best safeguard of morals and health."[12]

☞ "I feel very sensibly, in my old age, the absence of my children, though I recognise the necessity of every one's attending to his business, and admire him the more for so doing."[13]

☞ "Human virtues ought, in case of need, equal human calamities."[14]

☞ "I should prefer more quiet."[15]

☞ "Fame which does not result from good actions and achievements for the good of the whole people is not to be desired. Nero had fame (or rather notoriety). Who envies him?"[16]

☞ "No man can be so important in the world that he needs not the good-will and approval of others."[17]

☞ "I think it is better to do right, even if we suffer in so doing, than to incur the reproach of our consciences and posterity."[18]

☞ "'Charity should begin at home.' So says. No, charity should have no beginning or ending."[19]

☞ "I owe everything to my mother."[20]

☞ ". . . hope for the best, speak as little and act as discreetly as possible."[21]

☞ "What you do cultivate, do well."[22]

☞ "A farmer's motto should be *toil and trust*."[23]

☞ "You will have to get married if you wish to prosper. . ."[24]

To his daughter-in-law (wife of his son Fitzhugh), Mary Tabb (Bolling) Lee:
☞ "I hope . . . that you are becoming more and more interested in making those around you happy. That is the true way to secure your own happiness . . ."[25]

To his wife Mary regarding their daughter Agnes:
☞ "You know she is like her papa—always wanting something."[26]

To his daughter Mildred:
☞ "Experience will teach you that, notwithstanding all appearances to the contrary, you will never receive such a love as is felt for you by your father and mother."[27]

Though a devout Christian, General Lee had nothing but complete tolerance for other religions. Once, when a Jewish soldier sought permission from his captain to attend synagogue at Richmond, his superior responded with: "Disapproved: if such applications were granted the whole army would turn Jews or Shaking Quakers." The request eventually reached Lee's desk, who immediately rescinded the denial, writing:
☞ "Approved, and respectfully returned to Captain, with the advice that he should always respect the religious views and feelings of others."[28]

General Lee was a teetotaler who refused to promote officers who abused alcohol. More than one military man was denied advancement with Lee's stern admonition:

Robert E. Lee's wife, Mary Anne Randolph Custis. The author descends from Mary's second great-grandparents, Robert Bolling and Anne Mary Cocke of Prince George County, Virginia.

☞ "I will not put in control of others a man who cannot control himself."[29]

Whenever Lee's soldiers would denigrate their Yankee foes, he would say:
☞ "You forget that we are all Americans."[30]

An example of General Lee's gentle sense of humor occurred during the "Civil War," when one of his soldiers complained that it would take some time for his regiment to change from the old Revolutionary War flintlocks to the more modern percussion cap guns. With a wry smile the General made the following suggestion:
☞ "Telegraph to Mr. Lincoln to have the war put off for three weeks."[31]

To a student at Washington College who he found wantonly wasting his savings:
☞ "The money that you are squandering represents the sweat of your father's brow."[32]

Lee, who was always ready to set a good example for others, was a superb parent to his seven children—as can be seen from the following quote. One Winter's day the General was walking with his "very little" son Custis in the snow, when he noticed that the boy had fallen behind. Looking over his shoulder he saw him laboriously imitating every detail of his father's movements, holding his head high while carefully stepping in each of his footprints. Lee later commented:
☞ "When I saw this, I said to myself, 'It behooves me to walk very straight, when this fellow is already following in my tracks.'"[33]

Lee hated war, particularly Lincoln's unjust, illegal, and unnecessary war on the South, as he noted in this Christmas Day (1862) letter to his wife:
☞ ". . . But what a cruel thing is war; to separate and destroy families and friends, and mar the purest joys and happiness God has granted us in this world; to fill our hearts with hatred instead of love for our neighbours, and to devastate the fair face of this beautiful world! I pray that, on this day when only peace and good-will are preached to mankind, better thoughts may fill the hearts of our enemies and turn them to peace."[34]

In a June 8, 1863, letter from near Brandy Station, Virginia, Lee said something similar to his wife:

☞ "The country here looks very green and pretty, notwithstanding the ravages of war. What a beautiful world God, in His loving kindness to His creatures, has given us! What a shame that men endowed with reason and knowledge of right should mar His gifts. . . ."[35]

The General was widely known for his ever present positive attitude. One morning at camp breakfast he overheard one of his soldiers complaining about the hardness of the biscuits, to which Lee remarked:
☞ "You ought not to mind that; they will stick by you the longer!"[36]

Captain Robert E. Lee, in 1852, beginning his position as superintendent of West Point Military Academy.

Lee authored the following short but little known essay called, "The Test of a True Gentleman," illustrating his innate Christianity:
☞ "The forbearing use of power does not only form a touchstone, but the manner in which an individual enjoys certain advantages over others is the test of a true gentleman.

"The power which the strong have over the weak, the magistrate over the citizen, the employer over the employed, the educated over the unlettered, the experienced over the confiding, even the clever over the silly—the forbearing or inoffensive use of all this power or authority, or a total absence from it when the case admits it, will show the gentleman in plain light. The gentleman does not needlessly or unnecessarily remind an offender of a wrong he may have committed against him. He can not only forgive, he can forget; and he strives for that nobleness of self and mildness of character which impart sufficient strength to let the past be the past.

"A true gentleman of honor feels humbled himself when he cannot help humbling others."[37]

In early April 1865, as the War's end was drawing near and Lee was trying to decide whether to continue fighting or capitulate, he was asked by a fellow officer how history would record "the surrender of an army in the field." Lee replied:

☞ "Yes, I know they will say hard things of us; they will not understand that we were overwhelmed by numbers; but that is not the question, colonel. The question is, is it right to surrender this army? If it is right, then I will take all of the responsibility."[38]

Advice to his son Robert, Jr., from an August 5, 1867, letter:

☞ "Be prudent. I am very sorry that your harvest promises a poor yield. It will be better next year, but you must continue systematically the improvement of the land. I know of no better method than by liming, and if you wish to prosecute it, and are in need of help, I will aid you to the extent of last year or more. So make your arrangements, and let me know your wishes. A farmer's life is one of labour, but it is also one of pleasure, and the consciousness of steady improvement, though it may be slow, is very encouraging.

"I think you had better also begin to make arrangements to build yourself a house. If you can do nothing more than prepare a site, lay out a garden, orchard, etc., and get a small house partly finished, so as to inhabit it, it will add to your comfort and health. I can help you in that too. Think about it. Then, too, you must get a nice wife. I do not like you being so lonely. I fear you will fall in love with celibacy."[39]

Like the "true gentleman" he was, General Lee was very much in control of his emotions. He was particularly against any display of anger, and was quick to reprimand any soldier who violated this rule. On one occasion during the War, a subordinate brought some documents to him to look over and sign, a task he was well-known for greatly disliking. Seeing his temper beginning to rise, in sympathy the soldier imitated Lee, showing obvious disdain for the paperwork ahead. Looking up at his subordinate from his desk, the General said in a tranquil and steady voice:

☞ "Colonel, when I lose my temper, don't you let it make you angry."[40]

Once, when a faculty member at Washington College spoke disparagingly about Yankee General Ulysses S. Grant, Lee said calmly but firmly:

☞ "Sir, if you ever presume again to speak disrespectfully of General Grant in my presence, either you or I will sever his connection with this university."⁴¹

During the Sewell Mountain campaign, Lee had refused to send his troops against Union General William S. Rosecrans, which for a time tarnished Lee's sterling reputation as a courageous and brilliant leader. Denounced by the newspapers for backing away from a much needed Confederate victory, Lee was asked for the reasoning behind his decision, to which he replied:
☞ "I could not afford to sacrifice the lives of five or six hundred of my people to silence public clamor."⁴²

Shortly after the War, in 1866, a company in Baltimore, Maryland, offered to give General Lee a new hat. Here is his reply:
☞ "I am much obliged to you for your kind offer to send me a hat, and I appreciate most highly the motives which prompted it. When so many are destitute, I dislike to have more than I actually require, and yet am unwilling to appear insensible to your sentiments of friendship and sympathy. I have a very good hat, which will answer my purpose the whole year, and I would, therefore, prefer that you would give to others what I really do not require."⁴³

Robert E. Lee shortly after Lincoln's War.

Though one of the humblest of men, Lee once took time to brag about his new beard in a November 15, 1861, letter to his daughter Mildred:
☞ "I have a beautiful white beard. It is much admired. At least, much remarked on."⁴⁴

As he was at all times during his life, during Lincoln's War Lee was the

embodiment of humility, and early on accepted positions, without complaint, that many other officers would have scoffed at. When asked what his "guiding sentiment" was in this regard, he said:

☞ "I will accept every position to which the country appoints me, and will do my best in it."⁴⁵

After the War for Southern Independence, General Lee read few if any newspapers and was known to have rigorously avoided all study of military matters.⁴⁶ He wanted, in short, to re-immerse himself in everyday civilian life—which is not surprising after having lived through the horrors of Lincoln's War for four years. Later, this feeling inspired the following statement:

☞ "For my own part, I much enjoy the charms of civil life, and find too late that I have wasted the best years of my existence."⁴⁷

In this same letter the General gives some age-old fatherly advice to his sixteen year old daughter Mildred, then away at school in Winchester, Virginia:

☞ "You know I have told you not to believe what the young men tell you."⁴⁸

When he was asked to write a book about his war experiences, Lee replied with his usual modesty:

☞ "I shall write this history, not to vindicate myself, or to promote my own reputation. I want that the world shall know what my poor boys, with their small numbers and scant resources, succeeded in accomplishing."⁴⁹

On education:

☞ "In its broad and comprehensive sense, education embraces the physical, moral and intellectual instruction of a child from infancy to manhood."⁵⁰

☞ "[The best educational system] abases the coarse animal emotions of human nature and exalts the higher faculties and feelings."⁵¹

☞ "[Good school teachers] embrace morals and religion as well as the intellect. The teacher should be the example to the pupil. He should

Stratford Hall, Stratford, Virginia, Robert E. Lee's birthplace, built between 1730 and 1738 by Robert's great-granduncle, Thomas Lee. Two signers of the Declaration of Independence were also born here: Francis Lightfoot Lee and Richard Henry Lee, General Lee's first cousins.

aim at the highest attainable proficiency, and not at a pleasing mediocrity."[52]

From a May 30, 1858, to his son concerning alcoholic drink:
☞ "I think it better to avoid it altogether, as its temperate use is so difficult."[53]

When, after the War, Washington College tried to increase Lee's salary as president, he refused, saying:
☞ "I already receive a larger amount from the college than my services are worth."[54]

On hearing the news that the author's cousin, the esteemed Confederate General Jeb Stuart, had been killed during the raid at Yellow Tavern in May 1864, Lee exclaimed:
☞ "I can scarcely think of him without weeping."[55]

Once, during Lincoln's War, when a "saddle of mutton" had been given to the General as a present from a local citizen, he wrote to his wife:

☞ "If the soldiers get it, I shall be content. I can do very well without it. In fact, I should rather they should have it than I."⁵⁶

Lee felt true compassion for his sick soldiers, but sometimes little patience, as can be seen in this September 17, 1861, letter to his wife from the Virginia battlefield:
☞ "Our poor sick, I know, suffer much. They bring it on themselves by not doing what they are told [that is, bundle up]. They are worse than children, for the latter can be forced."⁵⁷

When it was suggested that the remains of the Confederate dead at Gettysburg, Pennsylvania, be removed and brought South, Lee disagreed, saying:
☞ "I know of no fitter resting-place for a soldier than the field on which he has nobly laid down his life."⁵⁸

When the Confederate capital was moved from Montgomery, Alabama, to Richmond, Virginia, in early 1861, the Virginia forces, of which Lee was then commander-in-chief, were merged with the Confederate army. As a result, Lee lost his independent command and his rank was lowered. Not one to be concerned with such matters, when Confederate Vice President Alexander H. Stephens asked him how he felt about it, Lee replied:
☞ "Mr. Stephens, I am willing to serve anywhere where I can be useful."⁵⁹

Lee loved to tease his four daughters with this expression:
☞ "You are all very helpless; I don't know what you will do when I am gone."⁶⁰

In November 1863 the City Council of Richmond, Virginia, offered to purchase an "elegant mansion" for Lee, a replacement for the two family estates he lost to the Yankees: Arlington House *(located on the Virginia Heights, it was thoroughly gutted then pilfered by Union soldiers of its furniture and invaluable family heirlooms, then later made part of Arlington National Cemetery) and the* White House *(located on the Pamunkey River, and the site of Lee's wife's great-grandmother's marriage to President George Washington, while under Union control it had been "burned to the ground"). Lee's reply to the Council's president reveals yet another aspect of the General's character:*

☞ "I assure you, sir, that no want of appreciation of the honor conferred upon me by this resolution, or insensibility to the kind feelings which prompted it, induces me to ask, as I most respectfully do, that no further proceedings be taken with reference to the subject. The house is not necessary for the use of my family, and my own duties will prevent my residence in Richmond. I should therefore be compelled to decline the generous offer, and I trust that whatever means the City Councils may have to spare for this purpose may be devoted to the relief of the families of our soldiers in the field, who are more in want of assistance, and more deserving of it, than myself."[61]

After the War, an English nobleman kindly offered Lee a mansion and an estate where he could have easily lived out his life in magnificent ease and quiet repose. The General, however, would not desert his beloved state, the Old Dominion, particularly now as she lay prostrate from Lincoln's illegal and bloody four year assault. Lee's reply to the royal concerning leaving Virginia:

☞ "I must abide her fortune and share her fate."[62]

While he was president of Washington College, Lee was continually offered money, fame, honors, and gifts, all which he declined, saying:

☞ "I feel that I have no claim to such oblation, and have a general disinclination to be brought before the public without good and sufficient reason."[63]

General Lee must have liked this image of himself: he gave autographed copies of it to his close friends.

After Lincoln's War a woman asked Lee if she could write his biography. This is his reply:
☞ "I am sensible of the implied compliment in your proposal to write a history of my life. I should be happy to see you in Lexington, but not on the errand you propose, for I know of nothing good I could tell of myself, and I fear I should not like to say any evil. The few incidents of interest in which I have been engaged are as well known to others as to

myself, and I know of nothing I could say in addition. With great respect, your obedient servant, R. E. Lee."[64]

Lee's response to a Southern minister who, during a sermon, bitterly berated the North for her illicit war on the South:
☞ "Doctor, there is a good old book which I read and you preach from which says, 'Love your enemies, bless them that curse you, do good to them that hate you, and pray for them which despitefully use you.' Do you think your remarks this evening were quite in the spirit of that teaching? . . . I have fought against the people of the North because I believed they were seeking to wrest from the South her dearest rights, but I have never cherished toward them bitter or vindictive feelings, and have never seen the day when I did not pray for them."[65]

What follows is General Lee's standard reply to all who offered him food, money, clothing, housing, job positions, and presents:
☞ "Give to the Confederate soldiers; or, if you wish, to the college. As for myself, I have enough and am content."[66]

Unlike many officers, General Lee was against even a hint of military nepotism—despite the fact that he had three sons in the Confederate army. Once, in February 1864, when his wife Mary made the motherly suggestion that their youngest son Robert, Jr., serve with either his father or his cousin General Fitzhugh Lee, the General made this reply:
☞ "In reference to Rob, his company would be a great pleasure and comfort to me, and he would be extremely useful in various ways, but I am opposed to officers surrounding themselves with their sons and relatives. It is wrong in principle, and in that case selections would be made from private and social relations, rather than for the public good. There is the same objection to his going with Fitz Lee. I should prefer Rob's being in the line, in an independent position, where he could rise by his own merit and not through the recommendation of his relatives. I expect him soon, when I can better see what he himself thinks. The young men have no fondness for the society of the old general. He is too heavy and sombre for them."[67]

Although the General loved to laugh and was not above gently pranking others,

The formidable Fifteen-inch Gun was greatly feared on the Civil War battlefield.

when it came to Lincoln's War his mood was usually quite serious. Thus, when his son Robert, Jr., sent him an invitation to a ball in the winter of 1864, he replied with this sharp letter:
☞ "I inclose a letter for you, which has been sent to my care. I hope you are well and all around you are so. Tell [your cousin] Fitz I grieve over the hardships and sufferings of his men, in their late expedition. I should have preferred his waiting for more favourable weather. He accomplished much under the circumstances, but would have done more in better weather. I am afraid he was anxious to get back to the ball. This is a bad time for such things. We have too grave subjects on hand to engage in such trivial amusements.

"I would rather his officers should entertain themselves in fattening their horses, healing their men, and recruiting their regiments. There are too many Lees on the committee. I like all to be present at battles, but can excuse them at balls. But the saying is, 'Children will be children.' I think he had better move his camp farther from Charlottesville, and perhaps he will get more work and less play. He and I are too old for such assemblies. I want him to write me how his men are, his horses, and what I can do to fill up the ranks."[68]

One day "Custis Morgan," Lee's daughter Mildred's pet squirrel, escaped out of their home. Though he loved animals, the General did not really approve of this particular houseguest, as he intimated in a July 10, 1864, letter to Mildred:
☞ "I was pleased on the arrival of my little courier to learn that you were better, and that 'Custis Morgan' was still among the missing. I think the farther he gets from you the better you will be."[69]

While he was president of Washington College, Lee was offered "an immense sum of money" and a large house if he would head a business in New York. Characteristically the General declined, saying:
☞ "I am grateful, but I have a self-imposed task which I must accomplish. I have led the young men of the South in battle; I have seen many of them die on the field; I shall devote my remaining energies to training young men to do their duty in life."[70]

Robert E. Lee during Lincoln's War. While he was widely noted for his dashing appearance, the General himself thought little of his looks, once observing that he wore a hat to shield "my ugly face, which is masked by a white beard as stiff and wiry as the teeth of a [wool] card."

2

PERSONAL LETTERS

In chronological order

Nowhere do we learn more about Lee the soldier, the man, the husband, the father, the sibling, and the friend than we do through his personal letters. For it is only here, through his correspondences with family and friends, that he allowed his full true personality and character to shine through. As was typical with the General, it is said that "he always answered all letters addressed to him, from whatever source, if it was possible."[71]

This, the earliest known portrait of Robert E. Lee, shows him, at twenty-two, as second lieutenant of the U.S. army's Topographical Engineers in 1829.

An early letter from St. Louis, Missouri (where the General was then stationed with orders to "improve the Mississippi River"), to his wife Mary, dated October 16, 1837, concerns the problems of child-rearing and their five year old son George Washington Custis Lee, whom they called "Custis":

☞ "The improved condition of the children, which you mention, was a source of great comfort to me; and as I suppose, by this time, you have all returned to Arlington, you will be able to put them under a proper restraint, which you were probably obliged to relax while visiting among strangers, and which that indulgence will now render more essential. Our dear little boy seems to have among his friends the reputation of being hard to manage,—a distinction not at all desirable, as it indicates self-will and obstinacy.

"Perhaps these are qualities which he really possesses, and he may have a better right to them than I am willing to acknowledge; but it is our duty, if possible, to counteract them, and assist him to bring them under his control. I have endeavored, in my intercourse with him, to require nothing but what was in my opinion necessary or proper, and to explain to him temperately its propriety, at a time when he could listen to my arguments, and not at the moment of his being vexed, and his little faculties warped by passion. I have also tried to show him that I was firm in my demands and constant in their enforcement, and that he must comply with them; and I let him see that I looked to their execution in order to relieve him, as much as possible, from the temptation to break them.

"Since my efforts have been so unsuccessful, I fear I have altogether failed in accomplishing my purpose, but I hope to be able to profit by my experience. You must assist me in my attempts, and we must endeavor to combine the mildness and forbearance of the mother with the sternness and, perhaps, unreasonableness of the father. This is a subject on which I think much, though M_____ may blame me for not reading more. I am ready to acknowledge the good advice contained in the text-books, and believe that I see the merit of their reasoning generally; but what I want to learn is, to apply what I already know.

"I pray God to watch over, and direct our efforts in guarding our dear little son, that we may bring him up in the way he should go. . . . Oh what pleasure I lose in being separated from my children. Nothing can compensate me for that; still I must remain here, ready to perform what little service I can, and hope for the best."[72]

Lee's love of children, including those not his own, was legendary. And children were drawn to him as well, naturally viewing him as a friendly, fatherly, Santa Claus-like figure. Here is an excerpt from a letter to his wife from around 1838 or 1839, while the General was still stationed at St. Louis:

☞ ". . . I saw a number of little girls all dressed up in their white frocks and pantalets, their hair plaited and tied up with ribbons, running and chasing each other in all directions. I counted twenty-three nearly the same size. As I drew up my horse to admire the spectacle, a man appeared at the door with the twenty-fourth [child] in his arms.

"'My friend,' said I, 'are all these your children?'

"'Yes,' he said, 'and there are nine more in the house, and this is the youngest.'

"Upon further inquiry, however, I found that they were only temporarily his, and that they were invited to a party at his house. He said, however, he had been admiring them before I came up, and just wished that he had a million of dollars, and that they were all his in reality. I do not think the eldest exceeded seven or eight years old. It was the prettiest sight I have seen in the west, and, perhaps, in my life."[73]

In a letter to his wife, dated June 5, 1839, Lee again touches on the topic of child socialization:

☞ "You do not know how much I have missed you and the children, my dear Mary. To be alone in a crowd is very solitary. In the woods, I feel sympathy with the trees and birds, in whose company I take delight, but experience no pleasure in a strange crowd. I hope you are all well and will continue so, and, therefore, must again urge you to be very prudent and careful of those dear children. If I could only get a squeeze at that little fellow, turning up his sweet mouth to 'keeze baba!' You must not let him run wild in my absence, and will have to exercise firm authority over all of them. This will not require severity or even strictness, but constant attention and an unwavering course. Mildness and forbearance will strengthen their affection for you, while it will maintain your control over them."[74]

George Washington Custis Lee, known as "Custis" by his family, he was Robert E. Lee's oldest son. A lifelong bachelor and a general during Lincoln's War, he served on the staff of Confederate President Jefferson Davis, a position so influential that even his own father sometimes sought his advice. In 1870 George succeeded his father as president of Washington College, where he remained until 1897.

An 1847 letter from the General to his two eldest sons, George ("Custis") and William ("Fitzhugh"), written from aboard a ship off Vera Cruz, Mexico, where

he was stationed at the time:
☞ "My dear boys: I received your letters with the greatest pleasure, and, as I always like to talk to you both together, I will not separate you in my letters, but write one to you both. I was much gratified to hear of your progress at school, and hope that you will continue to advance, and that I shall have the happiness of finding you much improved in all your studies on my return. I shall not feel my long separation from you, if I find that my absence has been of no injury to you, and that you have both grown in goodness and knowledge, as well as stature.

"But, ah! how much I will suffer on my return if the reverse has occurred. You enter all my thoughts, into all my prayers; and on you, in part, will depend whether I shall be happy or miserable, as you know how much I love you. You must do all in your power to save me from pain. . . . Tell [your brother] Rob he must think of me very often, be a good boy, and always love papa . . . . The ship rolls so that I can scarcely write. You must write to me very often. I am always very glad to hear from you. Be sure that I am thinking of you, and that you have the prayers of your affectionate father, R. E. Lee."[75]

After a particularly difficult battle, in April 1847 Lee wrote to his then fourteen year old son Custis from the front lines of the Mexican-American War:
☞ "I thought of you, my dear Custis, on the 18th, in the battle, and wondered, when the musket balls and grape were whistling over my head in a perfect shower, where I could put you, if with me, to be safe. I was truly thankful that you were at school, I hope learning to be good and wise. You have no idea what a horrible sight a battlefield is."[76]

Another letter from the Mexican-American War, this one from Lee to his wife Mary concerning the Mexican city of Jalapa (or Xalapa):
☞ "[It is] the most beautiful country I have seen in Mexico, and will compare with any I have seen elsewhere. I wish it was in the United States, and that I was located with you and the children around me in one of its rich bright valleys."[77]

From a February 1848 letter concerning formulating a peace treaty with Mexico:
☞ "I would not exact now more than I would have taken before the commencement of hostilities, as I should wish nothing but what was just,

The Lee family home, Arlington House, Arlington, Virginia. The antebellum estate, built by Lee's wife's father, George Washington Parke Custis, was overtaken by Yankee troops during Lincoln's War. Ransacked and "captured" in May 1861 for use as a Union headquarters, it is today part of Arlington National Cemetery.

and that I would have sooner or later. . . . It is true we bullied her. For that I am ashamed, for she was the weaker party, but we have since, by way of set-off, drubbed her handsomely and in a manner no man might be ashamed of. They begin to be aware how entirely they are beaten, and are willing to acknowledge it."[78]

Around this same period it was suggested that he would be handsomely decorated for his service in the Mexican-American War, to which Lee replied:

☞ "I hope my friends will give themselves no annoyance on my account, or any concern about the distribution of favours. I know how those things are awarded at Washington and how the President [James Knox Polk] will be besieged by clamourous claimants. I do not wish to be numbered among them. Such as he can conscientiously bestow, I shall gratefully receive, and have no doubt that those will exceed my deserts."[79]

Here is Lee's marriage advice, from a letter he wrote to a young female cousin, dated April 12, 1848:

☞ "It seems that all in Alexandria are progressing as usual, and that nothing will stop their marrying and being given in marriage. Tell Miss

_____ she had better dismiss that young divine [clergyman] and marry a soldier. There is some chance of the latter being shot, but it requires a particular dispensation of Providence to rid her of the former."[80]

After returning to Virginia from the Mexican-American War in 1848, Lee wrote this letter to his brother, navy Captain Sydney Smith Lee (whom the General referred to as "Smith"), on June 30:

☞ "Here I am once again, my dear Smith, perfectly surrounded by [my wife] Mary and her precious children, who seem to devote themselves to staring at the furrows in my face and the white hairs in my head. It is not surprising that I am hardly recognisable to some of the young eyes around me and perfectly unknown to the youngest. But some of the older ones gaze with astonishment and wonder at me, and seem at a loss to reconcile what they see and what was pictured in their imaginations. I find them, too, much grown, and all well, and I have much cause for thankfulness, and gratitude to that good God who has once more united us."[81]

Lee had a well-known passion for animals, especially horses, all which he spoke to as if they were people and which he regarded as literal family members. The Lee family dogs even went to church with them every Sunday, obediently sitting at their feet among the pews. Among the long list of horses owned by the General was one named Grace Darling, which he bought in Texas in 1846 and rode throughout the Mexican-American War. According to his son Robert, Jr.: "My father was very much attached to and proud of her, always petting her and talking to her in a loving way, when he rode her or went to see her in her stall."[82] Unfortunately for the Lee family, Grace Darling was stolen by Yankee soldiers in the Spring of 1862 while Union General George B. McClellan was headquartered at the White House, one of the Lee family estates. After returning from the Mexican-American War in 1848, Lee wrote about Grace Darling as if she were a human traveling companion:

☞ "I only arrived yesterday, after a long journey up the Mississippi, which route I was induced to take, for the better accommodation of my horse, as I wished to spare her as much annoyance and fatigue as possible, she already having undergone so much suffering in my service. I landed her at Wheeling and left her to come over with Jim [Connally, the Lee's Irish servant, who had been with the General in Mexico]."[83]

THE QUOTABLE ROBERT E. LEE ✤ 37

Once, when he was forced to be away from his beloved Civil War horse Traveller, the General wrote back to his keeper:
☞ "How is Traveller? Tell him I miss him dreadfully, and have repented of our separation but once—and that is the whole time since we parted."[84]

Lee later wrote to the same individual:
☞ "I hope Traveller is well and wants for nothing. I want him more than ever now that I shall be alone."[85]

These excerpts are from a letter Lee wrote to his wife Mary sometime before 1850:
☞ "I pray God to watch over and direct our efforts in guarding our dear little son. . . . Oh, what pleasure I lose in being separated from my children! Nothing can compensate me for that. . . ."[86]

To his son Fitzhugh the General wrote:
☞ "I cannot go to bed, my dear son, without writing you a few lines, to thank you for your letter, which gave me great pleasure. . . . You and [your brother] Custis must take great care of your kind mother and dear sisters when your father is dead. To do that you must learn to be good. Be true, kind and generous, and pray earnestly to God to enable you to keep His Commandments 'and walk in the same all the days of your life.' I hope to come on soon to see that little baby you have got to show me. You must give her a kiss for me, and one to all the children, to your mother, and grandmother."[87]

Robert E. Lee, Jr., the General's youngest son, in 1862. A farmer, businessman, and author, Robert wrote a wonderful book about his father in 1904 entitled: *Recollections and Letters of General Robert E. Lee*.

What follows is a letter from Superintendent Robert E. Lee to his daughter Anne, dated February 25, 1853, from West Point Military Academy, where he was working as a supervisor at the time. "The Mim" referred to here was Lee's pet name for his wife Mary:

☞ "My Precious Annie: I take advantage of your gracious permission to write to you, and there is no telling how far my feelings might carry me were I not limited by the conveyance furnished by the Mim's letter which lies before me, and which must, the Mim says so, go in this morning's mail. But my limited time does not diminish my affection for you, Annie, nor prevent my thinking of you and wishing for you. I long to see you through the dilatory nights. At dawn when I rise, and all day, my thoughts revert to you in expressions that you cannot hear or I repeat. I hope you will always appear to me as you are now painted on my heart, and that you will endeavour to improve and so conduct yourself as to make you happy and me joyful all our lives. Diligent and earnest attention to all your duties can only accomplish this.

"I am told you are growing very tall, and I hope very straight. I do not know what the Cadets will say if the Superintendent's children do not practice what he demands of them. They will naturally say he had better attend to his own before he corrects other people's children, and as he permits his to stoop it is hard he will not allow them. You and [your sister] Agnes must not, therefore, bring me into discredit with my young friends, or give them reason to think that I require more of them than of my own.

"I presume your mother has told all about us, our neighbours and our affairs. And indeed she may have done that and not said much either, so far as I know. But we are all well and have much to be grateful for. To-morrow we anticipate the pleasure of [Custis] your brother's company, which is always a source of pleasure to us. It is the only time we see him, except when the Corps come under my view at some of their exercises, when my eye is sure to distinguish him among his comrades and follow him over the plain. Give much love to your dear grandmother, grandfather, Agnes, Miss Sue, Lucretia, and all friends, including the servants. Write sometimes, and think always of your affectionate father, R. E. Lee."[88]

In the Spring of 1853 Lee's wife's mother, Mary (Fitzhugh) Custis, died. She was the wife of Washington Custis, who was the grandson of Martha Washington—the wife of U.S. President George Washington. Lee wrote the following to his wife:

☞ "She was to me all that a mother could be, and I yield to none in admiration for her character, love for her virtues, and veneration for her memory. . . . May God give you strength to enable you to bear and say, 'His will be done.' She has gone from all trouble, care and sorrow to a holy immortality, there to rejoice and praise forever the God and Saviour she so long and truly served. Let that be our comfort and that our consolation. May our death be like hers, and may we meet in happiness in Heaven. . . ."[89]

Henry "Light Horse" Lee, the father of Robert E. Lee. "Harry," as he was known, was a celebrated officer in the American Revolutionary War, a member of the U.S. House of Representatives, and the governor of Virginia.

Well respected Lee was much sought after by the younger generation for help with their questions and problems. Here, from a letter dated August 6, 1853, are the General's words to a young friend seeking advice on the start of his working career:

☞ "I am glad to find that you have also a prospect of employment with Mr. Manning. Choose between them that which best affords a prospect of advancement and improvement. You are perhaps aware that a young man entering on railroad service, and bringing no experience, is expected to take a subordinate position, no matter what his qualifications, at the bottom of the ladder, and to prove by his work his capabilities for advancement. Bear this constantly in mind, my dear Conny, and work your own promotion. Recollect what depends on your exertions, and how much you owe your mother's love, sister's affection, the expectations of family and friends. You must excuse my anxiety on your behalf, my interest in your welfare, and my ardent desire to see you do justice to yourself and credit to your name."[90]

The following is from an 1855 letter Lee wrote to his son George, whom, as mentioned, the family called "Custis":
☞ "You must study to be frank with the world: frankness is the child of

honesty and courage. Say just what you mean to do on every occasion, and take it for granted you mean to do right. If a friend asks a favor, you should grant it if it is reasonable; if not, tell him plainly why you cannot: you will wrong him and wrong yourself by equivocation of any kind. Never do a wrong thing to make a friend or keep one; the man who requires you to do so is dearly purchased at a sacrifice.

"Deal kindly but firmly with all your classmates; you will find it the policy which wears best. Above all, do not appear to others what you are not. If you have any fault to find with any one, tell him, not others, of what you complain; there is no more dangerous experiment than that of undertaking to be one thing before a man's face and another behind his back. We should live, act, and say nothing to the injury of any one. It is not only better as a matter of principle, but it is the path of peace and honor."[91]

More from Lee's letter to his son Custis:
☞ "In regard to duty, let me, in conclusion of this hasty letter, inform you that nearly a hundred years ago there was a day of remarkable gloom and darkness, still known as 'the Dark Day' —a day when the light of the sun was slowly extinguished as if by an eclipse. The legislature of Connecticut was in session, and as its members saw the unexpected and unaccountable darkness coming on they shared in the general awe and terror. It was supposed by many that the Last Day, the day of judgment, had come. Some one, in the consternation of the hour, moved an adjournment.

"Then there arose an old Puritan legislator, [Abraham] Davenport of Stamford [Connecticut], and said that if the Last Day had come he desired to be found at his place doing his duty, and therefore moved that candles be brought in, so that the House could proceed with its duty. There was quietness in that man's mind—the quietness of heavenly wisdom and inflexible willingness to obey present duty. Duty, then, is the sublimest word in our language. Do your duty in all things, like the old Puritan. You cannot do more—you should never wish to do less. Never let me and your mother wear one gray hair for any lack of duty on your part."[92]

During the summer of 1856 Lee was stationed along the Brazos River in Texas.

The sun was formidable, the heat unbearable, the dry choking dust a daily nightmare. Daydreaming of his idyllic home and family back at Arlington, Lee, then a U.S. lieutenant colonel, was often forced to seek shelter under the shade of his army blanket during the hottest part of the day. His abject misery at this time may explain his uncharacteristically grumpy reply to his wife, who had written to him encouragingly about several open positions in the rank of brigadier general:

☛ "Do not give yourself any anxiety about the appointment of the brigadier. If it is on my account that you feel an interest in it, I beg you will discard it from your thoughts. You will be sure to be disappointed; nor is it right to indulge improper and useless hopes. It, besides, looks like presumption to expect it."⁹³

Like most Southerners then as today, Lee loved nature, as is evidenced in the following excerpt from a letter to a relative, written in early 1857 while he was stationed at Fort Brown on the Rio Grande:

George Washington, first president of the U.S. and the step great-grandfather of Robert E. Lee's wife, Mary Anne Randolph Custis. The author descends from Washington's great-grandparents, John Washington and Ann Pope of Westmoreland County, Virginia.

☛ "My daily walks are alone, up and down the banks of the river, and my pleasure is derived from my own thoughts and from the sight of the flowers and animals I there meet with. The birds of the Rio Grande form a constant source of interest, and are as numerous as they are beautiful in plumage. I wish I could get for you the roots of some of the luxuriant vines that cover everything, or the seeds of the innumerable flowers."⁹⁴

After suppressing the John Brown Raid (in which the Connecticut madman had illegally and violently tried to instigate a failed slave rebellion in Virginia) on October 17, 1859, then capturing its anti-South leader, Lee wrote the following to his wife Mary from Harper's Ferry. It is dated December 1:

☛ "I arrived here, dearest Mary, yesterday about noon, with four companies from Fort Monroe, and was busy all the evening and night getting accommodation for the men, etc., and posting sentinels and piquets [a still popular two-handed card game for two players, played with a reduced deck of thirty-two cards] to insure timely notice of the approach of the enemy. The night has passed off quietly. The feelings of the community seem to be calmed down, and I have been received with every kindness. Mr. Fry is among the officers from Old Point. There are several young men, former acquaintances of ours, as cadets, Mr. Bingham of Custis's class, Sam Cooper, etc., but the senior officers I never met before, except Captain Howe, the friend of our Cousin Harriet R_____.

"I presume we are fixed here till after the 16th. Tomorrow will probably be the last of Captain Brown [John Brown was indeed hanged the next day]. There will be less interest for the others, but still I think the troops will not be withdrawn till they are similarly disposed of.

"[Our son] Custis will have informed you that I had to go to Baltimore the evening I left you, to make arrangements for the transportation for the troops. . . . This morning I was introduced to Mrs. [John] Brown, who, with a Mrs. Tyndall and a Mr. and Mrs. McKim, all from Philadelphia, had come on to have a last interview with her husband. As it is a matter over which I have no control I referred them to General [William B.] Taliaferro.

"You must write to me at this place. I hope you are all well. Give love to everybody. Tell [my brother] Smith that no charming women have insisted on taking care of me as they are always doing of him—I am left to my own resources. I will write you again soon, and will always be truly and affectionately yours, R. E. Lee."[95]

On April 20, 1861, three days after Virginia seceded from the Union, Lee resigned from the U.S. army and wrote the following letter to his sister Anne in Baltimore, Maryland. Just days earlier, on April 9, big government liberal, President Abraham Lincoln, had launched his diabolical war against the South:[96]

☞ "My Dear Sister: I am grieved at my inability to see you. I have been waiting for a more convenient season, which has brought to many before me deep and lasting regret. Now we are in a state of war which will yield to nothing. The whole South is in a state of revolution, into which

Virginia, after a long struggle, has been drawn; and, though I recognize no necessity for this state of things, and would have forborne and pleaded to the end for redress of grievances, real or supposed, yet in my own person I had to meet the question whether I should take part against my native State.

"With all my devotion to the Union, and the feeling of loyalty and duty of an American citizen, I have not been able to make up my mind to raise my hand against my relatives, my children, my home. I have therefore resigned my commission in the army, and, save in defence of my native State, with the sincere hope that my poor services may never be needed, I hope I may never be called on to draw my sword. I know you will blame me, but you must think as kindly of me as you can, and believe that I have endeavored to do what I thought right.

"To show you the feeling and struggle it has cost me I send a copy of my letter to General Scott which accompanied my letter of resignation. I have no time for more. May God guard and protect you and yours, and shower upon you every blessing, is the prayer of your devoted brother, R. E. Lee."[97]

Martha Washington, the great-grandmother of Robert E. Lee's wife, Mary Anne Randolph Custis. Martha, the daughter of John Dandridge and Francis Jones, was the only wife of U.S. President George Washington, her second husband. Martha's first husband was Daniel Parke Custis, Mary's biological great-grandfather.

On April 26, 1861, only weeks after the Battle of Fort Sumter, Lee wrote the following to his wife Mary at their beautiful home Arlington House:
☞ ". . . I am very anxious about you. You have to move and make arrangements to go to some point of safety, which you must select. The Mount Vernon plate and pictures ought to be secured. Keep quiet while you remain and in your preparation. War is inevitable, and there is no telling when it will burst around you. Virginia, yesterday, I understand, joined the Confederate States [Virginia officially seceded April 17]. What policy they may adopt I cannot conjecture. May God bless and

preserve you, and have mercy upon all our people, is the constant prayer of your affectionate husband, R. E. Lee."[96]

On April 30, 1861, Lee wrote this letter to his wife:
☞ "On going to my room last night I found my trunk and sword there, and opening them this morning discovered the package of letters and was very glad to learn you were all well and as yet peaceful. I fear the latter state will not continue long. . . . I think therefore you had better prepare all things for removal [from Arlington House], that is, the plate, pictures, etc., and be prepared at any moment. Where to go is the difficulty. When the war commences no place will be exempt, in my opinion, and indeed all the avenues into the State will be the scenes of military operations.

"There is no prospect or intention of the [U.S.] Government to propose a truce. Do not be deceived by it. . . . May God preserve you all and bring peace to our distracted country."[97]

Around this same time, as the Southern states were quickly seceding and Lincoln's War was growing in severity, Lee wrote the following to his wife concerning whether their oldest son Custis should follow the South or the North:
☞ "Tell Custis he must consult his own conscience as to the course he may take. I do not wish him to be guided by my wishes or example; if I have done wrong, let him do better. The present question is one which every man must settle for himself."[98]

On May 2, 1861, an anxious Lee wrote again to his wife:
☞ "My dear Mary: I received last night your letter of the 1st, with contents. It gave me great pleasure to learn that you were all well and in peace. You know how pleased I should be to have you and my dear daughters with me. That I fear cannot be. There is no place that I can expect to be but in the field, and there is no rest for me to look to. But I want you to be in a place of safety. . . . We have only to be resigned to God's will and pleasure, and do all we can for our protection. . . . I have just received [our son] Custis's letter of the 30th, inclosing the acceptance of my resignation. It is stated that it will take effect April 25th. I resigned on the 20th, and wished it to take effect that day. I cannot consent to its running on further, and he must receive no pay, if they

tender it, beyond that day, but return the whole, if need be. . . ."⁹⁹

On May 8, 1861, Lee once again wrote to his spouse:
☞ ". . . I grieve at the necessity that drives you from your home. I can appreciate your feelings on the occasion, and pray that you may receive comfort and strength in the difficulties that surround you. When I reflect upon the calamity impending over the country, my own sorrows sink into insignificance. . . . Be content and resigned to God's will. I shall be able to write seldom. Write to me, as your letters will be my greatest comfort. I send a check for $500 [today's equivalent of about $13,000]; it is all I have in bank. Pay the children's school expenses. . . ."¹⁰⁰

Lee sent this letter to his wife on May 11, 1861:
☞ "I have received your letter of the 9ᵗʰ from Arlington. I had supposed you were at Ravensworth. . . . I am glad to hear that you are at peace, and enjoying the sweet weather and beautiful flowers. You had better complete your arrangements and retire further from the scene of war. It may burst upon you at any time. It is sad to think of the devastation, if not ruin, it may bring upon a spot so endeared to us. But God's will be done. We must be resigned. May He guard and keep you all, is my constant prayer."¹⁰¹

Colonel Robert E. Lee, as he looked in 1853 while serving as superintendent of West Point Military Academy.

On May 24, 1861, as socialistic Lincoln's full scale assault on the South and states' rights continued to escalate,¹⁰² Yankee troops invaded and occupied the Lee's grand family home, Arlington House. Mary and her children were callously thrown into the street, instantly becoming homeless refugees. The house was trashed then stripped of its valuables, some which were family heirlooms that had belonged to President George Washington. This came during a conflict that pro-North supporters still call a "war over slavery"! Lee sent ever more frantic letters to his wife, as this example from the following day, May 25, illustrates:

☞ "I have been trying, dearest Mary, ever since the receipt of your letter by [our son] Custis, to write to you. I sympathise deeply in your feelings at leaving your dear home. I have experienced them myself, and they are constantly revived. I fear we have not been grateful enough for the happiness there within our reach, and our heavenly Father has found it necessary to deprive us of what He has given us. I acknowledge my ingratitude, my transgressions, and my unworthiness, and submit with resignation to what he thinks proper to inflict upon me. We must trust all then to him, and I do not think it prudent or right for you to return there, while the United States troops occupy that country. I have gone over all this ground before, and have just written to Cousin Anna on the subject.

". . . I must now leave the matter to you, and pray that God may guard you. I have no time for more. I know and feel the discomfort of your position, but it cannot be helped, and we must bear our trials like Christians. . . . If you and Cousin Anna choose to come here, you know how happy we shall be to see you. I shall take the field as soon now as I can. . . . Ever yours truly and devotedly, R. E. Lee."[103]

Lee to his wife, dated June 9, 1861, from Richmond, Virginia:
☞ "I have just returned from a visit to the batteries and troops on James and York rivers, etc., where I was some days. I called a few hours at the White House [one of the Lee's family homes]. Saw Charlotte [Wickham, his son Fitzhugh's first wife] and Annie [their daughter]. Fitzhugh was away, but got out of the cars [trains] as I got in. Our little boy looked very sweet and seemed glad to kiss me a good-bye. Charlotte said she was going to prepare to leave for the summer, but had not determined where to go. I could only see some of the servants about the house and the stables. They were all well. . . .

"You may be aware that the Confederate Government is established here. Yesterday I turned over to it the command of the military and naval forces of the State, in accordance with the proclamation of the Government and the agreement between the State and the Confederate States. I do not know what my position will be. I should like to retire to private life, if I could be with you and the children, but if I can be of any service to the State or her cause I must continue. Mr. [Jefferson] Davis and all his Cabinet are here. . . .

"Good-bye. Give much love to kind friends. May God guard and bless you, them, and our suffering country, and enable me to perform my duty. I think of you constantly. Write me what you will do. Direct here. Always yours, R. E. Lee."[104]

The following is Lee's reply to his wife in a letter dated July 12, 1861. The General is responding to the suggestion by some that he be made military commander-in-chief of the entire Confederate forces. Being inherently conservative, many Southerners were extremely wary of this new position, however, as they felt it could lead to a military dictatorship. Lee himself says here that he has never heard of the position and has no interest in it:

☞ "I am very anxious to get into the field, but am detained by matters beyond my control. I have never heard of the appointment, to which you allude, of Commander-in-Chief of the Confederate States Army, nor have I any expectation or wish for it. President Davis [a civilian] holds that position. Since the transfer of the military operations in Virginia to the authorities of the Confederate States, I have only occupied the position of a general in that service, with the duties devolved on me by the President.

"I have been labouring to prepare and get into the field the Virginia troops, and to strengthen, by those from the other States, the threatened commands of Johnston, Beauregard, Huger, Garnett, etc. Where I shall go I do not know, as that will depend upon President Davis. As usual in getting through with a thing, I have broken down a little and had to take my bed last evening, but am at my office this morning and hope will soon be right again. . . . Always yours, R. E. Lee."[105]

"Tom Tita," one of the Lee family's many pet cats. The General dearly loved them all, along with the rest of the clan's menagerie of animals, including horses, dogs, and even pet squirrels.

On July 27, 1861, six days after the Confederates trounced the Yankees at the Battle of Manassas I (at which Lee was not present), he wrote this letter to his wife:

☞ "That indeed was a glorious victory and has lightened the pressure upon our front amazingly. Do not grieve for the brave dead. Sorrow for those they left behind—friends, relatives, and families. The former are at rest. The latter must suffer. The battle will be repeated there in greater force. I hope God will again smile on us and strengthen our hearts and arms. I wished to partake in the former struggle, and am mortified at my absence, but the President thought it more important I should be here. I could not have done as well as has been done, but I could have helped, and taken part in the struggle for my home and neighbourhood. So the work is done I care not by whom it is done. . . . Give love to all, and for yourself accept the constant prayers and love of truly yours, R. E. Lee."[106]

Lee predicted the loss of the Lee family home, Arlington House, as noted in this Christmas Day (1861) letter to his wife:
☞ "As to our old home, if not destroyed, it will be difficult ever to be recognised. Even if the enemy had wished to preserve it, it would almost have been impossible. With the number of troops encamped around it, the change of officers, etc., the want of fuel, shelter, etc., and all the dire necessities of war, it is vain to think of its being in a habitable condition. I fear, too, books, furniture, and the relics of Mount Vernon will be gone. It is better to make up our minds to a general loss. They cannot take away the remembrance of the spot, and the memories of those that to us rendered it sacred. That will remain to us as long as life will last, and that we can preserve.

"In the absence of a home, I wish I could purchase [my birthplace] 'Stratford [Hall].' That is the only other place that I could go to, now accessible to us, that would inspire me with feelings of pleasure and local love. You and the girls could remain there in quiet. It is a poor place, but we could make enough cornbread and bacon for our support, and the girls could weave us clothes. I wonder if it is for sale and at how much. Ask [our son] Fitzhugh to try to find out, when he gets to Fredericksburg."[107]

To his daughter Anne, from Savannah, South Carolina, dated March 2, 1862:
☞ "My Precious Annie: It has been a long time since I have written to you, but you have been constantly in my thoughts. I think of you all,

separately and collectively, in the busy hours of the day and the silent hours of the night, and the recollection of each and every one whiles away the long night, in which my anxious thoughts drive away sleep. But I always feel that you and Agnes at those times are sound asleep, and that it is immaterial to either where the blockaders are or what their progress is in the river. . . . Goodbye, my dear child. May God bless you and our poor country. Your devoted father, R. E. Lee."[108]

To his wife, dated March 14, 1862:
☞ "My Dear Mary: I have been trying all the week to write to you, but have not been able. I have been placed on duty here to conduct operations under the direction of the [Confederate] President [Jefferson Davis]. It will give me great pleasure to do anything I can to relieve him and serve the country, but I do not see either advantage or pleasure in my duties. But I will not complain, but do my best. I do not see at present either that it will enable me to see much more of you. In the present condition of affairs no one can foresee what may happen, nor in my judgment is it advisable for any one to make arrangements with a view to permanency or pleasure. We must all do what promises the most usefulness."[109]

Robert E. Lee with his second son William Henry Fitzhugh Lee in 1845.

During Lincoln's War, Yank General John Pope committed a wide array of what Lee rightly called "atrocities" against "defenceless citizens."[110] *From the battlefield during the Summer of 1862, an obviously disappointed Lee sent the following to his wife concerning Louis Marshall, a family relative who had sided with the Union and was serving under Pope—to this day still considered a war criminal across the South:*

☞ "In the prospect before me I cannot see a single ray of pleasure during this war; but so long as I can perform any service to the country I am content.

"When you write to [our son] Rob [of Stonewall Jackson's artillery] again, tell him to catch Pope for me, and also to bring in his cousin Louis Marshall, who, I am told, is on his staff. I could forgive the latter fighting against us, but not his joining Pope."[111]

An August 17, 1862, letter to family reflects Lee's near perpetual state of composure, even during times of intense duress:

☞ "Here I am in a tent instead of my comfortable quarters at Dobbs's. The tent, however, is very comfortable and of that I have nothing to complain. [Union] General Pope says he is very strong, and seems to feel so, for he is moving apparently up to the Rapidan. I hope he will not prove stronger than we are. I learn since I have left, that [Union] General McClellan has moved down the James River with his whole army. I suppose he is coming here too, so we shall have a busy time. [Union Generals Ambrose Everett] Burnside and [Rufus] King from Fredericksburg have joined Pope, which, from their own report, has swelled Pope to ninety-two thousand. I do not believe it, though I believe he is very big. Johnny Lee saw Louis Marshall [General Lee's nephew, who, as mentioned above, had turned against the South and joined Pope's staff] after Jackson's last battle, who asked him kindly after his old uncle, and said his mother was well. Johnny said Louis looked wretchedly himself. I am sorry he is in such bad company, but I suppose he could not help it."[112]

After the terrible Battle of Sharpsburg (Antietam to Yanks) on September 17, 1862—considered by many to be the bloodiest engagement of the entire War—Lee sent this epistle to his wife:

☞ "I have not laid eyes on [our son] Rob since I saw him in the battle of Sharpsburg going in with a single gun of his battery for the second time after his company had been withdrawn, in consequence of three of its guns having been disabled. [Our other son] Custis has seen him, and says he is very well and apparently happy and content. My hands are improving slowly [after an accident with a horse], and with my left hand I am able to dress and undress myself, which is a great comfort. My right is becoming of some assistance, too, though it is still swollen and sometimes painful. The bandages have been removed. I am now able to sign my name. It has been six weeks to-day since I was injured, and I have at last discarded the sling."[113]

Lee's second daughter, Anne, died unexpectedly on October 20, 1862, at the age of twenty-three, prompting this letter from the General to his wife on October 26:

☞ ". . . I cannot express the anguish I feel at the death of our sweet Annie. To know that I shall never see her again on earth, that her place in our circle, which I always hoped one day to enjoy, is forever vacant, is agonising in the extreme. But God in this, as in all things, has mingled mercy with the blow, in selecting that one best prepared to leave us. May you be able to join me in saying 'His will be done!' . . .

"I know how much you will grieve and how much she will be mourned. I wish I could give you any comfort, but beyond our hope in the great mercy of God, and the belief that He takes her at the time and place when it is best for her to go, there is none. May that same mercy be extended to us all, and may we be prepared for His summons."[114]

Confederate General Fitzhugh Lee, Robert E. Lee's famous nephew. Fitzhugh served gallantly at such battles as First Manassas and Spotsylvania Court House, and after the War, in 1885, he was elected governor of Virginia.

Just prior to the Battle of Fredericksburg (December 11-15, 1862), Lee sent the following to his wife. He need not have doubted himself, however, for the Confederates won:

☞ "I tremble for my country when I hear of confidence expressed in me. I know too well my weakness, and that our only hope is in God."[115]

On December 10, 1862, the General wrote to his daughter-in-law Charlotte (Wickham) Lee, concerning the passing of her second child, Charlotte Carter Lee, on December 6 (her first child, Robert E. Lee, III, had died only months earlier, on June 30, 1862):

☞ "I heard yesterday, my dear daughter, with the deepest sorrow, of the death of your infant. I was so grateful at her birth. I felt that she would be such a comfort to you, such a pleasure to my dear [son] Fitzhugh, and would fill so full the void still aching in your hearts. But you have now two sweet angels [babies Charlotte and Robert] in heaven. What joy there is in the thought! What relief to your grief! What suffering and sorrow they have escaped! I can say nothing to soften the anguish you must feel, and I know you are assured of my deep and affectionate sympathy. May God give you strength to bear the affliction He has imposed, and produce future joy out of your present misery, is my earnest prayer.

". . . My horse is waiting at my tent door, but I could not refrain from sending these few lines to recall to you the thought and love of your devoted father, R. E. Lee."[116]

Toward the end of 1862 Lee wrote a number of letters to family members. This one, dated December 25, 1862, was written to his daughter Mildred:

☞ "I cannot tell you how I long to see you when a little quiet occurs. My thoughts revert to you, your sisters and mother; my heart aches for our reunion. Your brothers I see occasionally. This morning [your brother] Fitzhugh rode by with his young aide-de-camp (Rob) at the head of his brigade, on his way up the Rappahannock.

"You must study hard, gain knowledge, and learn your duty to God and your neighbor: that is the great object of life. I have no news, confined constantly to camp and my thoughts occupied with its necessities and duties. I am, however, happy in the knowledge that [Union] General [Ambrose Everett] Burnside and his army will not eat their promised Xmas dinner in Richmond to-day."[117]

On December 26, 1862, Lee wrote this letter to his daughter Agnes:

☞ "My Precious Little Agnes: I have not heard of you for a long time. I wish you were with me, for, always solitary, I am sometimes weary, and long for the reunion of my family once again. But I will not speak of myself, but of you. . . .

"I have only seen the ladies in this vicinity when flying from the enemy, and it caused me acute grief to witness their exposure and suffering. But a more noble spirit was never displayed anywhere. The faces of old and young were wreathed with smiles and glowed with happiness at their sacrifices for the good of their country. Many have lost everything. What the fire and shells of the enemy spared their pillagers destroyed. But God will shelter them, I know. So much heroism will not be unregarded.

Confederate General William Henry Fitzhugh Lee, Robert E. Lee's second son. He was generally known as "Rooney" to avoid confusion with his famous first cousin Fitzhugh Lee, but his immediate family called him "Fitzhugh." In 1859 William inherited his grandfather's beautiful estate, White House, on the Pamunkey River, where he settled down to begin farming. This was interrupted by Lincoln's War, during which Yankee troops illegally and unnecessarily burned White House to the ground. After the Battle of Brandy Station, where William was seriously injured, he was captured by the Union while recuperating and imprisoned from June 1863 to March 1864. After the War he served as president of the Virginia Agricultural Society, became a senator, and in 1887 was elected to the U.S. Congress.

"I can only hold oral communication with your sister, and have forbidden the scouts to bring any writing, and have taken back some that I had given them for her. If caught it would compromise them. They only convey messages. I learn in that way she is well, your devoted father, R. E. Lee."[118]

The following letter, written from father to daughter on February 6, 1863, was sent from Camp Fredericksburg:

☞ "To Agnes Lee: I read yesterday, my precious daughter, your letter, and grieved very much when last in Richmond at not seeing you. My movements are so uncertain that I cannot be relied on for anything. The only place I am to be found is in camp, and I am so cross now that I am not worth seeing anywhere. Here you will have to take me with the three stools—the snow, the rain, and the mud. The storm of the last twenty-four hours has added to our stock of all, and we are now in a floating condition. But the sun and wind will carry all off in time, and then we shall appreciate our relief.

"Our horses and mules suffer the most. They have to bear the cold and rain, tug through the mud, and suffer all the time with hunger. The roads are wretched, almost impassable. . . . I wish you were here with me to-day. You would have to sit by this little stove, look out at the rain, and keep yourself dry. But here come, in all their wet, the adjutant generals with the papers. I must stop and go to work. See how kind God is: we have plenty to do in good weather and bad. . . . Your devoted father, R. E. Lee."[119]

Lee penned this letter to his wife Mary on February 23, 1863, from the field:
☞ "The weather now is very hard upon our poor bushmen. This morning the whole country is covered with a mantle of snow fully a foot deep. It was nearly up to my knees as I stepped out this morning, and our poor horses were enveloped. We have dug them out and opened our avenues a little, but it will be terrible and the roads impassable. No cars [trains] from Richmond yesterday. I fear our short rations for man and horse will have to be curtailed.

"Our enemies have their troubles too. They are very strong immediately in front, but have withdrawn their troops above and below us back toward Acquia Creek. I owe [Union General] Mr. Joseph Hooker no thanks for keeping me here. He ought to have made up his mind long ago what to do.—Feb. 24th. The cars [trains] have arrived, and brought me a young French officer full of vivacity, and ardent for service with me. I think the appearance of things will cool him. If they do not, the night will, for he brought no blankets. R. E. Lee."[120]

It is not generally known by the public, but after the disastrous Battle of Gettysburg (July 1-3, 1863), Lee resigned the command of his army with the following letter to Confederate President Jefferson Davis (who wisely turned down the General's request):
☞ "Mr. President: Your letters of the 28th July and 2d August have been received, and I have waited for a leisure hour to reply, but I fear that will never come. I am extremely obliged to you for the attention given to the wants of this army and the efforts made to supply them. Our absentees

are returning, and I hope the earnest and beautiful appeal made to the country in your proclamation may stir up the whole people, and that they may see their duty and perform it. Nothing is wanted but that their fortitude should equal their bravery to ensure the success of our cause.

"We must expect reverses, even defeats. They are sent to teach us wisdom and prudence, to call forth greater energies, and to prevent our falling into greater disasters. Our people have only to be true and united, to bear manfully the misfortunes incident to war, and all will come right in the end. I know how prone we are to censure, and how ready to blame others for the nonfulfilment of our expectations. This is unbecoming in a generous people, and I grieve to see its expression. The general remedy for the want of success in a military commander is his removal. This is natural, and in many instances proper. For, no matter what may be the ability of the officer, if he loses the confidence of his troops disaster must sooner or later ensue.

"I have been prompted by these reflections more than once since my return from Pennsylvania to propose to Your Excellency the propriety of selecting another commander for this army. I have seen and heard of expressions of discontent in the public journals at the result of the expedition. I do not know how far this feeling extends in the army. My brother-officers have been too kind to report it, and so far the troops have been too generous to exhibit it. It is fair, however, to suppose that it does exist, and success is so necessary to us that nothing

Another image of Mary Anne Randolph Custis, Robert E. Lee's wife. The couple, friends since childhood, were third cousins once removed. Mary was the great-granddaughter of Martha Washington, the wife of U.S. President George Washington (Mary's step great-grandfather).

should be risked to secure it. I therefore, in all sincerity, request Your Excellency to take measures to supply my place. I do this with the more earnestness because no one is more aware than myself of my inability for the duties of my position. I cannot even accomplish what I myself desire. How can I fulfil the expectations of others?

"In addition, I sensibly feel the growing failure of my bodily strength. I have not yet recovered from the attack I experienced the past spring. I am becoming more and more incapable of exertion, and am thus prevented from making the personal examinations and giving the personal supervision to the operations in the field which I feel to be necessary. I am so dull that in making use of the eyes of others I am frequently misled. Everything, therefore, points to the advantages to be derived from a new commander, and I the more anxiously urge the matter upon Your Excellency from my belief that a younger and abler man than myself can readily be obtained. I know that he will have as gallant and brave an army as ever existed to second his efforts, and it would be the happiest day of my life to see at its head a worthy leader—one that could accomplish more than I could perform, and all that I have wished. I hope Your Excellency will attribute my request to the true reason, the desire to serve my country and to do all in my power to ensure the success of her righteous cause.

"I have no complaints to make of any one but myself. I have received nothing but kindness from those above me, and the most considerate attention from my comrades and companions-in-arms. To Your Excellency I am specially indebted for uniform kindness and consideration. You have done everything in your power to aid me in the work committed to my charge, without omitting anything to promote the general welfare.

"I pray that your efforts may at length be crowned with success, and that you may long live to enjoy the thanks of a grateful people. With sentiments of great esteem, I am very respectfully and truly yours, R. E. Lee, General."[121]

On August 23, 1863, Lee wrote to his wife. The letter included this interesting tidbit:

☞ ". . . My camp is near Mr. Erasmus Taylor's house, who has been very kind in contributing to our comfort. His wife sends us, every day,

This home, known as "President's House," was specially built for the General during his tenure as head of Washington College, Lexington, Virginia.

buttermilk, loaf bread, ice, and such vegetables as she has. I cannot get her to desist, though I have made two special visits to that effect."[122]

A November 5, 1863 to his wife contained this anecdote:

☞ "While on the ground, a man rode up to me and said he was just from Alexandria and had been requested to give me a box, which he handed me, but did not know who sent it. It contained a handsome pair of gilt spurs."[123]

On April 7, 1864, from the field, Lee wrote this letter to a female relative, which included a pincushion as a gift. On the top of the cushion was a picture of a Confederate Flag with the words "Conquer or Die" below it. On the reverse side was inscribed the word "Love":

☞ "My Dear Cousin Margaret: I send you a pincushion, made on the banks of the Ohio. The sentiment on its face I trust inspires the action of every man in the Confederacy, whilst their hearts overflow with the passion inscribed on its reverse. A soldier's heart, you know, is divided between love and glory. One goes to Richmond to-day who has his share of both. You will probably see him. Elevate his desire for the latter, but do not hearken to his words on the former.

"Soliciting your prayers for the safety of the army, the success of our cause, and the restoration of peace to our country, I am, with great affection, very truly yours, R. E. Lee."[124]

On July 5, 1864, during the Petersburg campaign, the General wrote this letter to his fourth and youngest daughter (and last child) Mildred Childe Lee, whom he nicknamed "Precious Life":

☞ "My Precious Life: I received this morning, by your brother, your note, and am very glad to hear your mother is better. I sent out immediately to try and find some lemons, but could only procure two—sent to me by a kind lady, Mrs. Kirkland, in Petersburg. These were gathered from her own trees; there are none to be purchased. I found one in my valise, dried up, which I also send, as it may be of some value. I also put up some early apples, which you can roast for your mother, and one pear. This is all the fruit I can get.

"You must go to market every morning and see if you cannot find some fresh fruit for her. There are no lemons to be had here. Tell her lemonade is not as palatable or digestible as buttermilk. Try and get some for her—with ice it is delicious, and very nutritious. I hope she will continue to improve, and be soon well and leave that heated city. It must be roasting now. Tell her I can only think of her and pray for her recovery. I wish I could be with her to nurse her and care for her. I want to see you all very much, but cannot now see the day when we shall be together once more. I think of you, long for you, pray for you: it is all I can do. Think sometimes of your devoted father, R. E. Lee."[125]

Dated November 6, 1864, here is another letter from Lee to his daughter Mildred:
☞ "My Precious Life: This is the first day I have had leisure to answer your letter. I enjoyed it very much at the time of its reception, and have enjoyed it since. But I have often thought of you in the mean time, and have seen you besides. Indeed, I may say you are never out of my thoughts. I hope you think of me often, and if you could know how earnestly I desire your true happiness, how ardently I pray you may be directed to every good and saved from every evil, you would as sincerely strive for its accomplishment. Now in your youth you must be careful to discipline your thoughts, words, and actions. Habituate yourself to useful employment, regular improvement, and to the benefit of all those around you.

"You have had some opportunity of learning the rudiments of your education—not as good as I should have desired, but I am much cheered by the belief that you availed yourself of it—and I think you are now prepared by diligence and study to learn whatever you desire. Do not allow yourself to forget what you have spent so much time and labor in acquiring, but increase it every day by extended application. I hope you will embrace in your studies all useful acquisitions.

"I was so much pleased to hear that while at 'Bremo' you passed much of your time in reading and music: all accomplishments will enable you to give pleasure, and thus exert a wholesome influence. Never neglect the means of making yourself useful in the world.

"I think you will not have to complain of [your brother] Rob again for neglecting your schoolmates. He has equipped himself with a new uniform from top to toe, and with a new and handsome horse is cultivating a marvellous beard and preparing for conquest.

"I went down on the lines to the right Friday, beyond Rowanty Creek, and pitched my camp within six miles of [your brother] Fitzhugh's that night. Rob came up and spent the night with me, and Fitzhugh appeared early in the morning. They rode with me till late that day. I visited the battlefield in that quarter, and General [Wade] Hampton in describing it said there had not been during the war a more spirited charge than Fitzhugh's division made that day up the Boydton plank road, driving cavalry and infantry before him, in which he was stopped by night. I did not know before that his horse had been shot under him.

Another image of Robert E. Lee's third and youngest son, Robert E. Lee, Jr. Known affectionately as "Rob," he rose to the rank of captain during Lincoln's War and served as his brother George's aide. Robert married twice and had two daughters with his second wife Juliet Carter.

"Give a great deal of love to your dear mother, and kiss your sisters for me. Tell them they must keep well, not talk too much, and go to bed early. Ever your devoted father, R. E. Lee."[126]

In January 1865, four months before the close of Lincoln's War, Lee wrote the following to his wife:
☞ "Yesterday afternoon three little girls walked into my room, each with a small basket. The eldest carried some fresh eggs, laid by her own hens; the second, some pickles made by her mother; the third, some popcorn grown in her garden. They were accompanied by a young maid with a block of soap made by her mother. They were the daughters of a Mrs. Nottingham, a [war] refugee from Northampton County, who lived near Eastville, not far from 'old Arlington.' The eldest of the girls, whose age did not exceed eight years, had a small wheel on which she spun for her mother, who wove all the cloth for her two brothers—boys of twelve and fourteen years. I have not had so pleasant a visit for a long time. I fortunately was able to fill their baskets with apples . . . and I begged them to bring me nothing but kisses and to keep the eggs, corn, etc., for themselves. I pray daily and almost hourly to our Heavenly Father to come to the relief of you and our afflicted country. I know He will order all things for our good, and we must be content."[127]

General Lee was always a farmer at heart and expressed as much on numerous occasions, as the following two examples illustrate. The first is from a letter to one of his sons, dated July 1865, four months after the end of the "Civil War":
☞ "[Someday] I shall endeavour to procure some humble, but quiet abode for your mother and sisters, where I hope they can be happy. As I before said, I want to get in some grass country where the natural product of the land will do much for my subsistence. . . ."[128]

Upon receiving an invitation from Washington College to become its next president, Lee declined the offer in this August 24, 1865, reply from Powhatan County, Virginia (the school ignored Lee's letter and gave him the position):
☞ "Gentlemen: I have delayed for some days replying to your letter of the 5th inst., informing me of my election by the board of trustees to the presidency of Washington College, from a desire to give the subject due consideration. Fully impressed with the responsibilities of the office, I have feared that I should be unable to discharge its duties to the

satisfaction of the trustees or to the benefit of the country. The proper education of youth requires not only great ability, but I fear more strength than I now possess, for I do not feel able to undergo the labour of conducting classes in regular courses of instruction. I could not, therefore, undertake more than the general administration and supervision of the institution.

"There is another subject which has caused me serious reflection, and is, I think, worthy of the consideration of the board. Being excluded from the terms of amnesty in the proclamation of the President of the United States, of the 29th of May last, and an object of censure to a portion of the country, I have thought it probable that my occupation of the position of president might draw upon the college a feeling of hostility; and I should, therefore, cause injury to an institution which it would be my highest desire to advance. I think it the duty of every citizen, in the present condition of the country, to do all in his power to aid in the restoration of peace and harmony, and in no way to oppose the policy of the State or general government directed to that object.

"It is particularly incumbent on those charged with the instruction of the young to set them an example of submission to authority, and I could not consent to be the cause of animadversion upon the college. Should you, however, take a different view, and think that my services in the position tendered to me by the board will be advantageous to the college and country, I will yield to your judgment and accept it; otherwise, I must most respectfully decline the office. Begging you to express to the trustees of the college my heartfelt gratitude for the honour conferred upon me, and requesting you to accept my cordial thanks for the kind manner in which you have communicated their decision, I am, gentlemen, with great respect, your most obedient servant, R. E. Lee."[129]

This is from a letter to one of Lee's sons dated October 1865, just after starting his new career as president of Washington College in Lexington, Virginia:
☞ "I should have selected a more quiet life and a more retired abode than Lexington. I should have preferred a small farm, where I could have earned my daily bread."[130]

As a father, General Lee was always ready with offers of advice and encouragement

Another likeness of that important piece of American history, Stratford Hall, General Robert E. Lee's birthplace. The great plantation and its manor house have been preserved, and are today open for tours, shopping, dining, lodging, summer camp, field trips, symposia, and hiking.

to his children. An example is this March 16, 1866, letter to his son Robert, Jr., who had recently taken up farming in King William County, Virginia:

☞ "I am clear for your doing everything to improve your property and make it remunerative as far as you can. You know my objection to incurring debt. . . . I hope you will overcome your chills, and by next winter you must patch up your house, and get a sweet wife. You will be more comfortable, and not so lonesome. Let her bring a cow and a churn. That will be all you will want. . . . Give my love to [your brother] Fitzhugh. I wish he were regularly established [that is, employed]. He cannot afford to be idle. He will be miserable."[131]

After the War Lee had his choice of hundreds of job offers, many quite prestigious, with accompanying exorbitant salaries and lavish homes. Why then did he accept the relatively modest position of president of the then rundown Washington College at Lexington? The answer is to be found in the following excerpt from a letter he wrote to Reverend G. W. Leyburn on March 20, 1866:

☞ "So greatly have those [educational] interests been disturbed at the South, and so much does its future condition depend upon the rising generation, that I consider the proper education of its youth one of the most important objects now to be attained, and one from which the greatest benefits may be expected. Nothing will compensate us for the depression of the standard of our moral and intellectual culture, and each State should take the most energetic measures to revive the schools and colleges, and, if possible, to increase the facilities for instruction, and to elevate the standard of learning."[132]

Lee's wife Mary was incapacitated with rheumatism during the later stage of their marriage, requiring a "wheeled chair" and constant care. Once, while walking on crutches, she took the waters at Rockbridge Baths (near Lexington, Virginia) in the Summer of 1866, but fell, causing serious injury. Learning of the accident, the General wrote her this letter on August 10:

☞ "My Dear Mary: On receiving your note, yesterday, I had only time to get the arnica [a flowering herb used as an anti-inflammatory] and send it by the stage. I am very sorry that you received such a fall, and fear it must have been a heavy shock to you. I am, however, very thankful that you escaped greater injury, and hope it is no worse than you describe. I will endeavour to get down to see you to-morrow evening, and trust I may find you somewhat relieved from its effects. We are pretty well here [at Washington College]. Many people are out of town, and I have not seen those who are in. Love to the girls. Truly and affectionately yours, R. E. Lee."[133]

The General received a constant stream of offers to write his biography, all which he diplomatically turned down. The following September 5, 1866, letter, to a New Yorker, illustrates the usual manner in which Lee handled these types of situations:

☞ "Dear Sir: I return you my thanks for the compliment paid me by your proposition to write a history of my life. It is a hazardous undertaking to publish the life of any one while living, and there are but few who would desire to read a true history of themselves. Independently of the few national events with which mine has been connected, it presents little to interest the general reader, nor do I know where to refer you for the necessary materials. All my private, as well as public, records have been destroyed or lost, except what is to be found in published documents, and I know of nothing available for the purpose. Should you, therefore, determine to undertake the work, you must rely upon yourself, as my time is so fully occupied that I am unable to promise you any assistance. Very respectfully, R. E. Lee."[134]

Lee continued to hand out fatherly advice to his son Robert, Jr., throughout the year 1866, particularly in regards to the boy's new farm. With his deep love for Nature, the land, and the agrarian life, the General naturally paid close attention to the many details of his son's occupation, as he does in this October 18 letter:

☞ "Am glad to hear that you are well and progressing favourably. Your Uncle Smith [the General's brother, Sydney Smith Lee] says, in a letter just received in which he writes of his difficulties and drawbacks, 'I must tell you that if you desire to succeed in any matter relating to agriculture you must personally superintend and see to everything.' Perhaps your experience coincides with his.

Winter view of Washington College, Lexington, Virginia. Now known as Washington and Lee University, General Lee served as president here from 1865 until his death in 1870, after which the school was renamed in his honor.

"I hope your wheat will reimburse you for your labour and guano [bird manure used for fertilizer]. I think you are right in improving your land. You will gain by cultivating less and cultivating that well, and I would endeavour to manure every crop—as to the kind of manure which will be the most profitable, you must experiment. Lime acts finely on your land, and is more lasting than guano. If you can, get shells to burn on your land, or, if not, shell lime from Baltimore. I think you would thereby more certainly and more cheaply restore your fields. . . ."[135]

Lee could not bear to be without his daughters, and when they were away he missed them terribly. Here is another letter he wrote to Mildred during her stay with family relations in Baltimore, Maryland. Dated January 27, 1867, the General is concerned that she is underweight, and warns her about partying, staying up late, and dressing and acting immoderately in public:

☞ "My Precious Daughter: Your letter to your mother gave us the satisfactory information of your continued good health, for I feared that your long silence had been caused by indisposition of body, rather than that due to writing. I hope you will not let so long an interval between your letters occur again, for you know I am always longing to hear from you, when I cannot see you, and a few lines, if only to say you are well, will prevent unpleasant apprehensions. I am delighted at your increased bodily dimensions, and your diminished drapery. One hundred and twenty-eight avoirdupois is approximately a proper standard. Seven more pounds will make you all right. But I fear before I see you the unnatural life, which I fear you will lead in Baltimore, will reduce you to skin and bone. Do not go out to many parties, preserve your simple tastes and manners, and you will enjoy more pleasure. Plainness and simplicity of dress, early hours, and rational amusements, I wish you to practise. . . . You must bear in mind that it will not be becoming in a Virginia girl now to be fine or fashionable, and that gentility as well as self-respect requires moderation in dress and gaiety. While her people are suffering, she should practise self-denial and show her sympathy in their affliction. . . ."[136]

In a February 16, 1867, letter to Mildred, the General writes:
☞ "Everybody seems anxious for your return, and is surprised you can stay so long from your papa."[137]

After Lincoln's War, the noble President Jefferson Davis was hunted down like a rabid dog and thrown in prison, where he spent two wretched years (without benefit of a trial) and nearly died due to the often brutal conditions. Upon his release, Lee wrote this June 1, 1867, letter to the great Confederate leader:
☞ "My Dear Mr. Davis: You can conceive better than I can express the

Another view of General Lee's Lexington, Virginia, campus home during his time at Washington College. The Lee family stayed in the house to the right while the larger one in the foreground was being completed.

misery which your friends have suffered from your long imprisonment, and the other afflictions incident thereto. To no one has this been more painful than to me, and the impossibility of affording relief has added to my distress. Your release has lifted a load from my heart which I have not words to tell. My daily prayer to the great Ruler of the world is that He may shield you from all future harm, guard you from all evil, and give you that peace which the world cannot take away. That the rest of your days may be triumphantly happy is the sincere and earnest wish of your most obedient, faithful friend and servant, R. E. Lee."[138]

This is an excerpt from an October 1867 letter to his son Robert, Jr.:
☞ "I am clear for your marriage, if you select a good wife. Otherwise, you had better remain as you are for a time. An improvident or uncongenial woman is worse than the minks [an animal considered a pest by Southern farmers]."[139]

This is a letter Lee wrote to his daughter Mary (or perhaps Mildred)[140] from Lexington, Virginia. It is dated December 21, 1867:

☞ "My Dearest Life: I was glad to learn through your letter that you were well and happy. I was pleased to find, too, that while enjoying the kindness of your friends we were not forgotten. Experience will teach you that, notwithstanding all appearances to the contrary, you will never receive such love as is felt for you by your father and mother: that lives through absence, difficulties, and times. I hope you will find time to read and improve your mind. Read history and works of truth—not novels and romances. Get correct views of life, and learn to see the world in its true light.

"We are getting on in the usual way. [Your sister] Agnes takes good care of us, and is always thoughtful and attentive. It is very cold. The ground is covered with six inches of snow, and the mountains, as far as the eye can reach, elevate their white crests as monuments of winter. I must leave to your sisters a description of all the gayeties, and also an account of the 'Reading Club.' As far as I can judge, it is a great institution for the discussion of apples and chestnuts, but is quite innocent of the pleasures of literature.

"Our feline companions are flourishing. Young Baxter is growing in gracefulness and favor, and gives cat-like evidences of future worth. He indulges in the fashionable color of 'moonlight on the lake'—apparently a dingy hue of the kitchen— and is strictly aristocratic in appearance and conduct. Tom, surnamed the 'Nipper' from the manner in which he slaughters our enemies the rats and mice, is admired for his gravity and sobriety, as well as his strict attention to the pursuits of his race. They both feel your absence sorely. Traveller and Custis are both well, and pursue their usual dignified gait and habits, not led away by the frivolous entertainments of lectures and concerts. . . .

"Think always of your father, who loves you dearly. R. E. Lee."[141]

Lee penned this agriculturally oriented letter to his son Robert, Jr., March 12, 1868:
☞ "My Dear Rob:—I am sorry to learn from your letter of the 1st that the winter has been so hard on your wheat. I hope, however, the present good weather is shedding its influence upon it, and that it will turn out better than it promises. You must take a lesson from the past season. What you do cultivate, do well. Improve and prepare the land

in the best manner; your labor will be less, and your profits more. Your flat lands were always uncertain in wet winters. The uplands were more sure. Is it not possible that some unbidden guest may have been feasting on your corn? Six hundred bushels is a large deficit in casting up your account for the year. But you must make it up by economy and good management. A farmer's motto should be *toil and trust*. I am glad that you have got your lime and sown your oats and clover. Do you use the drill, or sow broadcast?

"I shall try and get down to see you if I go to Richmond, for I am anxious to know how you are progressing and to see if I can in any way aid you. Whenever I can, you must let me know. You must still think about your house, and make up your mind as to the site and kind, and collect the material. I can help you to any kind of a plan, and with some ready money to pay the mechanics. . . .

"I have recently had a visit from Dr. Oliver, of Scotland, who is examining lands for immigrants from his country. He seems to be a sensible and judicious man. From his account, I do not think the Scotch and English would suit your part of the country. It would require time

Lee's office at the Chapel at Washington College, with his papers and furniture just as he left them. Many a frightened delinquent student was called into this office, only to be treated by the General in a warm, kind, and fatherly manner.

for them to become acclimated, and they would probably get dissatisfied, especially as there is so much mountainous region where they could be accommodated. I think you will have to look to the Germans; perhaps the Hollanders, as a class, would be the most useful. When the railroad shall have been completed to West Point, I think there will be no difficulty in getting whites among you. I would try and get some of our own young men in your employ. . . .

"I rode out the other day to Mr. Andrew Cameron's, and went into the field where he was ploughing. I took great pleasure in following the ploughs around the circuit. He had four in operation. Three of them were held by his former comrades in the army, who are regularly employed by him, and much, he says, to his satisfaction and profit. People have got to work now. It is creditable to them to do so; their bodies and their minds are benefitted by it, and those who can and will, will be advanced by it."[142]

After Lincoln's War, while Lee was serving as president of Washington College, one of the students died tragically in a boating accident. As head of the school it was the General's responsibility to contact the parents. These diplomatic and religious excerpts are from his March 19, 1868, letter:

☞ "My Dear Sir: Before this you have learned the affecting death of your son. I can say nothing to mitigate your grief or to relieve your sorrow; but if the sincere sympathy of his comrades and friends and of the entire community can bring you any consolation, I can assure you that you possess it in its fullest extent. When one, in the pureness and freshness of youth, before having been contaminated by sin or afflicted by misery, is called to the presence of his Merciful Creator, it must be solely for his good. As difficult as this may be for you now to recognise, I hope you will keep it constantly in your memory and take it to your comfort; and I pray that He who in His wise Providence has permitted this crushing sorrow may sanctify it to the happiness of all.

"Your son and his friend, Mr. Birely, often passed their leisure hours in rowing on the river, and, on last Saturday afternoon, the 4th inst., attempted what they had more than once been cautioned against—to approach the foot of the dam, at the public bridge. Unfortunately, their boat was caught by the return-current, struck by the falling water, and was immediately upset. Their perilous position was at once seen from the shore, and aid was hurried to their relief, but before it could reach them both had perished. Efforts to restore your son's life, though long continued, were unavailing. . . . With great regard and sincere sympathy, I am, most respectfully, R. E. Lee."[143]

This excerpt is from a letter Lee wrote from White Sulphur Springs, Virginia, to family members on August 28, 1868:
☞ ". . . The place looks beautiful—the belles very handsome, and the beaux very happy. All are gay, and only I solitary. I am all alone. There was a grand fancy masked ball last night. The room was overflowing, the music good, as much spring in the boards as in the conversation, and the german continued till two o'clock this morning. I return to the Hot [Springs] next week, and the following to Lexington. [Our daughter] Mildred is much better, but says she has forgotten how to write. I hope that she will be strong enough to return with me. . . . I am, truly and affectionately yours, R. E. Lee."[144]

One of the many homes of the Lee family, this one—which still stands—is located at 707 East Franklin, St., Richmond, Virginia. Having been cruelly evicted from their estate Arlington House by invading Yankee troops, Mrs. Lee and her daughters were forced to flee from house to house throughout the War. The homeless refugees stayed at the East Franklin St. residence above during the latter part of the conflict.

By the Fall of 1868 the General had begun to feel his mortality, as this somber sentence from a September letter to one of his sons reveals:
☞ "My life is very uncertain."[145]

This is an excerpt from a letter to Lee's son Fitzhugh, dated October 19, 1868:
☞ ". . . We shall look anxiously for your visit. Do not put it off too late or the weather may be unfavourable. Our mountain country is not the most pleasant in cold weather, but we will try and make you warm. Give my love to [your wife] Tabb, and tell her

I am wanting to see her all the time. All unite in love to her and you. Your mother is about the same, very busy, and full of work. Mildred is steadily improving, and is able to ride on horseback, which she is beginning to enjoy. Mary and Agnes very well.

"We see but little of [your brother] Custis. He has joined the mess at the institute, which he finds very comfortable, so that he rarely comes to our table to breakfast now. The rest of the time he seems to be occupied with his classes and studies. Remember me to [your brother] Rob. I hear of a great many weddings, but his has not been announced yet. He must not forget his house. I have not, and am going to take up the plan very soon. Mildred says a good house is an effective card in the matrimonial game. She is building a castle in the air. . . . I wish I could spend this month with you. That lower country is delightful to me at this season, and I long to be on the water again, but it cannot be. With much love, R. E. Lee."[146]

Once, when it was suggested to him that he invite his old nemesis, now U.S. president, Ulysses S. Grant to Washington College, where Lee was presiding as president, the General gave this January 8, 1869, reply:
☞ "I am much obliged to you for your letter of the 29th ult., which I am sure has been prompted by the best motives. I should be glad if General Grant would visit Washington College, and I should endeavour to treat him with the courtesy and respect due the President of the United States; but if I were to invite him to do so, it might not be agreeable to him, and I fear my motives might be misunderstood at this time, both by himself and others, and that evil would result instead of good. I will, however, bear your suggestion in mind, and should a favourable opportunity offer I shall be glad to take advantage of it. Wishing you happiness and prosperity, I am, very respectfully, your obedient servant, R. E. Lee."[147]

As mentioned, the Lee's beautiful home, Arlington House, was captured and illegally pillaged by Yankee soldiers in the Spring of 1861. In the mansion at the time had been numerous family heirlooms passed down from Lee's wife's great-grandmother Martha Washington, the wife of President George Washington. In early 1869 the Lee's began to petition the U.S. government for the return of these invaluable items. All of their entreaties were rejected, however, and the stolen objects remained the property of the U.S. government until they were generously restored to the family by order of President William McKinley in 1903. What follows are two letters the General wrote to several individuals regarding this subject in 1869:

☞ "Lexington, Virginia, February 12, 1869. . . . Mrs. Lee has determined to act upon your suggestion and apply to President [Andrew] Johnson for such of the relics from Arlington as are in the Patent Office. From what I have learned, a great many things formerly belonging to General [George] Washington, bequeathed to her by her father, in the shape of books, furniture, camp equipage, etc., were carried away by individuals [that is, Yankee soldiers] and are now scattered over the land. I hope the possessors appreciate them and may imitate the example of their original owners, whose conduct must at times be brought to their recollection by these silent monitors. In this way they will accomplish good to the country. . . ."[148]

From the same period, this letter is addressed to the Honourable George W. Jones of Dubuque, Iowa:

☞ ". . . In reference to certain articles which were taken from [our home] Arlington [House], about which you inquire, Mrs. Lee is indebted to our old friend Captain James May for the order from the present administration for their restoration to her. Congress, however, passed a resolution forbidding their return. They were valuable to her as having belonged to her great-grandmother (Mrs. General Washington), and having been bequeathed to her by her father [George Washington Parke Custis]. But as the country desires them, she must give them up. I hope their presence at the capital will keep in the remembrance of all Americans the principles and virtues of [President George] Washington. . . ."[149]

Robert E. Lee's wife, Mary Anne Randolph Custis, as she appeared in 1855. A talented painter, Mary suffered from rheumatoid arthritis and was confined to a wheelchair during her latter years.

A March 21, 1869, letter to his son Robert, Jr. contains these lines:
☞ ". . . We are all pretty well. Your mother has been troubled by a cold, but is over it I hope. The girls are well, and have as many opinions with as few acts as ever; and [your brother] Custis is so-so. . . . I am tolerable and wish I could get down to see you. . . . Give much love to . . . my daughter [-in-law] Tabb [Mary Tabb Bolling], and grandson [probably Mary's son, Robert E. Lee, III, born February 11, 1869]. I wonder what he will think of his grandpa. All unite in love, and I am, as always, your affectionate father, R. E. Lee."[150]

A letter to his wife, dated August 10, 1869:
☞ "My Dear Mary: I received this morning your *addenda* to Annie Wickham's letter inclosing Custis's. I also received by same mail a letter from Mr. Richardson, reiterating his request to insert my portrait in my father's Memoirs, saying that it was by the desire 'of many mutual friends' on the ground of its 'giving additional interest to the work, and increasing its sale.' That may or may not be so; at any rate, I differ from them. Besides, there is no good portrait accessible to him, and the engraving in the 'Lee Family' I think would be an injury to any book. His recent proposition of inserting my portrait where the family history is given takes from it a part of my obligation, and if it were believed that such an addition would add to the interest of the book, I should assent. I have so told him, and that I would write to you for your suggestions, and to ask whether you could send him a portrait worth inserting. What do you think?

"There is to be a grand concert here to-night for the benefit of our church at Lexington. It is gotten up by Miss Mary Jones and other kind people here, and the proposition is so favourably received that I hope a handsome sum will be realised.

"The girls are well. I do not know how long they will continue so. They seem to be foot-free. A great many visitors were turned off [that is, turned away] last night—no room for them! A grand ball in honour of Mr. Peabody is to come off to-morrow, after which it is supposed there will be more breathing-space. I have seen Mr. and Mrs. Charles Ridgely of 'Hampton' since I wrote, also numerous other acquaintances. I should prefer more quiet. How is my daughter [in-law] Tabb? Mother and son are improving, I trust. I hope you and Markie [a

General Robert E. Lee on his equally famous warhorse Traveller, an American Saddlebred. The General would often take the horse on long solitary rides out into the country or up into the mountains, not returning home until after dark. Born in 1857 in Greenbrier County, VA, (now WV), Traveller, like his master, survived Lincoln's War, and the two were inseparable up until the General's death in October 1870. Traveller, draped in black crepe, rode in Lee's funeral procession behind the casket. In early 1871, after Traveller trod on a rusty nail and developed tetanus, he was put down to alleviate his pain. Thus ended this unusually long and intimate relationship between a man and his horse.

cousin of the family, Martha Custis Williams] are also doing well. No change in myself as yet. The girls would send love if I could find them. Affectionately yours, R. E. Lee."[151]

From a December 2, 1869, letter to his son Fitzhugh:
☞ "I want to see you all very much, and think the sight of my daughter and grandson would do me good. I have had a wretched cold, the effects of which have not left me, but I am better. The doctors still have me in hand, but I fear can do no good. The present mild weather I hope will be beneficial, enabling me to ride and be in the open air. But Traveller's trot is harder to me than it used to be and fatigues me. We are all as usual—the women of the family very fierce and the men very mild. [Your brother] Custis has been a little unwell, but is well regulated by his sisters. Neither gaiety nor extravagance prevails amongst us, and the town is quiet."[152]

From a March 1870 letter comes this glimmer of hope of a brighter future:
☞ "My health has been so feeble this winter that I am only waiting to see the effect of the opening spring before relinquishing my present position [at Washington College]. I am admonished by my feelings that my years of labour are nearly over and my inclinations point to private life."[153]

From an April 11, 1870, from Savannah, Georgia, to his wife regarding his health problems:
☞ "As regards myself, my general health is pretty good. I feel stronger than when I came. The warm weather has also dispelled some of the rheumatic pains in my back, but I perceive no change in the stricture in my chest. If I attempt to walk beyond a very slow gait, the pain is always there. It is all true what the doctors say about its being aggravated by any fresh cold, but how to avoid taking cold is the question. It seems with me to be impossible. Everything and anything seems to give me one. I meet with much kindness and consideration, but fear that nothing will relieve my complaint, which is fixed and old. I must bear it."[154]

From Norfolk, Virginia, Lee wrote this newsy letter to his wife on May 7, 1870:
☞ "My Dear Mary: We have reached this point on our journey. Mrs. Harrison and Miss Belle are well and very kind, and I have been up to see Mr. William Harrison and Mr. George and their families. The former is much better than I expected to find him, and I hope will recover his health as the spring advances. The ladies are all well, and Miss Gulie is very handsome. Agnes and I went over to see Warrenton Carter and his wife this morning. They are both very well, and everything around them looks comfortable and flourishing. They have a nice home, and, as far as I could see, everything is prospering. Their little boy was asleep, but we were invited in to see him. He is a true Carter.

"Mrs. Page, the daughter of General Richardson, is here on a visit, and Mrs. Murdock, wife of their former pastor, arrived this morning. We are to go up to Mr. George Harrison's this evening, where the children are to have some tableaux, and where we are expected to spend the evening. In Norfolk we saw all our friends, but I did not succeed in getting out to Richard Page's as I desired, on account of the heavy rain on the appointed day and engagements that interfered on others. Agnes and Mrs. Selden rode out, however, and saw all the family. Everybody inquired kindly after you, down to Bryan, and all sent their love. 'Brandon' [the home of the Harrison family on the James River] is looking very beautiful, and it is refreshing to look at the river. The garden is filled with flowers and abounds in roses. The yellow jasmine is still in bloom and perfumes the atmosphere.

"I have not heard from you or from Lexington since I left Savannah. I hope all are well. I am better, I trust; am getting fat and big, but am still rigid and painful in my back. On Tuesday night I expect to go to 'Shirley' [the childhood home of the General's mother], and on Thursday, 12th inst., to Richmond, and on Friday to the 'White House' [one of the Lee family homes, this one on the Pamunkey River], unless I hear that you are crowded, in which case I will submit myself to the doctors for two or three days, as they desire, and then go down. Agnes now says she will accompany me to the 'White House,' so that I shall necessarily pass through Richmond, as our baggage renders that route necessary. Therefore, unless something unforeseen prevents, I shall be with you on Friday next. All unite in love. Agnes, I hope, is better than

In this photo of the Lee's Washington College campus home, the quarters of the General's horse Traveller can be seen next door (to the left), attached to the family's house by a covered passageway.

when she left Lexington, but is not strong. You must give a great deal of love to Fitzhugh, Tabb, my grandson Robert, and all with you. Most truly and affectionately, R. E. Lee."[155]

A July 2, 1870, letter to his wife reveals further deterioration of the General's health:

☞ "My Dear Mary: I reached here yesterday evening at 9:15 P.M. Found Mr. Tagart at the depot waiting for me, where he had been since eight o'clock, thanks to his having a punctual wife, who regulates everything for him, so that he had plenty of time for reflection. I believe, however, the delay was occasioned by change of schedule that day, of which Mrs. Tagart was not advised. We arrived at Alexandria at 5:00 P.M., and were taken to Washington and kept in the [railroad] cars till 7:45, when we were sent on. It was the hottest day I ever experienced, or I was in the hottest position I ever occupied, both on board the packet and in the railroad cars, or I was less able to stand it, for I never recollect having suffered so much.

"Dr. Buckler came in to see me this morning, and examined me, stripped, for two hours. He says he finds my lungs working well, the action of the heart a little too much diffused, but nothing to injure. He is inclined to think that my whole difficulty arises from rheumatic excitement, both the first attack in front of Fredericksburg and the second last winter. Says I appear to have a rheumatic constitution, must guard against cold, keep out in the air, exercise, etc., as the other physicians prescribe. He will see me again. In the meantime, he has told me to try lemon juice and watch the effect.

"I will endeavour to get out to Washington Peter's on the 4th and to Goodwood as soon as Dr. B_____ is satisfied. Mr. and Mrs. Tagart are very well and send regards. The messenger is waiting to take this to the office. It is raining, and I have not been out nor seen any one out of the house. I hope all are well with you, and regret that I was obliged to come away. Tell the girls I was so overcome that I could not get up this morning till 8:00 A.M. Give much love to everybody, and believe me most truly, R. E. Lee."[156]

From Hot Springs (Bath County), Virginia, Lee sent this playful August 23, 1870, letter to his daughter Agnes:

White Sulphur Springs, Greenbrier County, in what is now West Virginia, as it looked in July 1867. The health retreat was often visited by the Lees, who, in the Victorian fashion of the day, used its healing mineral-rich waters for soothing various ailments. Other 19th-Century guests of note included U.S. Presidents John Tyler, James Buchanan, Franklin Pierce, Millard Fillmore, and Martin Van Buren, as well as Dolly Madison, Davy Crockett, John C. Calhoun, Colonel Wade Hampton II, Daniel Webster, Francis Scott Key, and Henry Clay.

☞ "My Dear Agnes: I have received both of your letters, the last the 17th, and thank you for them as well as for your care of my room and clothes. The former I understand is used for a multiplicity of purposes, and the cats and kittens have the full run of my establishment. Guard me against 'Miss Selden' [one of the family kittens] I pray you.

"I am sorry that you are not with me, as it possibly may have benefited your neuralgia. But if Miss Belle is with you, I am sure she will be of greater service, and tell her she must remain till I come, that she may cure me. That you may have some other inducements than your flowers and weeds to take you out of doors, I will write to your mother to send for the horses as soon as she can make arrangements to have them cared for, and then you and Mildred and Miss Belle, the one on Traveller, the other on Lucy, can scour the country and keep us in eggs and chickens. I am sorry for the death of our good cow, but glad that she is out of misery. . . .

"I do not think any of your friends are here. Mr. Washington has been vibrating between this place and the Healing, but does not seem to be well. Miss Alman, from Salem, Massachusetts, whom you may recollect as having been at the White [House on the Pamunkey River] last summer, is here with her father and mother. Miss Mollie Jourdan left to-day, and Colonel Robert Preston arrived. The Chestnuts and Le Verts are still here. I hope that you are well and that all is well with you. When [your brother] Custis comes, ask him to see to the horses and the cow and that they are gently treated and properly fed. I know nothing of Henry's [a family servant] capacity in that way. I hope to be home next week and am very anxious to get back. Your father, R. E. Lee."[157]

The following is the General's last known letter to his wife (as of 1904). It was

written from Hot Springs, Virginia, on August 27, 1870:
☞ "My Dear Mary: I have received your letter of the 22d. I should remain here a week longer if time permitted, as I have felt in the last few days better than I have yet, but I am obliged to be in Staunton on the 30th, and therefore must leave Monday, 29th. I should not have time to return here. The college opens on September 15th, and I wish to see that all things are prepared. Possibly the little improvement now felt will continue. If not, I shall have to bear my malady. I am truly sorry to hear of [our cousin Confederate Lieutenant Colonel] Edwin [Grey] Lee's death. He was a true man, and, if health had permitted, would have been an ornament as well as a benefit to his race. He certainly was a great credit to the name. Give my sincere sympathy to his wife and family.

"You have never mentioned anything of Dr. Grahame. I have heard that he was in a critical condition. I saw Colonels Allan and Johnston. They only stayed a day, and went on to the White. I have heard of them on their return, and presume they will reach Lexington to-morrow. Mr. George Taylor, who has been a month at the White, arrived here to-day. Both he and his wife are well. The company is thinning, though arrivals occur daily. Mr. Middleton and his daughter and son, from Washington, whom you may recollect, also came. But I hope to see you so soon that I will defer my narrative.

"I am glad that [our daughter] Mary is enjoying herself and that [our son] Rob is so happy. May both long continue so. I will endeavour to get the muslin, but fear I shall not succeed. I trust I may not be detained in Staunton more than a day or two. In that event, you may expect me Thursday, September 1st, but I cannot say as to time. I hope that I shall find you all well. Give my love to [our children] Agnes and Mildred, and Custis, if he has arrived. Colonel Turner is very well. Tell his wife that he was exhibited to-day at the Healing as a specimen of the health of the Hot. In my last [letter] I gave you my views about the servants and sent you a check for _____, which I hope that you have received. Most truly and affectionately, R. E. Lee."[158]

This is the last known letter written by General Lee (as of 1904). It was written to his friend Samuel Tagart, of Baltimore, Maryland, on September 28, 1870:
☞ "My Dear Mr. Tagart: Your note of the 26th reached me this

morning, and see how easy it is to inveigle me into a correspondence. In fact, when a man desires to do a thing, or when a thing gives a man pleasure, he requires but small provocation to induce him to do it. Now I wanted to hear how you and Mrs. Tagart were, what you were doing, and how you had passed the summer, and I desired to tell you so. That is the reason I write. In answer to your question, I reply that I am much better. I do not know whether it is owing to having seen you and Doctor Buckler last summer, or to my visit to the Hot Springs. Perhaps both. But my pains are less, and my strength greater. In fact, I suppose I am as well as I shall be. I am still following Doctor B_____'s directions, and in time I may improve still more.

"I expect to have to visit Baltimore this fall, in relation to the Valley Railroad, and in that event I hope to see you, if you will permit me. I am glad to hear that you spent a pleasant summer. Colonel _____ and I would have had a more agreeable one had you been with us at the Hot [Springs], and as every place agrees so well with Mrs. Tagart, I think she could have enjoyed as good health there as at Saratoga, and we should have done better. Give my sincere regards to Mrs. Tagart, and remember me to all friends, particularly Mr. _____. Tell _____ his brother is well and handsome, and I hope that he will study, or his sweethearts in Baltimore will not pine for him long. Captain _____ is well and busy, and joins in my remembrances. Mrs. Lee and my daughters unite with me in messages to you and Mrs. Tagart, and I am most truly yours, R. E. Lee."[159]

A July 1867 sketch of the Lee's family cottage in "Baltimore Row," at the White Sulphur Springs health retreat in what was then part of Virginia.

3

NATURE

Like so many other Victorian Virginians, General Lee had a deep and abiding love for the natural world, and an authentic appreciation for the great outdoors, the changing seasons, and animals of all kinds. A true "country boy," he much preferred the quiet of the mountains, long winding country roads, and little villages to the hustle and bustle of big cities, where he was forced to spend most of his postwar years.

One of the many sketches of Robert E. Lee.

One of Lee's favorite pastimes was to take his loyal steed Traveller out alone for long rides into the countryside. These journeys would sometimes last for many hours, or even a full day, with him returning home at night under the moon and stars. Only the General himself knows what he thought about during these breathtaking but lonesome rides out into the wilds of Virginia.

Nowhere is Lee's mystical passion for Nature and animals more evident than in the following statement:

☞ "Traveller is my only companion; I may also say my pleasure. He and I, whenever practicable, wander out in the mountains and enjoy sweet confidence."[160]

Though by now fully enveloped in Lincoln's War, Lee still took time to appreciate the natural world, as he did in this August 4, 1861, letter to his wife from the battlefield:

☞ ". . . I travelled from Staunton on horseback. A part of the road, as far as Buffalo Gap, I passed over in the summer of 1840, on my return to St. Louis, after bringing you home. If any one had then told me that the next time I travelled that road would have been on my present errand, I should have supposed him insane. I enjoyed the mountains, as I rode along. The views are magnificent—the valleys so beautiful, the scenery so peaceful. What a glorious world Almighty God has given us. How thankless and ungrateful we are, and how we labour to mar his gifts."[161]

Another letter from this period, this one dated August 29, 1861, shows Lee in the field amidst blood, flooding rains, mud, damp, disease, and general misery. However, he notes in a letter to two of his daughters:

☞ "The mountains are magnificent. The sugar-maples are beginning to turn already, and the grass is luxuriant."[162]

On February 23, 1862, from Savannah, South Carolina, Lee paused just long enough between planning his battles to write the following to his wife:

☞ "Here the yellow jasmine, red-bud, orange-tree, etc., perfume the whole woods, and the japonicas and azaleas cover the garden."[163]

When General Lee became president of Washington College after Lincoln's War, part of his plan to resuscitate the school was to re-landscape the property. As such, he directed the planting of numerous trees on the front campus. A student once asked him why he had placed the trees so randomly across the yards, to which Lee replied:

☞ "Not in rows. Nature never plants trees in rows. As far as possible imitate Nature."[164]

When it came time to put a required fence up around the college, Lee bristled, saying to the workers:

☞ "A fence is a blot on any lawn. We must have a fence; but select a color which will render the fence as inconspicuous as possible: one that will harmonize with the surrounding colors."[165]

4

RELIGION

In his correspondences Lee mentions God, sin, prayer, and the Afterlife more than any other Confederate that I have studied. Intensely religious, or rather highly spiritual, a strong church-going Episcopalian throughout his life, and president of the Rockbridge Bible Society after the War,[166] this is not surprising. What follows are some examples of Lee's soulful religiosity.

Lee's monument at Gettysburg, Pennsylvania.

From the battlefield, this is an excerpt from a December 2, 1861, letter to his wife:

☞ "If [our children] Mary and Rob get to you Christmas, you will have quite a family party, especially if Fitzhugh is not obliged to leave his home and sweet wife before that time. I shall think of you all on that holy day more intensely than usual, and shall pray to the great God of Heaven to shower His blessings upon you in this world, and to unite you all in His courts in the world to come. With a grateful heart I thank Him for His preservation thus far, and trust to His mercy and kindness for the future. Oh, that I were more worthy, more thankful for all He has done and continues to do for me!"[167]

From a Christmas Day, 1861, letter to his wife:
☞ "I cannot let this day of grateful rejoicing pass, dear Mary, without some communication with you. I am thankful for the many among the past that I have passed with you, and the remembrance of them fills me with pleasure. For those on which we have been separated we must not repine. If it will make us more resigned and better prepared for what is in store for us, we should rejoice. Now we must be content with the many blessings we receive. If we can only become sensible of our transgressions, so as to be fully penitent and forgiven, that this heavy punishment under which we labour [that is, Lincoln's War] may with justice be removed from us and the whole nation, what a gracious consummation of all that we have endured it will be!"[168]

From Savannah, South Carolina, on February 8, 1862, Lee wrote this to his wife:
☞ ". . . I hope God will at last crown our efforts [against the Yankees] with success. But the contest must be long and severe, and the whole country has to go through much suffering. It is necessary we should be humbled and taught to be less boastful, less selfish, and more devoted to right and justice to all the world."[169]

In this March 2, 1862, letter to his daughter Anne, Lee connects the successes and failures of the Confederacy to the Christian morality of the Southern people:
☞ "I hope you are all well, and as happy as you can be in these perilous times to our country. They look dark at present, and it is plain we have not suffered enough, laboured enough, repented enough, to deserve success. But they will brighten after awhile, and I trust that a merciful God will arouse us to a sense of our danger, bless our honest efforts, and drive back our enemies to their homes.

"Our people have not been earnest enough, have thought too much of themselves and their ease, and instead of turning out to a man, have been content to nurse themselves and their dimes, and leave the protection of themselves and families to others. To satisfy their consciences, they have been clamorous in criticising what others have done, and endeavoured to prove that they ought to do nothing. This is not the way to accomplish our independence. I have been doing all I can with our small means and slow workmen to defend the cities and coast here. Against ordinary numbers we are pretty strong, but against the hosts our enemies seem able to bring everywhere[,] there is no calculating. But if our men will stand to their work, we shall give them trouble and damage them yet."¹⁷⁰

From a March 15, 1862, letter to his wife:
☛ "As I have done all in the matter that seems proper and right, I must now leave the rest in the hands of our merciful God."¹⁷¹

Washington College, now known as Washington and Lee University, where the General spent the last five years of his life.

From a July 9, 1862, letter to his wife:
☛ ". . . I have returned to my old quarters and am filled with gratitude to our Heavenly Father for all the mercies He has extended to us. Our success has not been so great or complete as we could have desired, but God knows what is best for us. Our enemy met with a heavy loss, from which it must take him some time to recover, before he can recommence his operations. . . ."¹⁷²

During the Battle of Fredericksburg (December 11-15, 1862), Lee added these final words to an order to Stonewall Jackson:
☛ "I am truly grateful to the Giver of all victory for having blessed us thus far in our terrible struggle. I pray He may continue it."¹⁷³

On Christmas Day 1862, Lee penned this to his wife:
☞ ". . . I will commence this holy day by writing to you. My heart is filled with gratitude to Almighty God for His unspeakable mercies with which He has blessed us in this day, for those He has granted us from the beginning of life, and particularly for those He has vouchsafed us during the past year. What should have become of us without His crowning help and protection? Oh, if our people would only recognise it and cease from vain self-boasting and adulation, how strong would be my belief in final success and happiness to our country! . . .

"I pray that, on this day when only peace and good-will are preached to mankind, better thoughts may fill the hearts of our enemies and turn them to peace. Our army was never in such good health and condition since I have been attached to it. I believe they share with me my disappointment that the enemy did not renew the combat on the 13th. I was holding back all day and husbanding our strength and ammunition for the great struggle, for which I thought I was preparing. Had I divined that was to have been his only effort, he would have had more of it. My heart bleeds at the death of every one of our gallant men."[174]

On the battlefield in the Spring of 1863, after two years of war against Lincoln's ruthless invaders, Lee issued the following spiritual encouragement to his men:
☞ "Soldiers! no portion of our people have greater cause to be thankful to Almighty God than yourselves. He has preserved your lives amidst countless dangers; He has been with you in all your trials; He has given you fortitude under hardships, and courage in the shock of battle; He has cheered you by the example and by the deeds of your martyred comrades; He has enabled you to defend your country successfully against the assaults of a powerful oppressor. Devoutly thankful for His signal mercies, let us bow before the Lord of Hosts, and join our hearts with millions in our land in prayer that He will continue His merciful protection over our cause; that He will scatter our enemies and set at naught their evil designs, and that he will graciously restore to our beloved country the blessings of peace and security."[175]

After Stonewall Jackson's death at the Battle of Chancellorsville (April 30-May 6, 1863), Lee wrote to his wife:

☛ "Any victory would be dear at such a price. His remains go to Richmond to-day. I know not how to replace him, but God's will be done. I trust He will raise up some one in his place."[176]

Before one of his many military engagements, Lee wrote to his wife at the end of May 1863:
☛ "I pray that our merciful Father in Heaven may protect and direct us! In that case, I fear no odds and no numbers."[177]

In June of 1863, during an encounter with Union forces in Virginia, Lee's son Fitzhugh was wounded. On June 11, 1863, the General wrote a letter to Fitzhugh's wife at that time, Charlotte (Wickham) Lee:[178]
☛ "I am so grieved, my dear daughter, to send Fitzhugh to you wounded. But I am so grateful that his wound is of a character to give us full hope of a speedy recovery. With his youth and strength to aid him, and your tender care to nurse him, I trust he will soon be well again. I know that you will unite with me in thanks to Almighty God, who has so often sheltered him in the hour of danger, for his recent deliverance, and lift up your whole heart in praise to Him for sparing a life so dear to us, while enabling him to do his duty in the station in which He had placed him. Ask him to join us in supplication that He may always cover him with the shadow of His almighty arm, and teach him that his only refuge is in Him, the greatness of whose mercy reacheth unto the heavens, and His truth unto the clouds. As some good is always mixed with the evil in this world, you will now have him with you for a time, and I shall look to you to cure him soon and send him back to me. . . ."[179]

The Lee family's Coat of Arms, of Coton Hall, County Salop, England. The family motto, written here in Latin, means "Not Unmindful of the Future." The crest and motto are now used by Washington and Lee University, Lexington, Virginia, where General Lee was president when it was known as Washington College.

While he was recovering, the General's son Fitzhugh was seized and imprisoned by the Yanks, prompting this letter from Lee to his wife in July 1863:
☞ "I have heard with great grief that Fitzhugh has been captured by the enemy. Had not expected that he would be taken from his bed and carried off, but we must bear this additional affliction with fortitude and resignation, and not repine at the will of God. It will eventuate in some good that we know not of now. We must bear our labours and hardships manfully. Our noble men are cheerful and confident. I constantly remember you in my thoughts and prayers."[180]

On July 12, 1863, Lee wrote to his wife from Hagerstown, Virginia:
☞ "The consequences of war are horrid enough at best, surrounded by all the ameliorations of civilisation and Christianity.... I am very sorry for the injuries done the family at Hickory Hill, and particularly that our dear old Uncle Williams, in his eightieth year, should be subjected to such treatment. But we cannot help it, and must endure it. You will, however, learn before this reaches you that our success at Gettysburg was not so great as reported—in fact, that we failed to drive the enemy from his position, and that our army withdrew to the Potomac. Had the river not unexpectedly risen, all would have been well with us; but God, in His all-wise providence, willed otherwise, and our communications have been interrupted and almost cut off.

"The waters have subsided to about four feet, and, if they continue, by to-morrow, I hope, our communications will be open. I trust that a merciful God, our only hope and refuge, will not desert us in this hour of need, and will deliver us by His almighty hand, that the whole world may recognise His power and all hearts be lifted up in adoration and praise of His unbounded loving-kindness. We must, however, submit to His almighty will, whatever that may be. May God guide and protect us all is my constant prayer."[181]

On July 15, 1863, following the terrible onslaught at the Battle of Gettysburg, Lee sent this to his wife:
☞ "... I hope we will yet be able to damage our adversaries when they meet us. That it should be so, we must implore the forgiveness of God for our sins, and the continuance of His blessings. There is nothing but His almighty power that can sustain us. God bless you all...."[182]

On July 26, 1863, Lee once again wrote to Fitzhugh's first wife Charlotte, this time with his Christian explanation of how to deal with the evil deeds of Lincoln's soldiers, who had recently "kidnaped" Fitzhugh:

☞ ". . . we must bear it, exercise all our patience, and do nothing to aggravate the evil. This, besides injuring ourselves, would rejoice our enemies and be sinful in the eyes of God. In His own good time He will relieve us and make all things work together for our good, if we give Him our love and place in Him our trust."[183]

In the summer of 1863, during the Great Religious Revival that was then sweeping through the Confederate armies, Lee issued the following, General Orders No. 83:

☞ "The President of the Confederate States has, in the name of the people, appointed August 21st as a day of fasting, humiliation, and prayer. A strict observance of the day is enjoined upon the officers and soldiers of this army. All military duties, except such as are absolutely necessary, will be suspended. The commanding officers of brigades and regiments are requested to cause divine services, suitable to the occasion, to be performed in their respective commands.

"Soldiers! we have sinned against Almighty God. We have forgotten His signal mercies, and have cultivated a revengeful, haughty, and boastful spirit. We have not remembered that the defenders of a just cause should be pure in His eyes; that 'our times are in His hands,' and we have relied too much on our own arms for the achievement of our independence. God is our only refuge and our strength. Let us humble ourselves before Him. Let us confess our many sins, and beseech Him to give us a higher courage, a purer patriotism, and more determined will; that He will convert the hearts of our

A drawing of General Lee wearing his colonel's uniform. Confederate generals wore four stars on their collar, but modest Lee bucked the trend.

enemies; that He will hasten the time when war, with its sorrows and sufferings, shall cease, and that He will give us a name and place among the nations of the earth. R. E. Lee, General."[184]

From a December 3, 1863, letter to his wife Mary:
☞ "I believe a kind God has ordered all things for our good."[185]

On December 26, 1863, Fitzhugh's (first) wife Charlotte (Wickham) Lee suddenly passed away from sickness.[186] General Lee, who had loved Charlotte like his own daughter, asked Union General Benjamin "the Beast" Butler if Fitzhugh could be released from prison for 48 hours to see to her burial. In exchange, another one of the General's sons, Custis, would take Fitzhugh's place. Butler, of course, cruelly refused (Fitzhugh would not return home from prison until April 1864), prompting a thoroughly distraught General Lee to write the following to his wife on the 27th. Bear in mind that Fitzhugh had now lost both of his children and his wife to illness (probably typhoid fever):
☞ "Custis's despatch which I received last night demolished all the hopes, in which I had been indulging during the day, of dear Charlotte's recovery. It has pleased God to take from us one exceedingly dear to us, and we must be resigned to His holy will. She, I trust, will enjoy peace and happiness forever, while we must patiently struggle on under all the ills that may be in store for us. What a glorious thought it is that she has joined her little cherubs [her two children, Robert E. Lee, III, and Charlotte Carter Lee, had both passed away earlier as infants] and our angel [the General's daughter] Annie in Heaven [Anne had died a year earlier on October 20, 1862]. Thus is link by link the strong chain broken that binds us to earth, and our passage soothed to another world.

"Oh, that we may be at last united in that heaven of rest, where trouble and sorrow never enter, to join in an everlasting chorus of praise and glory to our Lord and Saviour! I grieve for our lost darling [Charlotte] as a father only can grieve for a daughter, and my sorrow is heightened by the thought of the anguish her death will cause our dear son [Fitzhugh] and the poignancy it will give to the bars of his [Yankee] prison. May God in His mercy enable him to bear the blow He has so suddenly dealt, and sanctify it to his everlasting happiness!"[187]

An excerpt from Lee's letter to a cousin, Margaret Stuart, on April 28, 1864:

☞ "I dislike to send letters within reach of the enemy, as they might serve, if captured, to bring distress on others. But you must sometimes cast your thoughts on the Army of Northern Virginia, and never forget it in your prayers. It is preparing for a great struggle, but I pray and trust that the great God, mighty to deliver, will spread over it His almighty arms, and drive its enemies before it."[188]

On June 30, 1864, Lee wrote to his wife in commemoration of their thirty-third anniversary:
☞ "Do you recollect what a happy day thirty-three years ago this was? How many hopes and pleasures it gave birth to! God has been very merciful and kind to us, and how thankless and sinful I have been. I pray that He may continue His mercies and blessings to us, and give us a little peace and rest together in this world, and finally gather us and all He has given us around His throne in the world to come."[189]

Near the end of Lincoln's War Lee was asked how he felt about the conflict, if he was satisfied with "the result," to which he replied:
☞ "At present I am not concerned with results. God's will ought to be our aim, and I am quite contented that His designs should be accomplished and not mine."[190]

Once, after the War, a minister happened to make some deprecating remarks about Yankees and their indictment of the General for "treason." Lee replied:
☞ "Doctor, there is a good book, which I read and you preach from, which says: 'Love your enemies, bless them that curse you, do good to them that hate you and pray for them that spitefully use you.'"[191]

On April 11, 1867, after the death of a male relative, Lee wrote this to the grief stricken widow:
☞ "It is the survivors of the sad event whom I commiserate, and not him whom a gracious God has called to himself; and whose tender

An engraving of General Lee as he appeared during Lincoln's War.

heart and domestic virtues make the pang of parting the more bitter to those who are left behind. . . . For what other purpose can a righteous man be summoned into the presence of a merciful God than to receive his reward? However, then, we lament we ought not to deplore him, or wish him back from his peaceful happy home. . . .

"Mrs. Lee and my daughters, while they join in unfeigned sorrow for your bereavement, unite with me in sincere regards, and fervent prayers to Him who can alone afford relief, for His gracious support, and continued protection to you. May His abundant mercies be showered upon you, and may His almighty arm guide and uphold you."[192]

Few statements capture Lee's religiosity more than the following, from one of his personal letters:
☞ "We are all in the hands of a kind God, who will do for us what is best, and more than we deserve, and we have only to endeavor to deserve more and to do our duty to Him and to ourselves. May we all deserve His mercy, His care, and His protection."[193]

As is still traditional across the South, Lee's favorite book was the Bible. Here is what he said about it:
☞ "It is a book which supplies the place of all others, and one that cannot be replaced by any other."[194]

After the War, General Lee, an Episcopalian, was approached by a Baptist youngster who said: "I wish you were a member of my church, so you could be my Sunday School teacher." Charmed, Lee replied with a beaming smile:
☞ "Son, we must all try and be good Christians—this is the most important thing."[195]

Words of spiritual wisdom from a May 21, 1867, letter:
☞ "I know that in pursuing the path dictated by prudence and wisdom, and in endeavouring honestly to accomplish only what is right, the darkness which overshadows our political horizon will be dissipated, and the true course to pursue will, as we advance, become visible and clear."[196]

Another view of the Lee's campus home at Washington College, Lexington, Virginia.

While president of Washington College, Lee spoke to a faculty member concerning the school's students, saying:
☞ "I shall be disappointed,—I shall fail in the leading object that brought me here, unless these young men all become consistent Christians."[197]

During a faculty meeting at Washington College one of the non-church-going members gave a speech on how to coerce students into attending chapel. Afterward, General Lee, who was against forced attendance, said:
☞ "The best way that I know of to induce students to attend is to set them the example of always attending ourselves."[198]

Lee penned this letter to his son Fitzhugh on June 8, 1867:
☞ "I . . . can anticipate for you many years of happiness and prosperity, and in my daily prayers to the God of mercy and truth I invoke His choicest blessings upon you. May He gather you under the shadow of His almighty wing, direct you in all your ways, and give you peace and everlasting life. It would be most pleasant to my feelings could I again, as you propose, gather you all around me, but I fear that will not be in this world. Let us all so live that we may be united in that world where there is no more separation, and where sorrow and pain never come."[199]

Shortly after his brother Sydney Smith Lee's death on July 22, 1869, the General ended a July 25 letter to his wife with these words:
☞ "May God bless us all and preserve us for the time when we, too, must part, the one from the other, which is now close at hand, and may we all meet again at the footstool of our merciful God, to be joined by His eternal love never more to separate."[200]

Before a trip south for health reasons, Lee wrote the following in a March 22, 1870, letter to his son Fizthugh:
☞ "I shall go first to Warrenton Springs, North Carolina, to visit the grave of my dear [daughter] Annie, where I have always promised myself to go, and I think, if I am to accomplish it, I have no time to lose. I wish to witness her quiet sleep, with her dear hands crossed over her breast, as it were in mute prayer, undisturbed by her distance from us, and to feel that her pure spirit is waiting in bliss in the land of the blessed."[201]

Confederate artillery holding off Yankee invaders in Virginia in the Summer of 1864.

From Savannah, Georgia, Lee wrote this letter on April 18, 1870, after visiting the original burial site of his father, Revolutionary War hero and Virginia Governor, Henry "Light Horse" Lee:
☞ "We visited Cumberland Island, and [our daughter] Agnes decorated my father's grave with beautiful fresh flowers. I presume it is the last time I shall be able to pay it my tribute of respect. The cemetery is unharmed and the graves are in good order, though the house of 'Dungeness' has been burned and the island devastated. I hope I am better. I know that I am stronger, but I still have the pain in my chest whenever I walk. I have felt it, too, occasionally recently when quiescent."[202]

5

THE UNION AND SECESSION

Lee as he looked while serving as captain of the U.S. engineer's corps, beginning in 1838.

Lee—like Jefferson Davis, Alexander H. Stephens, Nathan Bedford Forrest, and nearly every other Southerner of note—had an undying love for the Union and was, at first, vehemently against the secession of the Southern states. Indeed, he believed that maintaining the Union was far more important than anything else, including Southern slavery.[203] This chapter examines some of General Lee's thoughts on the United States and the constitutional right of secession.

Here, on January 23, 1861, on the eve of Lincoln's War, is what then U.S. Colonel Lee wrote to his wife from Texas, where he was stationed at the time:
☞ "I received Everett's *Life of General Washington*, which you sent me, and enjoyed its perusal. How his spirit would be grieved could he see the wreck of his mighty labors! I will not, however, permit myself to believe, until all the ground for hope has gone, that the fruit of his noble deeds will be destroyed and that his precious advice and virtuous example will so soon be forgotten by his countrymen.

"As far as I can judge from the papers, we are between a state of anarchy and civil war. May God avert both of these evils from us! I fear that mankind for years will not be sufficiently Christianized to bear the absence of restraint and force. I see that four States have declared themselves out of the Union: four more will apparently follow their example. Then, if the Border States are brought into the gulf of revolution, one half of the country will be arrayed against the other. I must try and be patient and await the end, for I can do nothing to hasten or retard it."[204]

What follows are some excerpts from a January 23, 1861, letter from Fort Mason, Texas. Written to his son Fitzhugh, it expresses similar views:

☞ "The South, in my opinion, has been aggrieved by the acts of the North, as you say. I feel the aggression, and am willing to take every proper step for redress. It is the principle I contend for, not individual or private benefit."[205]

☞ "As an American citizen I take great pride in my country, her prosperity, and her institutions, and would defend any State if her rights were invaded. But I can anticipate no greater calamity for the country than a dissolution of the Union. It would be an accumulation of all the evils we complain of, and I am willing to sacrifice everything but honor for its preservation. I hope, therefore, that all constitutional means will be exhausted before there is a resort to force."[206]

☞ "Secession is nothing but revolution. The framers of our Constitution never exhausted so much labor, wisdom, and forbearance in its formation, and surrounded it with so many guards and securities, if it was intended to be broken by every member of the Confederacy at will. It is intended for 'perpetual union,' so expressed in the preamble, and for the establishment of a government, not a compact, which can only be dissolved by revolution or the consent of all the people in convention assembled."[207]

☞ "It is idle to talk of secession. Anarchy would have been established, and not a government, by Washington, Hamilton, Jefferson, Madison, and all the other patriots of the Revolution."[208]

☞ "... a Union that can only be maintained by swords and bayonets, and in which strife and civil war are to take the place of brotherly love and kindness, has no charm for me."[209]

☞ "[If Virginia secedes] I shall mourn for my country and for the welfare and progress of mankind. If the Union is dissolved and the Government disrupted, I shall return to my native State and share the miseries of my people, and save in defence will draw my sword on none."[210]

At the start of the "Civil War," U.S. President Abraham Lincoln offered the position of general-in-chief of all Union armies to Lee. Lee, of course, turned it down, and went on to serve as both general-in-chief and commander-in-chief of all Confederate States armies. Anti-South proponents, however, such as Lincoln's Secretary of War Simon Cameron, began spreading the rumor that Lee had actually sought the original Yankee command offered by Lincoln. Years later, on February 25, 1868, Lee responded strongly to this fiction in a letter to Reverdy Johnson:

Lee fighting Indians in the American southwest in the mid 1850s.

☞ "My Dear Sir: My attention has been called to the official report of the debate in the Senate of the United States, on the 19th instant, in which you did me the kindness to doubt the correctness of the statement made by the Honourable Simon Cameron, in regard to myself. I desire that you may feel certain of my conduct on the occasion referred to, so far as my individual statement can make you.

"I never intimated to any one that I desired the command of the United States Army; nor did I ever have a conversation with but one gentleman, Mr. Francis Preston Blair, on the subject, which was at his invitation, and, as I understood, at the instance of President Lincoln.

After listening to his remarks, I declined the offer he made me, to take command of the army that was to be brought into the field; stating, as candidly and as courteously as I could, that, though opposed to secession and deprecating war, I could take no part in an invasion of the Southern States. I went directly from the interview with Mr. Blair to the office of General Scott; told him of the proposition that had been made to me, and my decision.

"Upon reflection after returning to my home, I concluded that I ought no longer to retain the commission I held in the United States Army, and on the second morning thereafter I forwarded my resignation to General Scott. At the time, I hoped that peace would have been preserved; that some way would have been found to save the country from the calamities of war; and I then had no other intention than to pass the remainder of my life as a private citizen. Two days afterward, upon the invitation of the Governor of Virginia, I repaired to Richmond; found that the Convention then in session had passed the ordinance withdrawing the State from the Union; and accepted the commission of commander of its forces, which was tendered me.

"These are the simple facts of the case, and they show that Mr. Cameron has been misinformed. I am with great respect, your obedient servant, R. E. Lee."[211]

When Lee was begged by Union officials not to resign from the U.S. armed forces and join the Southern Confederacy, he replied:
☞ "I am compelled to: I cannot consult my own feelings in this matter."[212]

Lee sent his letter of resignation from the U.S. army to General Winfield Scott on April 20, 1861. It reads:
☞ "General: Since my interview with you on the 18th instant I have felt that I ought not longer to retain my commission in the army. I therefore tender my resignation, which I request you will recommend for acceptance. It would have been presented at once, but for the struggle it has cost me to separate myself from a service to which I have devoted the best years of my life and all the ability I possessed.

"During the whole of that time, more than a quarter of a century, I have experienced nothing but kindness from my superiors and

Lee (second from right) commanding the successful takedown of Yankee lunatic John Brown at Harper's Ferry on October 17, 1859. Brown's attempt to start a slave insurrection in the South was so absurd that even Lincoln and black leader Frederick Douglass scoffed at it. Not a single Southern servant left his home to follow Brown and there were no slave riots during the entire "Civil War." In fact, the first victim of the senseless raid was Heyward Shepard, a black man who Brown viciously murdered because he refused to join his gang of outlaws. Despite Brown's failure and his execution shortly thereafter, his sectional hatred spread across the North like wildfire, helping to ignite the flames of Lincoln's War a year and a half later. It was all pointless, however. At the start of conflict only 4.8 percent of Southerners owned slaves (note that a great many of Dixie's slave owners were black and Native-American), while Virginia, the site of Brown's attack, was the birthplace of the American abolition movement, a state where its residents, like Lee, Jefferson, and Washington, had been planning the inevitable destruction of slavery for nearly one-hundred years.

a most cordial friendship from my comrades. To no one, general, have I been as much indebted as to yourself for uniform kindness and consideration, and it has always been my ardent desire to merit your approbation. I shall carry to the grave the most grateful recollections of your kind consideration, and your name and fame will always be dear to me.

"Save in the defence of my native State, I never desire again to draw my sword. Be pleased to accept my most earnest wishes for the continuance of your happiness and prosperity, and believe me most truly yours, R. E. Lee."[213]

Upon being appointed commander-in-chief of Virginia's military forces by the governor of Virginia, John Letcher, on April 23, 1861, Lee was presented with his commission by John Janney, president of the Virginia Convention. Lee responded in his typically humble manner:

☞ "Deeply impressed with the solemnity of the occasion on which I appear before you, and profoundly grateful for the honour conferred upon me, I accept the position your partiality has assigned me, though I would greatly have preferred your choice should have fallen on one more capable.

"Trusting to Almighty God, an approving conscience, and the aid of my fellow-citizens, I will devote myself to the defense and service of my native State, in whose behalf alone would I have ever drawn my sword."[214]

A portrait of Confederate Generals (from left to right) Thomas J. "Stonewall" Jackson, Joseph E. Johnston, and Robert E. Lee. Until Jackson's untimely death on May 10, 1863, the trio fought closely together in an attempt to repel Lincoln's illegal interlopers. After he was wounded at the Battle of Seven Pines and his command was turned over to Lee, Johnston had a particularly but inadvertently large impact on the outcome of the War. Just prior to the Battle of Atlanta on July 22, 1864, Johnston's strategies came to displease President Davis, who replaced him with someone unequal to the task: the author's cousin, Confederate General John Bell Hood. Hood went on to lose Atlanta, which not only rekindled war fever and anti-South sentiment in the North, but helped Lincoln get reelected for a second term. Hood then inexplicably broke off from Sherman (whom he was supposed to drive from the region) to pursue Union General John M. Schofield north into Tennessee. There Hood lost consecutively at the Battles of Columbia, Spring Hill, Franklin II, and finally Nashville (December 15-16, 1864). With the Army of Tennessee in tatters, it was chased southward into Mississippi by Yankee troops. Hood was relieved of his command and demoted, and Confederate strength in the Western theater came to an end. Lee's "surrender" at Appomattox came less than four months later.

6

THE CAUSE AND PURPOSE OF THE WAR

While pro-North writers delight in perpetuating the lie that the "Civil War" was fought over slavery, the educated know better. For one thing, both President Lincoln and President Davis themselves repeatedly denied this claim: the former said the North fought to "preserve the Union,"[215] while the latter stated that the South fought for "constitutional liberty"[216]—a phrase used by General Lee's family as well.[217] This chapter contains examples of Lee's views regarding the causes leading up to the War.

Years before Lincoln's unconstitutional War fell like a dark cloud upon the land, Lee was already highly aware of the ominous signs coming from his meddlesome neighbors to the North. Here, for instance, in a December 27, 1856, letter from Texas, is what the General had to

Lee's campaign in Western Virginia.

say about the Yankees' plans to abolish slavery across the South:

☞ "I have just received the *Alexandria Gazette* from the 20th of November to the 18th of December, inclusive. Besides the usual good reading matter, I am interested in the relation of local affairs, and infer from the quiet and ordinary course of events that all is going on well, especially (I hope) at Arlington.

"The steamer also brought the President's [Franklin Pierce] Message, the reports of the various heads of departments, etc., so that we are assured that the Government is in operation and the Union in existence. . . . I was much pleased with the President's Message. His views of the systematic and progressive efforts of certain people at the North to interfere with and change the domestic institutions of the South are truthfully and faithfully expressed. The consequences of their plans and purposes are also clearly set forth. These people must be aware that their object is both unlawful and foreign to them and to their duty, and that this institution, for which they are irresponsible and non-accountable, can only be changed by them through the agency of a civil and servile war."²¹⁸

A Union battery at the Battle of Gettysburg.

During John Brown's insane attempt to start a slave insurrection in Virginia, he found himself in an engine house, surrounded by Lee, then a U.S. army colonel, and his men. With Brown's group were a number of innocent hostages who he threatened to kill if he was not allowed to escape. Among the hostages was a brave U.S. army officer, Colonel Lewis Washington of Virginia, who, during the heated exchange between Lee and Brown, yelled out to Lee from inside the engine house: "Never mind us—fire!" Colonel Washington's display of Southern courage and righteousness prompted Lee to turn to a subordinate and say:

☞ "The old Revolutionary blood does tell."²¹⁹

Lee was able to defeat Brown using a lightning fast "shock and awe" attack, as he notes in his memorandum book from the period:

☞ "October 17, 1859. Received orders from the [then U.S.] Secretary of War [John Buchanan Floyd] in person,[220] to repair in evening train to Harper's Ferry. Reached Harper's Ferry at 11 P.M. . . . Posted marines in the United States Armory. Waited until daylight, as a number of citizens were held as hostages, whose lives were threatened. Tuesday about sunrise, with twelve marines, under Lieutenant Green, broke in the door of the engine-house, secured the insurgents, and relieved the prisoners unhurt. All the insurgents killed or mortally wounded, but four, John Brown, Stevens, Coppie, and Shields."[221]

In a February 10, 1866, letter, Lee refers to the true purpose for which the South fought:

☞ ". . . my countrymen, who struggled for constitutional government."[222]

Lee felt that Lincoln's illegal War was one that could and should have been averted:

☞ "I did believe at the time that it was an unnecessary condition of affairs and might have been avoided if forbearance and wisdom had been practised on both sides."[223]

During Lincoln's War General Lee was fond of riding up to the front lines to survey the battle, which always horrified his adoring troops. Fearing for his life and wishing to protect him, they would grab his horse and yell out, "Lee to the rear!", as shown in this illustration depicting the Battle of the Wilderness, May 5-7, 1864.

Generals Robert E. Lee and Stonewall Jackson confer during operations near Chancellorsville, Virginia, in May 1863. Jackson would be shot down by friendly fire just days later. After the great commander's death on May 10, a sorrowful Lee told his troops: "Let officers and soldiers emulate his invincible determination to do everything in the defense of our beloved country."

7
SLAVERY

General Lee, like nearly 96 percent of other Southerners, was a non-slave owner who detested the institution and wished to rid Dixie of it as soon as possible. By trying to force the South to liberate her slaves before the complex details of emancipation could be worked out, Lincoln and his meddlesome overbearing Northern constituents interrupted the delicate process of Southern abolition—particularly in Lee's home state, Virginia, the cradle of the American abolition movement.

A born humanitarian, General Lee had nothing but disdain for slavery. He saw it, like fellow Virginian Thomas Jefferson, as a wolf that has been caught by the ears and can neither be safely held or let go;[224] an institution that had been inherited from their ancestors, who in turn had it forced on the original thirteen American colonies by the English monarchy in the 1600s.[225]

As a Southerner, Lee had every right to be offended by the American slave trade and American slavery: both had begun in the North, the former in Massachusetts in 1638, the latter in Massachusetts in 1641.[226] From the Bay State, the Yankee's "peculiar institution" propagated riotously across the Northeastern states, finally enveloping nearly all of them, including Rhode Island, Pennsylvania, Maryland, Connecticut,[227] and even our nation's capital city, Washington, D.C., where one of America's largest slave marts existed, operating in full view of the Congress right up until the middle of the "Civil War,"[228] when Lincoln reluctantly issued the District of Columbia Emancipation Act (a document that included his plan to deport all of Washington's freed blacks to colonies in Africa and South America).[229]

Slavery only found its way South when it was pushed there by the racist white North after it finally found the presence of blacks "intolerable"[230] and the institution unprofitable (due to the rocky sandy soil, small farms, and long harsh winters of the Northeast).[231] By forcing it southward, Northern businessmen, who owned and operated the entire American slavery system at the time, were hoping to continue reaping the enormous monetary benefits of slavery while not having to deal with black slaves themselves.[232] In this way, American slavery, originally the Yankees' "peculiar institution," was foisted on the South against her will.[233] It is little wonder that Lee and most other Southerners—only 4.8 percent who owned slaves at the start of the "Civil War"—hated slavery and wished to be rid of it.[234]

In a letter dated December 27, 1856, Lee writes:
☞ "There are few, I believe, in this enlightened age, who will not acknowledge that slavery as an institution is a moral and political evil in any country. It is useless to expatiate on its disadvantages. I think it a greater evil to the white than to the black race.

"While my feelings are strongly enlisted in behalf of the latter, my sympathies are more strong for the former. The blacks are immeasurably better off here than in Africa, morally, physically, and socially. The painful discipline they are undergoing is necessary for their further instruction as a race, and I hope will prepare them for better things. How long their servitude may be necessary is known and ordered by a merciful Providence. Their emancipation will sooner result from the mild and melting influences of Christianity, than from the storms and tempests of fiery controversy. This influence, though slow, is sure. The doctrines and miracles of our Saviour have required nearly two thousand years to convert but a small portion of the human race, and even among Christian nations what gross errors still exist."[235]

At the start of Lincoln's War, Lee told Francis Preston Blair, Sr.:
☞ "If I owned the four millions of slaves [in the South], I would cheerfully sacrifice them to the preservation of the Union, but to lift my hand against my own state and people is impossible."[236]

Lee had warm personal relationships with his family's black servants, as the following March 9, 1866, postwar letter reveals. It is from Lee to one of his house servants, Amanda Parks, who he had freed even before Lincoln issued his duplicitous Final Emancipation Proclamation on January 1, 1863. Amanda had tried, unsuccessfully, to visit the General while he was at Washington, D.C. in February 1866, prompting this reply:

☞ "Amanda: I have received your letter of the 27th ult., and regret very much that I did not see you when I was in Washington. I heard on returning to my room, Sunday night, that you had been to see me; and I was sorry to have missed you, for I wished to learn how you were, and how all the people [that is, the Lee family servants] from Arlington were getting on in the world. My interest in them is as great now as it ever was, and I sincerely wish for their happiness and prosperity.

"At the period specified in [my wife's father] Mr. Custis's will—five years from the time of his death [October 10, 1857]—I caused the liberation of all the people at Arlington [House], as well as those at the White House and Romancoke, to be recorded in the Hustings Court at Richmond; and letters of manumission to be given to those with whom I could communicate who desired them. In consequence of the war which then existed, I could do nothing more for them.

The title of this wonderful 19th-Century illustration is "Lee reconnoitering at Thoroughfare Gap."

"I do not know why you should ask if I am angry with you. I am not aware of your having done anything to give me offense, and I hope you would not say or do what was wrong. While you lived at Arlington [House] you behaved very well, and were attentive and faithful to your duties. I hope you will always conduct yourself in the same manner. Wishing you health, happiness, and success in life, I am truly, R. E. Lee."[237]

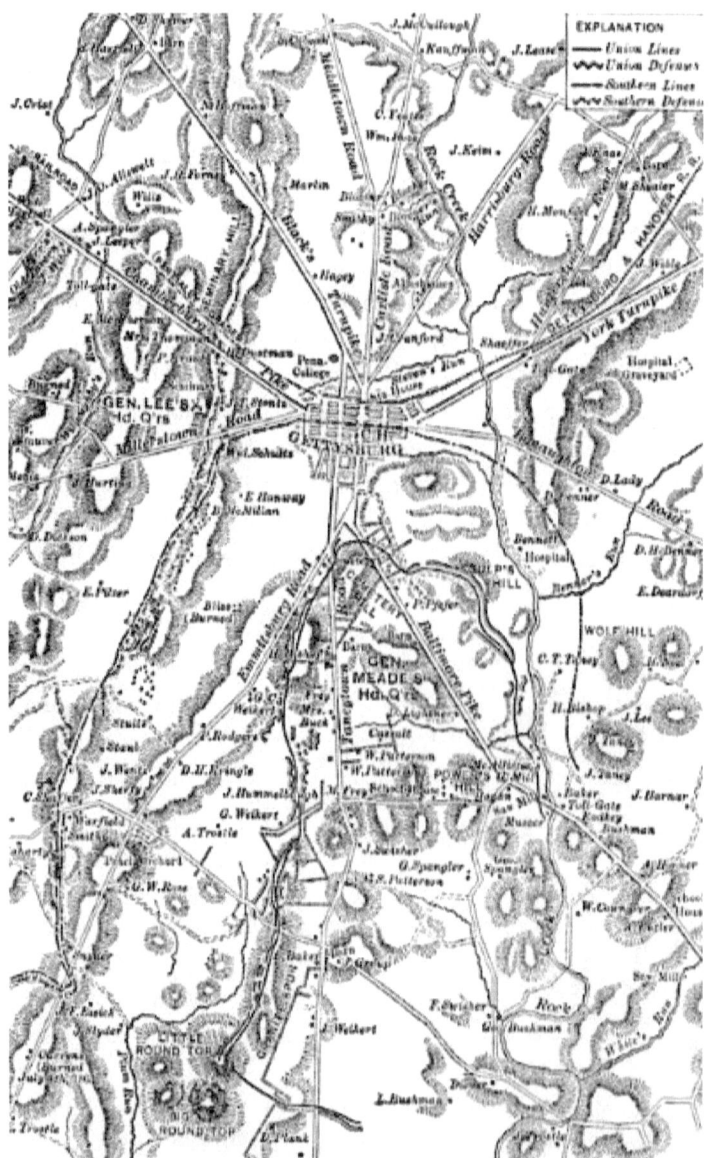

A map of the Battle of Gettysburg, July 1-3, 1863. Lee's loss here was a major turning point in Lincoln's War.

8
ABOLITION

As far back as his records go, it will be seen that General Lee was an abolitionist. This is not surprising: his home state, Virginia, was the veritable birthplace of the American abolition movement,[238] with native sons like George Washington, Thomas Jefferson, Fernando Fairfax, and George Mason, pushing for abolition as early as the late 1700s.[239] Contrary to Yankee mythology, Lee, an ardent member of this school, was joined by a majority of not only other Virginians, but other Southerners as well—nearly all who wished to see slavery abolished as soon as possible.[240]

Lee on his warhorse Traveller at the Battle of Gettysburg in the Summer of 1863.

The following excerpt from a December 27, 1856, letter is a fine example of Lee's thoughts on abolition:

☞ "While we see the course of the final abolition of human slavery is still onward, and give it the aid of our prayers, let us leave the progress as well as the results in the hand of Him who sees the end, who chooses to work by slow influences, and with whom a thousand years are but as a single day.

"Although the Abolitionist must know this—must know that he has neither the right nor the power of operating, except by moral means; that to benefit the slave he must not excite angry feelings in the master; that, although he may not approve the mode by which Providence accomplishes its purpose, the results will be the same; and that the reasons he gives for interference in matters he has no concern with holds good for every kind of interference with our neighbor,—still, I fear he will persevere in his evil course."[241]

I can find no record of Lee purchasing or selling slaves. In fact, as has been widely known across the South for generations, the General's immediate family did not personally own slaves, but instead had an assortment of black servants at their homes and farms they had inherited from their parents and grandparents.[242] All were treated humanely, fairly, and, as was the custom across the South, often like members of the Lee family, particularly the house servants. In 1862, five years after the death (on October 10, 1857) of Lee's wife's father George Washington Parke Custis, the General, who had been made the executor of Mr. Custis' will, immediately set about emancipating the family servants (who had originally belonged to Mr. Custis) as was set out in that document. Thus it is clear that the entire Lee clan was discussing personal abolition in their own household at least five years before the start of Lincoln's War, and that their servants were emancipated four months before Lincoln issued his fake and illegal Final Emancipation Proclamation (on January 1, 1863). What follows are excerpts from Lee's letters concerning this subject. The first is from December 16, 1862:

☛ ". . . As regards the liberation of the people [that is, the Lee family servants], I wish to progress in it as far as I can. Those hired in Richmond can still find employment there if they choose. Those in the country can do the same or remain on the farms. I hope they will all do well and behave themselves. I should like, if I could, to attend to their wants and see them placed to the best advantage. But that is impossible. All that choose can leave the State before the war closes. . . ."[243]

From a January 8, 1863, letter, Lee writes:
☛ ". . . I executed the deed of manumission sent me by Mr. Caskie, and returned it to him. I perceived that [our servants] John Sawyer and

The Battle of the Crater, July 30, 1864, pitted General Lee against Union General Ambrose E. Burnside. The Confederates won, but for a humanitarian like Lee it was a sad and hollow victory: when countless numbers of black Yankee soldiers were driven back into a thirty-foot deep bomb crater by the Rebels, they were ruthlessly bayoneted by their racist white Yankee comrades, who had said previously that they would not be "caught in the company of niggers." Afterward, Burnside's white troops bragged lustfully of the murders. Some 1,327 black Union soldiers were killed during the Battle of the Crater, the largest single loss of Federal African-Americans during the entire War—due in great part to the racism of Lincoln's white troops. General Grant later called it the "saddest affair" of the Civil War. Not because his white soldiers had mercilessly slaughtered their black brothers, but because Burnside lost a total of 4,000 men against Lee's 1,500. Lincoln led the way in intensifying white racism throughout his Northern armies by racially segregating his units, using black soldiers as shock troops, and paying blacks half that of their white associates. He also denied his black soldiers pensions, bonuses, support for dependents, and proper medical care, all which were provided to white Union soldiers.

James's names, among the Arlington [House] people, had been omitted, and inserted them. I fear there are others among the White House lot which I did not discover. As to the attacks of the Northern papers [on us and our servants], I do not mind them, and do not think it wise to make the publication you suggest.

"If all the names of the people at Arlington [House] and [the White House] on the Pamunkey [River] are not embraced in this deed I have executed, I should like a supplementary deed to be drawn up, containing all those omitted. They are entitled to their freedom and I wish to give it to them. Those that have been [forcibly] carried away [by the Yanks], I hope are free and happy; I cannot get their papers to them, and they do not require them. I will give them if they ever call for them. It will be useless to ask their restitution to manumit them. . . ."[244]

From a letter to one of his sons around the same time:
☞ "I hope we will be able to do something for the servants. I executed a deed of manumission embracing all the names sent me by your mother

and some that I recollected, but as I had nothing to refer to but my memory, I fear many were omitted. It was my desire to manumit all the people of your grandfather, whether present on the several estates or not. I believe your mother only sent me the names of those present at [our family homes] White House and Romancoke. Those that have left with the enemy may not require their manumission. Still, some may be found hereafter in the State, and, at any rate, I wished to give a complete list, and to liberate all to show that your grandfather's wishes, so far as I was concerned, had been fulfilled. . . .

"I shall [now begin to] pay wages to Perry [the General's body-servant], and retain him until he or I can do better. You can do the same with Billy. The rest that are hired out had better be furnished with their papers and be let go. But what can be done with those at the White House and Romancoke? Those at and about Arlington can take care of themselves, I hope, and I have no doubt but all are gone who desire to do so. At any rate, I can do nothing for them now."[245]

From a letter dated March 31, 1863, the General reveals his sympathetic nature. In this case concerning one of the family servants, Jim, a parentless black child who was too young to be emancipated:
☞ "But what can be done with poor little Jim? It would be cruel to turn him out on the world. He could not take care of himself."[246]

We will note here that General Lee never spoke of his black workers using the Yankee term: "slaves." He always referred to them, as was the custom across the Old South, as "servants."[247] *This was entirely correct as authentic slavery was never practiced in the American South. The proper word for the institution was servitude.*[248]

General Lee was a strong advocate of emancipating and enlisting Southern black servants as soldiers in the Rebel armies (see Appendix A), as the following February 18, 1865, letter to Confederate congressman Ethelbert Barksdale reveals. Lee's ideas were eventually adopted by the Rebel government, unfortunately far too late to affect the outcome of the War in the South's favor:
☞ "Sir: I have the honor to acknowledge the receipt of your letter of the 12th instant, with reference to the employment of negroes as soldiers. I think the measure not only expedient but necessary. The enemy will

certainly use them against us if he can get possession of them; and as his present numerical superiority will enable him to penetrate many parts of the country, I cannot see the wisdom of the policy of holding them to await his arrival, when we may, by timely action and judicious management, use them to arrest his progress. I do not think that our white population can supply the necessities of a long war without overtaxing its capacity and imposing great suffering upon our people; and I believe we should provide resources for a protracted struggle—not merely for a battle or a campaign.

"In answer to your second question, I can only say that in my opinion the negroes, under proper circumstances, will make efficient soldiers. I think we could at least do as well with them as the enemy, and he attaches great importance to their assistance. Under good officers and good instructions, I do not see why they should not become soldiers. They possess all the physical qualifications, and their habits of obedience constitute a good foundation for discipline. They furnish a more promising material than many armies of which we read in history, which owed their efficiency to discipline alone. I think those who are employed should be freed. It would neither be just nor wise, in my opinion, to require them to serve as slaves. The best course to pursue, it seems to me, would be to call for such as are willing to come with the consent of their owners. An impressment or draft would not be likely to bring out the best class, and the use of coercion would make the measure distasteful to them and to their owners.

Confederate General Thomas J. "Stonewall" Jackson. When Jackson was in hospital recovering from an amputation, Lee said of him: "He has lost his left arm, but I have lost my right arm." The two men had much in common, including a Virginia birth, gentlemanly manners, and a deep Christian faith. Jackson was only thirty-nine at the time of his death from pneumonia (brought on by his wounds and surgery).

"I have no doubt that if [the Confederate] Congress would authorize their reception into service, and empower the President to call upon individuals or States for such as they are willing to contribute, with the condition of emancipation to all enrolled, a sufficient number would be forthcoming to enable us to try the experiment. If it proved successful, most of the objections to the measure would disappear, and if individuals still remained unwilling to send their negroes to the army, the force of public opinion in the States would soon bring about such legislation as would remove all obstacles. I think the matter should be left, as far as possible, to the people and to the States, which alone can legislate as the necessities of this particular service may require. As to the mode of organizing them, it should be left as free from restraint as possible. Experience will suggest, the best course, and it will be inexpedient to trammel the subject with provisions that might, in the end, prevent the adoption of reforms suggested by actual trial. With great respect, your obedient servant, R. E. Lee, General."[249]

After Lincoln's War came to end, Lee said:
☞ "I have always been in favor of emancipation—gradual emancipation."[250]

In May 1870 Lee told John Leyburn of Baltimore, Maryland:
☞ "So far from engaging in a war to perpetuate slavery, I am rejoiced that slavery is abolished. I believe it will be greatly for the interests of the South. So fully am I satisfied of this as regards Virginia especially, that I would cheerfully have lost all I have lost by the war, and have suffered all I have suffered, to have this object attained."[251]

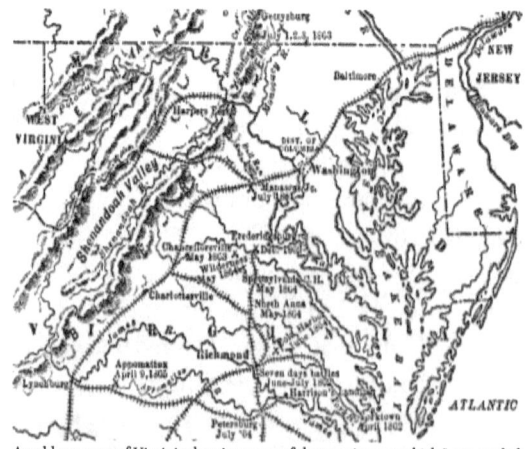

An old war map of Virginia showing some of the terrain over which Lee traveled and fought during Lincoln's illicit War against the South and states' rights.

9

CONFEDERATE

OFFICERSHIP

While Lee seems to have been born to be a military man, in his writings he chose to portray himself as a peace-loving farmer and country gentleman, not as a world famous Confederate commander.

Indeed, during Lincoln's War he repeatedly played down his rank, ignored or refused promotions, and even continued to wear his colonel's uniform after having been made general. His letters to his family throughout this period show a man who would rather have been almost anywhere but on the battlefield, and most preferably at home, surrounded by his adoring wife, children, and animals.

Despite his best efforts, Lee will no doubt always be remembered as the South's most beloved Civil War general, a brave and noble Southern gentleman who graduated with honors from West Point to become one of America's finest military tacticians.

The second Confederate Capitol, this one at Richmond, Virginia. The first was located at Montgomery, Alabama, but was moved to Richmond in early 1861 so the Confederate seat of power could be closer to the U.S. Capitol at Washington, D.C.

In this chapter I

provide some examples, from each year of the War, of Lee the Rebel officer, illustrating his day-to-day experiences and heavy responsibilities on the field of action. They range from the dull and routine to the terrifying and horrific, from the depressing and discouraging to the exciting and promising.

Lee certainly experienced every emotion between 1861 and 1865, a debilitating period that ended humiliatingly with the South's "surrender" and his physical health greatly depleted. His hard four year service in the Confederate States army would eventually contribute to his early death at age sixty-three just five years later, in 1870. All this so that liberal Lincoln could install big government in Washington, D.C.

At the beginning of Lincoln's War in April 1861, as a major general and the commander-in-chief of Virginia's military, Lee had to contend with innumerable problems, including requests from family members and friends alike for military positions. As would be expected of a man of his moral fiber and intelligence, he handled such occasions with aplomb and grace, as the following example shows:
☞ "My Dear _____: I have received your letter of 23d. I am sorry your nephew has left his college and become a soldier. It is necessary that persons on my staff should have a knowledge of their duties and an experience of the wants of the service to enable me to attend to other matters. It would otherwise give me great pleasure to take your nephew. I shall remember him if anything can be done. I am much obliged to you for Dr. M_____'s letter. Express to him my gratitude for his sentiments, and tell him that no earthly act could give me so much pleasure as to restore peace to my country.

"But I fear it is now out of the power of man, and in God alone must be our trust. I think our policy should be purely on the defensive—to resist aggression and allow time to allay the passions and permit Reason to resume her sway. Virginia has to-day, I understand, joined the Confederate States. Her policy will doubtless, therefore, be shaped by united counsels. I cannot say what it will be, but trust that a merciful Providence will not dash us from the height to which his smiles have raised us. I wanted to say many things to you before I left home, but the event was rendered so imperatively speedy that I could not. May God preserve you and yours! Very truly, R. E. Lee."[252]

Some of the generals of the Confederacy. From top, moving clockwise: Fitzhugh Lee, Richard Taylor, Earl Van Dorn, Joseph Wheeler, Alexander P. Stewart, Benjamin F. Cheatham. Center: Sterling Price.

As the following field dispatch reveals, General Lee had an inborn talent for stirring the patriotic passions of his men—who lovingly referred to their leader as "Marse Robert."[253] *It was written on September 8, 1861, during the campaign of western Virginia:*

☞ "The forward movement announced to the Army of the North-west in Special Order No. 28, from its headquarters, of this date, gives the general commanding the opportunity of exhorting the troops to keep steadily in view the great principles for which they contend, and to manifest to the world their determination to maintain them. The eyes of the country are upon you. The safety of your homes and the lives of all you hold dear depend upon your courage and exertions. Let each man resolve to be victorious, and that the right of self-government, liberty, and peace shall in him find a defender. The progress of this army must be forward. R. E. Lee, General commanding."[254]

A letter to Virginia Governor John Letcher from this same period, shows some of the tremendous difficulties General Lee faced during the beginning stages of the War for Southern Independence. It is dated September 17, 1861:

☞ "My Dear Governor: I received your very kind note of the 5th instant, just as I was about to accompany General [William W.] Loring's command on an expedition to the enemy's works in front, or I would have before thanked you for the interest you take in my welfare and your too flattering expressions of my ability. Indeed, you overrate me much, and I feel humbled when I weigh myself by your standard. I am, however, very grateful for your confidence, and I can answer for my sincerity in the earnest endeavor I make to advance the cause I have so much at heart, though conscious of the slow progress I make.

"I was very sanguine of taking the enemy's works on last Thursday morning. I had considered the subject well. With great effort the troops intended for the surprise had reached their destination, having traversed twenty miles of steep, rugged mountain-paths, and the last day through a terrible storm, which lasted all night, and in which they had to stand drenched to the skin in the cold rain. Still, their spirits were good. When morning broke I could see the enemy's tents on Valley River at the point on the Huttonsville road just below me. It was a tempting sight.

"We waited for the attack on Cheat Mountain, which was to be the signal, till 10 A.M.; the men were cleaning their unserviceable arms. But the signal did not come. All chance for surprise was gone. The provisions of the men had been destroyed the preceding day by the storm. They had nothing to eat that morning, could not hold out another day, and were obliged to be withdrawn. The party sent to Cheat Mountain to take that in the rear had also to be withdrawn. The attack to come off from the east side failed from the difficulties in the way; the opportunity was lost and our plan discovered.

"It is a grievous disappointment to me, I assure you. But for the rain-storm I have no doubt it would have succeeded. This, governor, is for your own eye. Please do not speak of it; we must try again. Our greatest loss is the death of my dear friend Colonel [John A.] Washington. He and my son were reconnoitering the front of the

Confederate generals. From top, moving clockwise: Wade Hampton, John Brown Gordon, Henry A. Wise, John B. Magruder, John C. Breckinridge, Turner Ashby. Center: Jubal A. Early.

enemy. They came unawares upon a concealed party, who fired upon them within twenty yards, and the colonel fell pierced by three balls. My son's horse received three shots, but he escaped on the colonel's horse. His zeal for the cause to which he had devoted himself carried him, I fear, too far.

"We took some seventy prisoners and killed some twenty-five or thirty of the enemy. Our loss was small besides what I have mentioned. Our greatest difficulty is the roads. It has been raining in these mountains about six weeks. It is impossible to get along. It is that which has paralyzed all our efforts. With sincere thanks for your good wishes, I am very truly yours, R. E. Lee."[255]

In this May 2, 1862, dispatch to Confederate General Edmund Kirby Smith, Lee mentions one of the many Native-American battalions that fought for the Confederacy:

☞ "General: Your letter of the 26th ultimo is received. The difficulties and embarrassments of your situation are fully appreciated. Everything in my power has been done for your assistance, and I only regret that I could do no more. Great reliance is placed in the judgment and vigor with which I am sure you will use the forces at your disposal. It will be necessary to hold yourself ready for rapid movements whenever the enemy may expose himself to a blow.

"You have already been informed by telegraph that a regiment of infantry and one of cavalry from Georgia have been ordered to Chattanooga for your support. These men will bring such arms as they have, and 1,000 improved arms have been ordered to the same place. All the arms that could be procured have been sent you, and I hope you will be able to supply some of the unarmed men with you, including the Indian battalion from North Carolina which was ordered to you.

"I have also informed you by telegram that I have applied to the Governor of Alabama to send you two additional regiments. These regiments are now at Talladega, and will be ordered to Chattanooga. They are not armed. I am, general, very respectfully, your obedient servant, R. E. Lee, General, Commanding."[256]

The day after the Rebel win at the Battle of Second Manassas on August 30, 1862, Lee sent this dispatch to his opponent Union General John Pope:

Confederate generals. From top, moving clockwise: Edmund Kirby Smith, John Bell Hood, Nathan Bedford Forrest, Leonidas Polk, John H. Morgan, William J. Hardee. Center: Braxton Bragg.

☞ "Sir: Consideration for your wounded induces me to consent to your sending ambulances to convey them within your lines. I cannot consent to a truce or a suspension of military operations of this army. If you desire to send for your wounded, should your ambulances report to Dr. Guild, medical director of this army, he will give directions for transportation.

"The wounded will be paroled, and it is understood that no delay will take place in their removal. I am, respectfully, etc., R. E. Lee, General."²⁵⁷

On June 11, 1862, Lee wrote the following to Confederate General Stonewall Jackson:
☞ "General: Your recent successes have been the cause of the liveliest joy in this army as well as in the country. The admiration excited by your skill and boldness has been constantly mingled with solicitude for your situation. The practicability of re-enforcing you has been the subject of earnest consideration. It has been determined to do so at the expense of weakening this army. Brigadier-General [Alexander Robert] Lawton, with six regiments from Georgia, is on the way to you, and Brigadier-General [William Henry Chase] Whiting, with eight veteran regiments, leaves here to-day. The object is to enable you to crush the forces opposed to you.

"Leave your enfeebled troops to watch the country and guard the passes covered by your cavalry and artillery, and with your main body, including Ewell's division and Lawton's and Whiting's commands, move rapidly to Ashland by rail or otherwise, as you may find most advantageous, and sweep down between the Chickahominy and Pamunkey, cutting up the enemy's communications, etc., while this army attacks [Union] General [George B.] McClellan in front. He will thus, I think, be forced to come out of his intrenchments, where he is strongly posted on the Chickahominy, and apparently preparing to move by gradual approaches on Richmond. Keep me advised of your movements, and, if practicable, precede your troops, that we may confer and arrange for simultaneous attack. I am, with great respect, your obedient servant, R. E. Lee, General."²⁵⁸

In this May 22, 1863, dispatch to Confederate General Arnold Elzey, Lee mentions 1,000 of the 300,000 to 1 million black Confederate soldiers (depending on how one defines a "private soldier")²⁵⁹ who fought for the Southern Cause:
☞ "General: Captain Capps, Fifteenth Virginia Cavalry, on duty in King William County, reports that Mr. Davis, whose home is at West Point, and who at this time is employed in the Confederate Navy, has been noticing the movements of the enemy, and states that they have left in

part. Three transports left on the 15th loaded with troops. There appears now to be there two squadrons of cavalry, one company artillery, and a small portion of infantry. About 1,000 negroes are at work on the intrenchments.[260] All the gunboats and transports have left except two. They appear to be ferry-boats.

"Have you received intelligence corroborating this, or can you ascertain what is the condition of things? It was reported yesterday that four gunboats were ascending the Rappahannock and had come within 12 miles of Tappahannock. Milroy has recrossed the mountains and returned to the valley. Our scouts north of the Rappahannock report indications of another move on the part of [Union] General [Joseph] Hooker. Seven pieces of artillery and some infantry have reached Stafford Court-House from Dumfries. Heintzelman is said to have joined him. Reports from Alexandria state that 30,000 new troops are to be sent to him. May I ask you to report these circumstances to the Secretary of War for his information? Very respectfully, your obedient servant, R. E. Lee, General."[261]

Generals Lee and Grant during the "surrender" at Appomattox. Grant behaved admirably: he let Lee keep his side-arms, horse, and baggage, allowed him to return home "unmolested," promised protection from the U.S. government, and even gave food rations to Lee's starving troops.

On June 18, 1863, Lee sent off this dispatch to Confederate President Jefferson Davis:
☞ "Mr. President: On the 10th, I put Ewell's corps in motion for the Valley. He reports, under date of the 13th, that, with [Confederate General Robert Emmett] Rodes' division, he drove the enemy out of Berryville, and, with [Confederate General Jubal Anderson] Early's and Johnson's, drove him within

his intrenchments at Winchester, where, it seems, he is more strongly fortified than supposed. According to our understanding, I presume he has advanced toward the Potomac, leaving a division in front of Winchester.

"General A. P. Hill reported yesterday that the Federal force in front of him withdrew from the south side of the Rappahannock on the night of the 13th, and by morning had nearly all disappeared, leaving strong pickets on the river. One division was seen going over the Stafford Hills, in the direction of Aquia, and he supposes the main body to have taken that route. Our scouts report a general movement of the enemy up the Rappahannock, but I have got no certain information on that point; I know a large force has been thrown toward Warrenton.

"The uncertainty of the reports as to threatened expeditions of the enemy along the coast of North Carolina, and between the Rappahannock and James Rivers in Virginia, has caused delay in the movements of this army, and it may now be too late to accomplish all that was desired. I am still ignorant as to the extent of the expedition said to be moving up the Peninsula, and hesitate to draw the whole of A. P. Hill's corps to me. Two of [Confederate General George Edward] Pickett's brigades are at Hanover Junction and Richmond, so that I am quite weak [as far as numerical strength]. I am, with great respect, your obedient servant, R. E. Lee, General."[262]

Two dispatches from Lee to President Davis after the disastrous Battle of Gettysburg show the General's calm reaction to the debacle. This first one is dated July 7, 1863:

☞ "Mr. President: My letter of the 4th instant will have informed you of the unsuccessful issue of our final attack on the enemy in the rear of Gettysburg. Finding the position too strong to be carried, and, being much hindered in collecting necessary supplies for the army, by the numerous bodies of local and other troops which watched the passes, I determined to withdraw to the west side of the mountains. This has been safely accomplished with great labor, and the army is now in the vicinity of this place.

"One of my reasons for moving in this direction, after crossing the mountains, was to protect our trains with the sick and wounded, which had been sent back to Williamsport, and which were threatened

After Lee's "surrender" at Appomattox he rode back through his troops. As his teary-eyed soldiers gathered around him for the last time, he said: "I have done the best I could for you men. My heart is too full to say more."

by the enemy's cavalry. Our advance reached here yesterday afternoon in time to support our cavalry in repulsing an attempt of the enemy to reach our trains. Before leaving Gettysburg, such of the sick and wounded as could be removed were sent back to Williamsport, but the rains that have interfered so much with our general movements have so swollen the Potomac as to render it unfordable, and they are still on the north side. Arrangements are being made to ferry them across to-day.

"We captured at Gettysburg about 6,000 prisoners, besides the wounded that remained in our hands after the engagements of the 1st and 2d. Fifteen hundred of these prisoners and the wounded were paroled, but I suppose that under the late arrangements these paroles will not be regarded. The rest have been sent to Williamsport, where they will cross. We were obliged to leave a large number of our wounded who were unable to travel, and many arms that had been collected on the field at Gettysburg.

"In addition to the general officers killed or wounded, of whom I sent you a list in my former letter, I have to mention General [Paul Jones] Semmes, General George Thomas Anderson, General [James Johnston] Pettigrew, and General John Marshall Jones, wounded; General [James Jay] Archer was made prisoner. General [Henry] Heth is again in command. In sending back our trains in advance, that of General Ewell was cut by the enemy's cavalry, and a number of wagons, said to be about 40, were captured. The enemys cavalry force, which attempted to reach our cavalry trains yesterday afternoon, was a large one. They came as far as Hagerstown, where they were attacked by General Stuart, and driven back rapidly toward Sharpsburg. Very respectfully, your obedient servant, R. E. Lee, General."[263]

The next day, July 8, 1863, from near Hagerstown, Maryland, the General sent off this missive to Davis. Though the Confederates had suffered terribly at Gettysburg, the ever optimistic Lee kept his spirits up:

☞ "Mr. President: My letter of yesterday will have informed you of the position of this army. Though reduced in numbers by the hardships and battles through which it has passed since leaving the Rappahannock, its condition is good, and its confidence unimpaired. Upon crossing the Potomac into Maryland, I had calculated upon the river remaining ford able during the summer, so as to enable me to recross at my pleasure, but a series of storms, commencing the day after our entrance into Maryland, has placed the river beyond fording stage, and the present storm will keep it so for at least a week. I shall, therefore, have to accept battle if the enemy offers it, whether I wish to or not, and as the result is in the hands of the Sovereign Ruler of the Universe, and known to Him only, I deem it prudent to make every arrangement in our power to meet any emergency that may arise.

"From information gathered from the papers, I believe that the troops from North Carolina and the Coast of Virginia, under Generals Foster and Dix, have been ordered to the Potomac, and that recently additional re-enforcements have been sent from the coast of South Carolina to General Banks. If I am correct in my opinion, this will liberate most of the troops in those regions, and should Your Excellency have not already done so, I earnestly recommend that all that can be spared be concentrated on the Upper Rappahannock, under General Beauregard, with directions to cross that river and make a demonstration upon Washington [D.C.].

"This command will answer the double purpose of affording protection to the capital at Richmond and relieving the pressure upon this army. I hope Your Excellency will understand that I am not in the

"Marse Robert," the nickname given to General Lee by his soldiers.

least discouraged, or that my faith in the protection of an all-merciful Providence, or in the fortitude of this army, is at all shaken. But, though conscious that the enemy has been much shattered in the recent battle, I am aware that he can be easily re-enforced, while no addition can be made to our numbers. The measure, therefore, that I have recommended is altogether one of a prudential nature. I am, most respectfully, your obedient servant, R. E. Lee, General.

"P.S. I see it stated in a letter from the special correspondent of the New York *Times* that a bearer of dispatches from Your Excellency to myself was captured at Hagerstown on the 2d July, and the dispatches are said to be of the greatest importance, and to have a great bearing on coming events. I have thought proper to mention this, that you may know whether it is so."[264]

This August 15, 1863, dispatch from Lee to Confederate General Jeb Stuart focuses on the Confederacy's lack of rifles and modern weaponry:
☞ "General: In reply to your different communications on the subject of the deficiency of good arms in the cavalry, I have to say that I have sent Colonel Baldwin to Richmond to see what can be done there. I have also issued an order that the infantry arms be thoroughly inspected, so as to obtain all the arms from among them which are better adapted for the cavalry service.

"There are many difficulties, however, in the way of arming the cavalry thoroughly, and keeping it in that condition. Few cavalry arms are imported, and those manufactured in the Confederacy are generally rejected. I fear there is great carelessness, too, in the preservation of arms in the whole army. Company and regimental officers do not hold their men to sufficient responsibility. Men who leave the camp on furlough should be compelled to turn in their arms and accouterments to the ordnance sergeant or brigade ordnance officer. Where infantry arms have been issued to the cavalry, it is stated that they have either been turned in or thrown away in nine cases out of ten. Before the army went into Maryland, 2,000 Austrian rifles were sent to Culpeper Court-House. Of these, very few were issued to the men, and after the fight at Brandy Station, nearly all that had been issued were returned or thrown away. Recently 600 Enfield rifles and Mississippi rifles were sent to Culpeper for the cavalry division. The brigade ordnance officer declined to receive them, saying the men would not take them.

"From the nature of the cavalry service, it is almost impossible for the ordnance officers to enforce the rules of the Department. Regimental and company commanders should be held to rigid account, and be required to make frequent returns. Where an arm or accouterment is missing and not properly accounted for, the soldier should not only be charged with it, but military punishment should be inflicted.

"Colonel Baldwin has ordered blank forms for cavalry armament returns to be prepared, which will be issued to every company commander in the division. To-day he reports having forwarded 220 Enfield rifles, and between 400 and 500 Sharps carbines, with some accouterments, ammunition, etc.; this on yesterday.

"I think your dismounted men should be speedily organized, and thoroughly drilled as infantry, and armed to be used as infantry, until they can be mounted.

"Your letter of August 14, with inclosed dispatches, was received. I thank you for the information of the enemy's position which it contains. Respectfully, etc., R. E. Lee, General."[265]

This January 16, 1864, dispatch was sent from Lee to Confederate General James Longstreet:

☞ "General: Your letters of the 10th and 11th instant were handed to me by Captain Goree last night. I am glad that you are casting about for some way to reach the enemy. If he could be defeated at some point before he is prepared to open the campaign it would be attended with the greatest advantages. Either of the points mentioned by you would answer. I believe, however, that if [Union General Ulysses S.] Grant could be driven back and Mississippi and Tennessee recovered, it would do more to relieve the country and inspirate our people than the mere capture of Washington. You know how exhausted the country is between here and the Potomac. There is nothing for man or horse. Everything must be carried. How is that to be done with weak transportation on roads in the condition we may expect in March? You know better than I how you will be off in that respect in the west.

"After you get into Kentucky I suppose provisions can be obtained. But if saddles, etc., could be procured in time, where can the horses or mules be? They cannot be obtained in this section of country, and as far as my information extends not in the Confederacy. But let us both quietly and ardently set to work; some good may result and I will institute inquiries.

"There is a part of your letter that gives me uneasiness; that is in relation to your position. Your cavalry, I hope, will keep you informed of any movement against you. After the completion of the Virginia and Tennessee Railroad you will be able to retire with ease, and you had better be prepared in case of necessity. If the enemy follow, with the assistance of General S. Jones you may be able to hit him a hard blow.

Another illustration of Lee after Appomattox, this one showing both the adoration and the despondency of his men.

I would suggest that you have the country examined, routes explored, and strong positions ascertained and improved.

"There is some report of a projected movement of the enemy next spring by the route from Knoxville and the abandonment of this to Richmond. It is believed that such a movement will be as successful as that by Grant on Vicksburg. As they have not been able yet to overcome the 80 miles between Washington and Richmond, by the shortest road, I hope they will not be able to accomplish the more circuitous route. Not knowing what they intended to do, and what [Confederate] General [Joseph Eggleston] Johnston can do, has prevented my recommending your return to this army. After hearing that you were in comfortable quarters and had plenty of provisions and forage, I thought it was best you should remain where you are until spring, or until it was determined what could be done. I hope you will be able to recruit your corps.

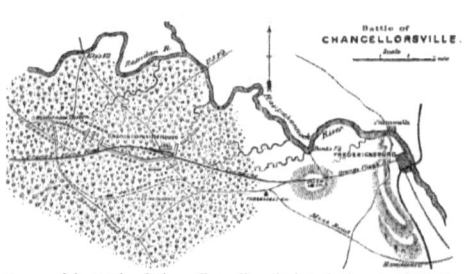

A map of the Battle of Chancellorsville, which took place April 30–May 6, 1863. Lee scored another victory for the Confederacy, this one over Union General Joseph Hooker. The win was marred, however, by the tragic death of General Stonewall Jackson, cut down by friendly fire.

"In reference to that, how would [Confederate] General [Simon Bolivar] Buckner answer for the command of [Confederate General John Bell] Hood's division, at least until it is seen whether he ever can return to it? You may recollect just before you went west certain promotions in the artillery of this army were agreed on, and that it was desired to promote Colonel Alexander, as chief of your corps, to the rank of brigadier-general, provided Colonel Walton could get service south. This I could not accomplish at the time, nor have I been able to do so since. Not wishing the officers in the other corps to be promoted without advancing those in yours, so that their relative rank might be preserved, I have refrained from sending in the recommendations, but the season of active operations is approaching, and I wish the organization perfected.

"I see by an order of yours that Colonel Alexander has been appointed chief of artillery of your corps. Is it permanent or temporary, and do you wish him promoted? As some change in your opinion as to the relative merits of the officers with you may have been made by your service west, I inclose a copy of the promotions proposed in your corps, as you may not have one. It was arranged upon the supposition that Colonel Walton could be assigned to other duty. If he cannot, he and Major Eshleman will be the field officers of the Washington Artillery. [Confederate] General [William Nelson] Pendleton has proposed an exchange between Colonel Cabell and Lieutenant-Colonel Lightfoot. I do not know whether that can be accomplished. Let me hear from you as soon as convenient. With kind regards to yourself and all with you, I am, very truly, yours, R. E. Lee, General."²⁶⁶

Lee wrote this July 2, 1864, dispatch to Confederate Secretary of War Seddon:
☞ "Sir: I have the honor to acknowledge the receipt of your letter of yesterday in relation to [Confederate] General [John Hunt] Morgan. If General Morgan could accomplish the object he proposes without endangering the lead and salt works in Southwest Virginia it would certainly be a valuable service, but I think it very important that the whole country in which his command now is should not be stripped of troops so as to invite an expedition of the enemy.

"I know of no troops that could replace General Morgan at this time, and his withdrawal would leave open the whole country from the lower Valley of Virginia to Northern Georgia. I think, however, that he might with advantage to Northwestern Virginia collect all the cattle and horses he can, and even threaten or enter Pennsylvania from that quarter, and if there is no force now threatening him should prefer such an expedition to the one he proposes. He would not then be out of reach of the interests with the defense of which he is specially charged, and at the same time would be likely to draw after him any force that may be in Western Virginia and make a diversion in favor of [Confederate] General [Jubal Anderson] Early.

"If there were any troops to take his place I should not object to his undertaking the movement against [Union General William T.] Sherman's communications, but the situation of affairs in the Valley makes it impossible at present to return any of those under General Breckinridge, and I know of no others. With great respect, your obedient servant, R. E. Lee, General."²⁶⁷

132 ～ THE QUOTABLE ROBERT E. LEE

For Southerners, this April 9, 1865, dispatch from Lee to Grant is one of the saddest documents in the history of the South:

☞ "General: I have received your letter of this date containing the terms of surrender of the Army of Northern Virginia as proposed by you. As they are substantially the same as those expressed in your letter of the 8th instant, they are accepted. I will proceed to designate the proper officers to carry the stipulations into effect. Very respectfully, your obedient servant, R. E. Lee, General."[268]

This document, entitled "Parole of General Robert E. Lee and Staff," was signed and issued on April 9, 1865 by the General and his officers:

☞ "We, the undersigned prisoners of war belonging to the Army of Northern Virginia, having been this day surrendered by General Robert E. Lee, C. S. Army, commanding said army, to Lieut. Gen. U. S. Grant, commanding Armies of the United States, do hereby give our solemn parole of honor that we will not hereafter serve in the armies of the Confederate states, or in any military capacity whatever, against the United States of America, or render aid to the enemies of the latter, until properly exchanged in such manner as shall be mutually approved by the respective authorities. Done at Appomattox Court-House, Va., this 9th day of April, 1865. R. E. Lee, General. W. H. Taylor, Lieutenant-Colonel and Assistant Adjutant-General. Charles S. Venable, Lieutenant-Colonel and Assistant Adjutant-General. Charles Marshall, Lieutenant-Colonel and Assistant Adjutant-General. H. E. Peyton, Lieutenant-Colonel, Adjutant and Inspector General. Giles B. Cooke, Major and Assistant Adjutant and Inspector General. H. E. Young, Major, Assistant Adjutant-General, and Judge-Advocate-General."[269]

General Lee, with Grant, preparing to sign the papers of "surrender" at Appomattox.

10

THE

SOUTHERN PEOPLE

After the Confederate victory at the Battle of Fredericksburg (December 11-15, 1862), Lee wrote this of the people of that fair Virginia city:

☞ "History presents no instance of a purer and more unselfish patriotism, or a higher spirit of fortitude and courage, than was evidenced by the citizens of Fredericksburg."[270]

In the winter of 1863 Lee wrote the following to his wife:

☞ "The kindness exhibited toward you as well as myself by our people, in addition to exciting my gratitude, causes me to reflect how little I have done to merit it, and humbles me in my own eyes to a painful degree."[271]

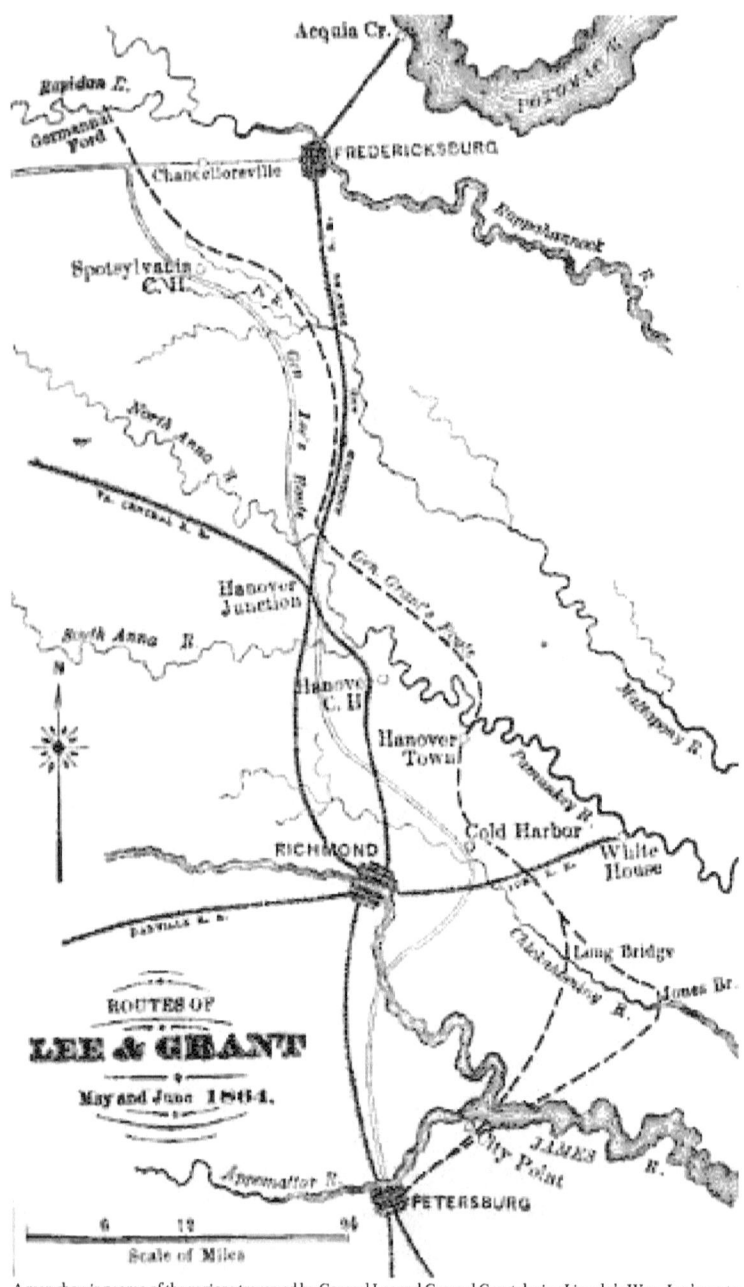

A map showing some of the regions traversed by General Lee and General Grant during Lincoln's War. Lee's route is marked with a set of double parallel lines, Grant's by a dashed line.

11

THE

NORTHERN PEOPLE

☞ "Is it not strange that the descendants of those Pilgrim Fathers who crossed the Atlantic to preserve their own freedom have always proved the most intolerant of the spiritual liberty of others ?"[272]

The U.S. Capitol at Washington, D.C. Pro-North historians have suppressed the fact, but it is well-known across the South that in the early 1860s Lincoln used Northern slaves (instead of free labor) to finish constructing the Capitol building, and that Northern slaves were used to build the White House, other Federal buildings, and many roads in and around the District of Columbia, as well. None of this is surprising. After he was elected president, Lincoln said he had no interest in freeing Washington, D.C.'s slaves, and put off issuing an emancipation proclamation for the city until April 16, 1862, nearly midway through his War. Worse still, the edict, known as the District of Columbia Emancipation Act, included Lincoln's diabolical racist plan calling for the immediate deportation of all freed blacks to colonies in South America, the Caribbean, and Africa. Northern abolitionists were not amused and began calling Lincoln "that damned idiot in the White House," and "that baboon at the other end of the avenue."

General Ulysses S. Grant, commander-in-chief of U.S. armies, was one of Lee's chief foes during Lincoln's War. To his credit, Grant treated Lee in a gentlemanly and diplomatic fashion during the Confederacy's "surrender" at Appomattox. Still, while we in the South may have forgiven Grant for the numerous and heinous war crimes he perpetuated against our people, we will never forget.

12

LINCOLN'S WAR ON THE SOUTH

In chronological order

Lee predicted Lincoln's War and its awful consequences for both the South and the Union. And he did his best to help prevent the conflict, but he was up against a truly implacable opponent: the Big Brother, states' rights-hating liberal, Abraham Lincoln.

Abraham Lincoln, dictatorial head of the Northern empire and the Yankee people between 1861 and 1865, he was directly responsible for starting the "Civil War," and for all of the misery, sorrow, carnage, death, and destruction that followed. Unbeknownst to most Northerners, and even many Southerners, the South is still recovering from Lincoln's War against states' rights.

Lincoln claims to have fought the South to "preserve the Union," an outright and demonstrable lie. His true agenda was to install big government in Washington, transform our confederate republic into socialized democracy, take over control of the U.S. military and the economy, and lord over the states with a tyrannical iron fist. None of this could be accomplished while the freedom-loving South was independent. So states' rights had to be crushed, and to do that Lincoln had to invade the South.

The question for him was, how to draw the peaceful agrarian South into war? Consulting with his advisors, Lincoln devised a way: he tricked the Confederates into firing the first shot at Fort Sumter on April 12, 1861, giving him full justification for sending 75,000 U.S. troops into Dixie. Though the act was unconstitutional and therefore illegal, the South had no choice but to defend herself, and thus was launched the so-called "Civil War."[273]

This chapter furnishes numerous examples of Lee's thoughts, feelings, and activities during the War Against Northern Aggression.

In early 1860, like most Southerners, Lee was at first against the secession of the Southern states and he strove to avoid bloodshed with the North at all costs. When asked what he thought of the United States' boast that if war came it would conquer the South in "ninety days," Lee gave the following emotional reply:

☞ "They do not know what they say. If it comes to a conflict of arms, the war will last at least four years. Northern politicians do not appreciate the determination and pluck of the South, and Southern politicians do not appreciate the numbers, resources, and patient perseverance of the North. Both sides forget that we are all Americans, and that it must be a terrible struggle if it comes to war. Tell [U.S.] General [Winfield] Scott that we must do all we can to avert war, and if it comes to the worst, we must then do every thing in our power to mitigate its evils."[274]

Lee was very much against the idea of pressuring male students to enlist in the Confederate military, as this April 1861 letter to his wife shows:

☞ "I wrote to [our son] Robert that I could not consent to take boys from their schools and young men from their colleges and put them in the ranks at the beginning of a war, when they are not wanted and when there were men enough for that purpose. The war may last ten years. Where are our ranks to be filled from then? I was willing for his company to continue at their studies, to keep up its organisation, and to perfect themselves in their military exercises, and to perform duty at the college; but not to be called into the field. I therefore wished him to remain. If the exercises at the college are suspended, he can then come home. . . ."[275]

General Lee and General Stonewall Jackson overseeing their troops at the Battle of Cold Harbor II, May 31-June 12, 1864

Though the War was only a few months old, Lee was already encouraging his soldiers with words like the following, from July 1861:
☞ "Our brave troops must bear up against misfortune. Reverses must happen, but they ought only to stimulate us to greater efforts."[276]

Lee held wartime journalists and newspapermen with little regard, particularly those who pretended to know more than the generals in the field, as this July 21, 1861, letter to his wife Mary reveals:
☞ "I inclose you a letter from Markie [Martha Custis Williams, a cousin of the family]. Write to her if you can and thank her for her letter to me. I have not time. My whole time is occupied, and all my thoughts and strength are given to the [Confederate] cause to which my life, be it long or short, will be devoted. Tell her not to mind the reports she sees in the papers [about me]. They are made to injure and occasion distrust. Those that know me will not believe them. Those that do not will not care for them. I laugh at them."[277]

A letter from Lee to his wife, dated September 1, 1861, from Valley Mountain, gives a glimpse into Lincoln's War as it was experienced by Confederate soldiers in Virginia:
☞ "We have a great deal of sickness among the soldiers, and now those

on the sick-list would form an army. The measles is still among them, though I hope it is dying out. But it is a disease which though light in childhood is severe in manhood, and prepares the system for other attacks. The constant cold rains, with no shelter but tents, have aggravated it. All these drawbacks, with impassable roads, have paralysed our efforts."²⁷⁸

During a discussion with the Honorable Benjamin H. Hill of Georgia, Lee displayed his attitude toward the newspapers, adding his own brand of gentle humor:
☞ "We made a great mistake, Mr. Hill, in the beginning of our struggle, and I fear, in spite of all we can do, it will prove to be a fatal mistake. . . . In the beginning we appointed all our worst generals to command the armies, and all our best generals to edit the newspapers. As you know, I have planned some campaigns and quite a number of battles. I have given the work all the care and thought I could, and sometimes, when my plans were completed, as far as I could see they seemed to be perfect. But when I have fought them through I have discovered defects, and occasionally wondered I did not see some of the defects in advance. When it was all over I found by reading a newspaper that these best editor-generals saw all the defects plainly from the start. Unfortunately, they did not communicate their knowledge to me until it was too late.

"I have no ambition but to serve the Confederacy, and do all I can to win our independence. I am willing to serve in any capacity to which the authorities may assign me. I have done the best I could in the field, and have not succeeded as I should wish. I am willing to yield my place to these best generals, and I will do my best for the cause in editing a newspaper."²⁷⁹

On September 9, 1861, Lee once again mentions the press in a letter to his wife:
☞ ". . . . For military news, I must refer you to the papers. You will see there more than ever occurs, and what does occur the relation must be taken with some allowance. Do not believe anything you see about me. There has been no battle, only skirmishing with the outposts, and nothing done of any moment."²⁸⁰

Conditions for the Confederacy often went suddenly from bad to worse, as this September 26, 1861, letter from Lee (camped on Sewell's Mountain) to his wife indicates:

☞ "It is raining heavily. The men are all exposed on the mountain, with the enemy opposite to us. We are without tents, and for two nights I have lain buttoned up in my overcoat. To-day my tent came up and I am in it. Yet I fear I shall not sleep for thinking of the poor men. I wrote about socks for myself. I have no doubt the yarn ones you mention will be very acceptable to the men here or elsewhere. If you can send them here, I will distribute them to the most needy."[281]

Lee as a young officer in the U.S. army, years before Lincoln's War.

During Lee's campaign in western Virginia, a September 1861 order to his soldiers contained these moving words:
☞ "The forward movement . . . gives the General commanding the opportunity of exhorting the troops to keep steadily in view the great principles for which they contend, and to manifest to the world their determination to maintain them. The eyes of the country are upon you. The safety of your homes and the lives of all you hold dear, depend upon your courage and exertions. Let each man resolve to be victorious, and that the right of self-government, liberty, and peace shall in him find a defender. The progress of this army must be forward."[282]

In an October 7, 1861, letter to his wife, Lee further elucidates on his feelings of the newspapers:
☞ "I am sorry, as you say, that the movements of our armies cannot keep pace with the expectations of the editors of the papers. I know they can regulate matters satisfactory to themselves on paper. I wish they

could do so in the field. No one wishes them more success than I do, and would be happy to see them have full swing. [Confederate] General [John Buchanan] Floyd has three editors on his staff. I hope something will be done to please them."[283]

The following letter from Lee to two of his daughters, Agnes and Anne, illustrates his state of mind during the close of the first year of the War. It is dated November 22, 1861:

☞ "My Darling Daughters: I have just received your joint letter of October 24th, from 'Clydale.' It was very cheering to me, and the affection and sympathy you expressed were very grateful to my feelings. I wish indeed I could see you, be with you, and never again part from you. God only can give me that happiness. I pray for it night and day. But my prayers I know are not worthy to be heard.

"I received your former letter in western Virginia, but had no opportunity to reply to it. I enjoyed it, nevertheless. I am glad you do not wait to hear from me, as that would deprive me of the pleasure of hearing from you often. I am so pressed with business. I am much pleased at your description of Stratford [Hall, the General's birth home] and your visit. It is endeared to me by many recollections, and it has been always a great desire of my life to be able to purchase it. Now that we have no other home, and the one we so loved has been so foully polluted [by the Yanks], the desire is stronger with me than ever.

"The horsechestnut you mention in the garden was planted by my mother. I am sorry the vault is so dilapidated. You did not mention the spring, one of the objects of my earliest recollections. I am very glad, my precious Agnes, that you have become so early a riser. It is a good habit, and in these times for mighty works advantage should be taken of every hour. I much regretted being obliged to come from Richmond without seeing your poor mother. . . .

"This is my second visit to Savannah. I have been down the coast to Amelia Island to examine the defenses. They are poor indeed, and I have laid off work enough to employ our people a month. I hope our enemy will be polite enough to wait for us. It is difficult to get our people [across the South] to realise their position. . . . Good-bye, my dear daughters. Your affectionate father, R. E. Lee."[284]

In December 1861, when the Yanks tried to illegally and immorally block off the shipping channel carrying supplies to the citizens of Charleston, South Carolina, an infuriated and disappointed Lee fired off this dispatch:

☞ "It has been reported to me by [Confederate] General [Roswell Sabine] Ripley that the enemy brought his stone fleet to the entrance of Charleston Harbour to-day [December 20], and sunk between thirteen and seventeen vessels in the main ship channel. The North Channel and Maffit's Channel are still open. This achievement, so unworthy any nation, is the abortive expression of the malice and revenge of a people which it wishes to perpetuate by rendering more memorable a day hateful in their calendar [that is, the secession of South Carolina].

"It is also indicative of their despair of ever capturing a city they design to ruin, for they can never expect to possess what they labour so hard to reduce to a condition not to be enjoyed. I think, therefore, it is certain that an attack on the city of Charleston is not contemplated, and we must endeavour to be prepared against assaults elsewhere on the Southern Coast."[285]

In the Winter of 1861 Lee wrote to the South Carolina Convention:

☞ "The Confederate States have now but one great object in view, the successful issue of their war for independence. Everything worth their

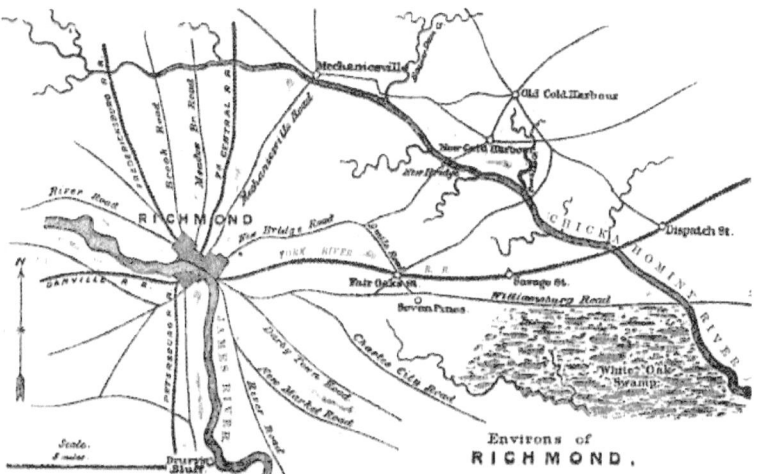

A 19th-Century map of Richmond, Virginia, showing the roads and rivers leading in and out of the town. General Lee was very familiar with these routes.

possessing depends on that. Everything should yield to its accomplishment."²⁸⁶

A portion of a personal letter to his family from the same period:
☞ "Among the calamities of war, the hardest to bear, perhaps, is the separation of families and friends. Yet all must be endured to accomplish our independence, and maintain our self-government. . . .

"Your old home [Arlington House], if not destroyed by our enemies, has been so desecrated that I cannot bear to think of it. I should have preferred it to have been wiped from the earth, its beautiful hill sunk, and its sacred trees buried, rather than to have been degraded by the presence of those [Yankees] who revel in the ill they do for their own selfish purposes. You see what a poor sinner I am, and how unworthy to possess what has been given me; for that reason it has been taken away. I pray for a better spirit, and that the hearts of our enemies may be changed."²⁸⁷

During Lincoln's War, Lee's cousin Martha Custis "Markie" Williams wanted to paint a portrait of his famous dark gray warhorse, Traveller, who not only survived the conflict but served his owner for many years afterward. Lee, of course, obliged, sending her the following interesting and descriptive letter:
☞ "If I was an artist like you, I would draw a true picture of 'Traveller,' representing his fine proportions, muscular figure, deep chest and short back, strong haunches, flat legs, small head, broad forehead, delicate ears, quick eye, small feet, and black mane and tail. Such a picture would inspire a poet, whose genius could then depict his worth and describe his endurance of toil, hunger, thirst, heat, cold, and the dangers and suffering through which he has passed. He could dilate upon his sagacity and affection and his invariable response to every wish of his rider. He might even imagine his thoughts through the long night-marches and days of battle through which he has passed. But I am no artist, and can only say he is a Confederate gray.

"I purchased him in the mountains of [Greenbrier County] Virginia in the autumn of 1861, and he has been my patient follower ever since—to Georgia, the Carolinas, and back to Virginia. He carried me through the seven days' battle around Richmond, the Second Manassas, at Sharpsburg, Fredericksburg, the last day at Chancellorsville, to

General Lee, surrounded by some of his officers, surveying the field of action at the Battle of Fredericksburg I, December 11-15, 1862.

Pennsylvania, at Gettysburg, and back to the Rappahannock. From the commencement of the campaign in 1864 at Orange till its close around Petersburg the saddle was scarcely off his back, as he passed through the fire of the Wilderness, Spottsylvania, Cold Harbor, and across the James River. He was almost in daily requisition in the winter of 1864-65 on the long line of defences from the Chickahominy north of Richmond and Hatcher's Run south of the Appomattox. In the campaign of 1865 he bore me from Petersburg to the final days at Appomattox Court-house.

"You must know the comfort he is to me in my present retirement. He is well supplied with equipments. Two sets have been sent to him from England, one from the ladies of Baltimore, and one was made for him in Richmond; but I think his favorite is the American saddle from St. Louis. Of all his [equine] companions in toil, 'Richmond,' 'Brown Roan,' 'Ajax,' and quiet 'Lucy Long,' he is the only one that retained his vigor to the last. The first two expired under their onerous burden, and the last two failed. You can, I am sure, from what I have said, paint his portrait."[288]

Once, when asked who he thought the greatest of the Yankee generals was, Lee immediately slapped his hand down on the table and said:
☞ "McClellan, by all odds!"[289]

On Christmas Day 1861 Lee wrote to his wife about the Trent Affair, in which the United States illegally arrested and imprisoned two Confederate commissioners on their way to England aboard the British mail steamer Trent *on November 8, 1861:*
☞ "You must not build your hopes on peace on account of the United States going into a war with England [over the Trent Affair]. She will be very loath to do that, notwithstanding the bluster of the Northern papers. Her rulers are not entirely mad, and if they find England is in earnest, and that war or a restitution of their captives must be the consequence, they will adopt the latter. We must make up our minds to fight our battles and win our independence alone. No one will help us. We require no extraneous aid, if true to ourselves. But we must be patient. It is not a light achievement and cannot be accomplished at once. . . .

"I wrote a few days since, giving you all the news, and have now therefore nothing to relate. The enemy is still quiet and increasing in strength. We grow in size slowly but are working hard. I have had a day of labour instead of rest, and have written at intervals to some of the children. I hope they are with you, and inclose my letters. . . . Affectionately and truly, R. E. Lee."

From a February 23, 1862, letter to his wife:
☞ "I fear our soldiers have not realised the necessity for the endurance and labour they are called upon to undergo, and that it is better to sacrifice themselves than our cause."[290]

Due to growing personal divisions in the Confederate military, in the Spring of 1862 Lee found himself having to be a diplomat among his own forces, saying to his fellow officers:
☞ "This is not a time to squabble about rank; every one must work, and do what he can to promote the cause."[291]

On June 1, 1862, when President Davis ordered Lee to take over command of the Army of Northern Virginia after the previous officer, Joseph Eggleston Johnston, had been injured in May at the Battle of Seven Pines, Lee said:
☞ "I wish . . . [Johnston's] mantle had fallen upon an abler man, or that I were able to drive our enemies back to their homes. I have no ambition

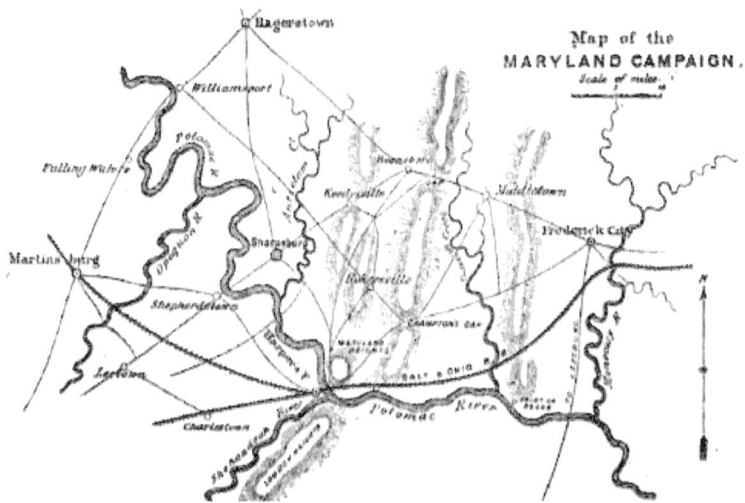

A Victorian map outlining General Lee's operations in Maryland. Lee tried to rescue the states' citizens from the iron grip of martial law placed over them by dictator Lincoln, but they rejected him. After his horrendous loss at Gettysburg, Pennsylvania, Lee headed back south to defend Dixie, giving up his noble but futile attempt to free the Northern people.

and no desire but for the attainment of this object."²⁹²

Around this period Lee issued his first general order as commander of the Army of Northern Virginia:

☞ "The presence of the enemy in front of the Capital, the great interests involved, and the existence of all that is dear to us, appeal in terms too strong to be unheard, and . . . [I feel] assured that every man has resolved to maintain the ancient fame of the Army of Northern Virginia, and the reputation of its general [J. E. Johnston] and to conquer or die in the approaching contest."²⁹³

On June 27, 1862, after the Battle of Gaines' Mill that same day, Lee wrote the following to President Davis, capturing a moment in the life of one of history's most important military officers:

☞ "Mr. President,—Profoundly grateful to Almighty God for the signal victory granted to us, it is my pleasing task to announce to you the success achieved by this army to-day.

"The enemy was this morning driven from his strong position behind Beaver Dam Creek, and pursued to that behind Powhite Creek, and finally, after a severe contest of five hours, entirely repulsed from the field. Night put an end to the contest. I grieve to state that our loss in officers and men is great.

"We sleep on the field, and shall renew the contest in the morning. I have the honour to be, very respectfully, R. E. Lee, General."[294]

After the hard-fought Confederate win at the ferocious Seven Days' Battle (June 25-July 1, 1862), where Lee's army suffered some 20,000 casualties, he spoke encouragingly to his men:
☞ "The immediate fruits of our success are the relief of Richmond from a state of siege; the rout of the great army that so long menaced its safety; many thousand prisoners, including officers of high rank; the capture or destruction of stores to the value of millions, and the acquisition of thousands of arms and forty pieces of superior artillery.

"The service rendered to the country in this short but eventful period can scarcely be estimated, and the General commanding cannot adequately express his admiration of the courage, endurance and soldierly conduct of the officers and men engaged. These brilliant results have cost us many brave men; but while we mourn the loss of our gallant dead, let us not forget that they died nobly in defence of their country's freedom, and have linked their memory with an event that will live forever in the hearts of a grateful people.

"Soldiers, your country will thank you for the heroic conduct you have displayed, conduct worthy of men engaged in a cause so just and sacred, and deserving a nation's gratitude and praise."[295]

On September 3, 1862, Lee wrote bravely to President Davis about the sorry condition of his troops:
☞ "The army is not properly equipped for an invasion of an enemy's territory. It lacks much of the material of war, is feeble in transportation, the animals being much reduced, and the men are poorly provided with clothes, and in thousands of instances are destitute of shoes. Still we cannot afford to be idle, and though weaker than our opponents in men and military equipments, must endeavour to harass if we cannot destroy them. I am aware that the movement is attended with much risk, yet I do not consider success impossible, and shall endeavour to guard it from loss."[296]

THE QUOTABLE ROBERT E. LEE 🖝 149

In another letter from September 1862, Lee again pleads with Confederate authorities for help in outfitting his soldiers:
🖝 "The number of barefooted men is daily increasing, and it pains me to see them limping over the rocky roads."²⁹⁷

After the people of Maryland failed to support Lee's attempt to free them from Lincoln's oppressive yolk of tyranny, and after the vicious and bloody Battle of Sharpsburg (September 17, 1862), the General found many of his men demoralized. To counteract this negative sentiment, on October 2, 1862, he issued the following speech to his troops at his headquarters near Bunker Hill, Virginia:
🖝 "In reviewing the achievements of the army during the present campaign, the commanding general cannot withhold the expression of his admiration of the indomitable courage it has displayed in battle and its cheerful endurance of privation and hardships on the march.

"Since your great victories around Richmond you have defeated the enemy at Cedar Mountain, expelled him from the Rappahannock, and after a conflict of three days utterly repulsed him on the plains of Manassas and forced him to take shelter within the fortifications around his capital. Without halting for repose, you crossed the Potomac,

General Lee at the Battle of Chancellorsville, where he won against an army over twice his size.

stormed the heights of Harper's Ferry, made prisoners of more than 11,600 men, and captured upward of seventy pieces of artillery, all their small-arms, and other munitions of war. While one corps of the army was thus engaged the other ensured its success by arresting at Boonsboro' the combined armies of the enemy, advancing under their favorite general to the relief of their beleaguered comrades.

"On the field of Sharpsburg, with less than one-third his numbers, you resisted from daylight until dark the whole army of the enemy, and repulsed every attack along his entire front of more than four miles in extent.

"The whole of the following day you stood prepared to resume the conflict on the same ground, and retired next morning without molestation across the Potomac.

"Two attempts subsequently made by the enemy to follow you across the river have resulted in his complete discomfiture and his being driven back with loss. Achievements such as these demanded much valor and patriotism. History records fewer examples of greater fortitude and endurance than this army has exhibited, and I am commissioned by the President to thank you in the name of the Confederate States for the undying fame you have won for their arms.

"Much as you have done, much more remains to be accomplished. The enemy again threatens us with invasion, and to your tried valor and patriotism the country looks with confidence for deliverance and safety. Your past exploits give assurance that this confidence is not misplaced. R. E. Lee, General Commanding."[298]

Also on October 2, 1862, Lee replied to a missive from President Davis with these words:

☞ "I wish I felt that I deserved the confidence you express in me. I am only conscious of an earnest desire to advance the interests of the country and of my inability to accomplish my wishes. The brave men of this army fully deserve your thanks, and I will take pleasure in communicating them."[299]

On the other hand, Lee had nothing but praise for most of his fellow officers, as noted in this excerpt from a Fall 1862 letter to President Davis concerning Stonewall Jackson:

☞ "My opinion of the merits of General Jackson has been greatly enhanced during this expedition. He is true, honest, and brave; has a single eye to the good of the service, and spares no exertion to accomplish his object."[300]

General Lee strongly disapproved of gambling in camp, as this order to his soldiers shows:
☞ "It was not supposed that a habit so pernicious and demoralising would be formed among men engaged in a cause, of all others, demanding the highest virtue and purest morality in its supporters."[301]

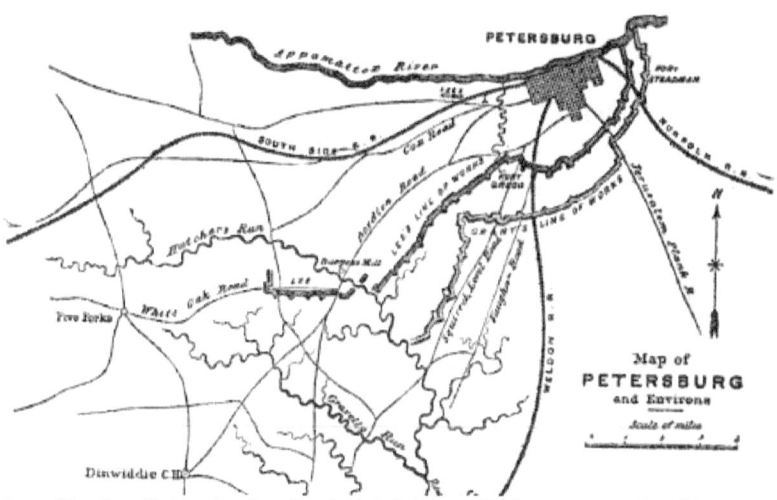

A map of Petersburg, Virginia, where General Lee fought in the Summer of 1864, winning against General Grant.

During the Battle of Fredericksburg (December 11-15, 1862), Lee said the following to his chief of ordnance General Edward Porter Alexander:
☞ "It is well war is so terrible or we would grow too fond of it."[302]

On December 16, 1862, after the Battle of Fredericksburg, Lee wrote of his enemy there, Union General Ambrose E. Burnside and the U.S. Army of the Potomac:
☞ "They suffered heavily as far as the battle went, but it did not go far enough to satisfy me."[303]

After the Confederate win at the Battle of Fredericksburg an officer recommended

to Lee that a "battalion of honour" be formed, to which he replied:
☞ "The fact is, General, we have now an army of brave men. The formation of a battalion of honour would reward a few and leave many, equally brave and equally faithful, unnoticed and, perhaps, with the feeling that an improper distinction had been made between themselves and their comrades."³⁰⁴

On January 10, 1863, Lee wrote the following to James Alexander Seddon, Confederate secretary of war at the time:
☞ "The success with which our efforts have been crowned, under the blessing of God, should not betray our people into the dangerous delusion that the armies now in the field are sufficient to bring this war to a successful and speedy termination. . . .

"The great increase of the enemy's forces will augment the disparity of numbers to such a degree that victory, if attained, can only be achieved by a terrible expenditure of the most precious blood of the country. This blood will be upon the heads of the thousands of able-bodied men who remain at home in safety and ease, while their fellow-citizens are bravely confronting the enemy in the field, or enduring with noble fortitude the hardships and privations of the march and camp. . . .

"In view of the vast increase of the forces of the enemy, of the savage and brutal policy he [Lincoln] has proclaimed [that is, the issuance of the Final Emancipation Proclamation on January 1, 1863], which leaves us no alternative but success or degradation worse than death, if we would save the honour of our families from pollution, our social system from destruction, let every effort be made, every means employed, to fill and maintain the ranks of our armies, until God, in His mercy, shall bless us with the establishment of our independence."³⁰⁵

From a March 3, 1863, letter to one of his children:
☞ "Your poor mamma has been a great sufferer this winter. I have not been able to see her and fear I shall not. She talks of coming to Hickory Hill this month, when the weather becomes more fixed. We are up to our eyes in mud now, and have but little comfort. [Yankee General] Mr. [Joseph] Hooker looms very large over the river. He has two [observation] balloons up in the day and one at night. I hope he is

gratified at what he sees.

"Your cousin, Fitz Lee, beat up his quarters the other day with about four hundred of his cavalry, and advanced within four miles of Falmouth, carrying off one hundred and fifty prisoners with their horses, arms, etc. The day after he recrossed the Rappahannock, they sent all their cavalry after him . . . but the bird had flown. . . . I hope these young Lees will always be too smart for the enemy."[306]

At the Battle of Chancellorsville, April 30-May 6, 1863, the Confederates scored another victory against the Yanks. However, the win was tempered by the fact that the beloved Rebel General Stonewall Jackson was mortally wounded by friendly fire. He did not die at once, but succumbed to pneumonia eight days later after having his left arm amputated. After the initial injury, as Jackson tried to recover, Lee sent the bedridden officer several notes to perk up his spirits, one of the more famous which reads:

☞ "Give him my affectionate regards, and tell him to make haste and get well, and come back to me as soon as he can. He has lost his left arm, but I have lost my right arm."[307]

General Lee commanding his forces at the Battle of Petersburg II, also known as the Assault on Petersburg, June 15-18, 1864.

Another note included this statement to Jackson:
☞ "I cannot express my regret at the occurrence [of you being wounded]. Could I have directed events, I should have chosen for the good of the country to have been disabled in your stead. I congratulate you on the victory, which is due to your skill and energy."[308]

When Lee heard that Jackson's condition was worsening, he said:
☞ "Tell him that I am praying for him as I believe I have never prayed for myself."[309]

After Jackson's passing on May 10, Lee announced the tragedy to his men in the following dispatch. Known as "General Orders No. 61," it is dated May 11, 1863:
☞ "With deep grief, the commanding general announces to the army the death of Lieutenant-general T. J. Jackson, who expired on the 10th instant at 3:15 P.M. The daring, skill, and energy of this great and good soldier, by the decree of an all-wise Providence, are now lost to us. But while we mourn his death, we feel that his spirit still lives, and will inspire the whole army with his indomitable courage and unshaken confidence in God as our hope and our strength. Let his name be a watchword to his corps, who have followed him to victory on so many fields. Let officers and soldiers emulate his invincible determination to do everything in the defense of our beloved country. R. E. Lee, General."[310]

On May 21, 1863, Lee wrote to Confederate General John Bell Hood about Jackson's passing:
☞ "I grieve much over the death of General Jackson. For our sakes not his. He is happy and at peace. But his spirit lives with us. I hope it will raise up many Jacksons in our ranks."[311]

After the Confederate win at the Battle of Chancellorsville (May 30-April 6, 1863), Lee wrote in his official report concerning:
☞ ". . . the dangers and difficulties which under God's blessing, were surmounted by the fortitude and valour of our army. The conduct of the troops cannot be too highly praised. Attacking largely superior numbers in strongly intrenched positions, their heroic courage overcame every

A map of the Battle of Sharpsburg, known as the Battle of Antietam to Yanks, September 16-18, 1862. Here, Lee went up against Union General George B. McClellan and a Federal army twice the size of his own. Though the conflict was widely considered a draw, dictator Lincoln decided to see it as a Yankee win, using it not only as an excuse to issue his Preliminary Emancipation Proclamation (on September 22), but also to whip up the flames of sectional hatred and racial discord. And indeed, this is precisely what occurred. For Lincoln's edict was nothing more than a "military emancipation," issued solely for the purposes of replacing his ever decreasing numbers of white troops with blacks, attempting to start slave riots across the South, and pushing Congress to give him more money to fund his overtly racist campaign to have all African-Americans shipped out of the country—preferably, as he put it on August 21, 1858, during a speech at Ottawa, Illinois, "back to their native land" (Africa). The plan, known as "black colonization," backfired, and he was denounced from coast to coast by both white and black abolition leaders. One from the latter group, Frederick Douglass, correctly observed that Lincoln's view of African-Americans "lacks the genuine spark of humanity."

obstacle of nature and art and achieved a triumph most honourable to our arms. . . .

"Among them will be found some who have passed by a glorious death beyond the reach of praise, but the memory of whose virtues and devoted patriotism will ever be cherished by their grateful countrymen. . . . To the skilful and efficient management of the artillery the successful issue of the contest is in great measure due."[312]

In 1863 General Lee penned the following to Confederate General John Bell Hood:
☞ "I agree with you in believing that our army would be invincible if it could be properly organized and officered. There were never such men in an army before. They will go anywhere and do anything if properly led. But there is the difficulty—proper commanders. Where can they

be obtained? But they are improving, constantly improving. Rome was not built in a day, nor can we expect miracles in our favor."[313]

In June 1863 Lee had this to say about the growing antiwar party in the North:
☞ "We should not . . . conceal from ourselves that our resources in men are constantly diminishing, and the disproportion in this respect between us and our enemies, if they continue united in their efforts to subjugate us, is steadily augmenting. . . .

"Under these circumstances, we should neglect no honourable means of dividing and weakening our enemies, that they may feel some of the difficulties experienced by ourselves. It seems to me that the most effectual mode of accomplishing this object now within our reach, is to give all the encouragement we can, consistently with truth, to the rising peace party of the North.[314]

From his headquarters at Chambersburg, Pennsylvania, on June 27, 1863, Lee issued the following "General Orders No. 72" to his soldiers. Here we see not only the General's standing prohibition against committing outrages against noncombatants, but his opinion of the many heinous crimes perpetuated by Lincoln's armies:
☞ "The commanding general has observed with marked satisfaction the conduct of the troops on the march, and confidently anticipates results commensurate with the high spirit they have manifested. No troops could have displayed greater fortitude or better performed the arduous marches of the past ten days. Their conduct in other respects has, with few exceptions, been in keeping with their character as soldiers, and entitles them to approbation and praise.

"There have, however, been instances of forgetfulness on the part of some that they have in keeping the yet unsullied reputation of the [Confederate] army, and that the duties exacted of us by civilization and Christianity are not less obligatory in the country of the enemy than in our own. The commanding general considers that no greater disgrace could befall the army, and through it our whole people, than the perpetration of the barbarous outrages upon the innocent and defenceless and the wanton destruction of private property that have marked the

Confederate generals. From top, moving clockwise: Pierre G. T. Beauregard, James Longstreet, Jeb Stuart, Albert S. Johnston, Ambrose P. Hill, Richard S. Ewell. Center: Thomas J. "Stonewall" Jackson.

course of the enemy in our own country. Such proceedings not only disgrace the perpetrators and all connected with them, but are subversive of the discipline and efficiency of the army and destructive of the ends of our present movements.

"It must be remembered that we make war only on armed men, and that we cannot take vengeance for the wrongs our people have suffered without lowering ourselves in the eyes of all whose abhorrence has been excited by the atrocities of our enemy, and offending against Him to whom vengeance belongeth, without whose favor and support our efforts must all prove in vain.

"The commanding general therefore earnestly exhorts the troops to abstain, with most scrupulous care, from unnecessary or wanton injury to private property, and he enjoins upon all officers to arrest and bring to summary punishment all who shall in any way offend against the orders on this subject. R. E. Lee, General."[315]

While Lee's many admirers had nothing but compliments and praise pertaining to his physical appearance, his own view of himself could not have been more different, as noted in the following self description the General penned during the War for Southern Independence:

☞ "My coat is of gray, of the regulation style and pattern, and my pants of dark blue, as is also prescribed, partly hid by my long boots. I have the same handsome hat which surmounts my gray head (the latter is not prescribed in the regulations), and shields my ugly face, which is masked by a white beard as stiff and wiry as the teeth of a [wool] card. In fact, an uglier person you have never seen, and so unattractive is it to our enemies that they shoot at it whenever visible to them."[316]

Just prior to the Battle of Gettysburg, July 1-3, 1863:
☞ "The enemy is here and if we do not whip him, he will whip us."[317]

After Pickett's Charge on July 3, 1863—in which Confederate General George E. Pickett's division was nearly destroyed during Lee's failed assault against Union troops on the last day of the Battle of Gettysburg—Lee told an inconsolable Pickett:
☞ "Never mind, general; all this has been my fault. It is *I* who have lost this fight, and you must help me out of it the best way you can."[318]

About the same time Lee penned the following to a female relative:
☞ "I cannot tell how often and much I have thought of you the past winter, how I have grieved over your restraint and ill-usage by our enemies, and how I have regretted my inability to relieve you. . . . I knew that crossing the Potomac would draw them [the Yankees at the

Battle of Gettysburg] off, and if we could only have been strong enough we should have detained them. But God willed otherwise, and I fear we shall soon have them all back. The [Confederate] army did all it could. I fear I required of it impossibilities. But it responded to the call nobly and cheerfully, and, though it did not win a victory, it conquered a success. We must now prepare for heavier blows and harder work. But my trust is in Him who favors the weak and relieves the oppressed, and my hourly prayer is that He will 'fight for us once again.'"319

On July 11, 1863, immediately following Gettysburg, Lee issued the following address to his gallant troops:

☞ "After long and trying marches, endured with the fortitude that has ever characterised the soldiers of the Army of Northern Virginia, you have penetrated the country of our enemies, and recalled to the defence of their own soil those who were engaged in the invasion of ours. You have fought a fierce and sanguinary battle, which, if not attended with the success that has hitherto crowned your efforts, was marked by the same heroic spirit that has commanded the respect of your enemies, the gratitude of your country, and the admiration of mankind.

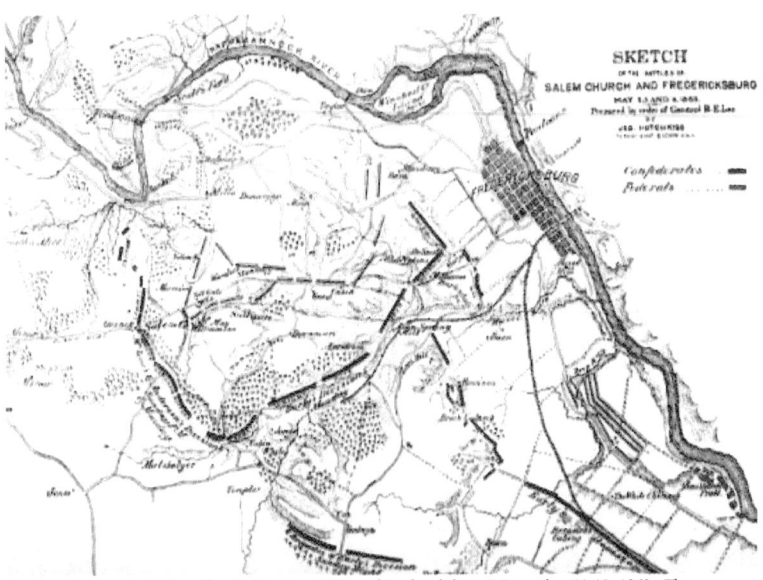

A map of the Battles of Salem Church, May 3-4, 1863, and Fredericksburg I, December 11-15, 1862. The Confederates won both.

"Once more you are called upon to meet the army from which you have won on so many fields a name that will never die. . . . Let every soldier remember that on his courage and fidelity depends all that makes life worth having—the freedom of his country, the honour of his people, and the security of his home. . . ."³²⁰

Despite such positive statements, Lee never got over his loss at Gettysburg. In 1868, when he was asked by Major William M. McDonald about some of his greatest battles, Lee explained the Pennsylvania conflict this way:
☞ "As to the battle of Gettysburg, I must again refer you to the official accounts. Its loss was occasioned by a combination of circumstances. It was commenced in the absence of correct intelligence. It was continued in the effort to overcome the difficulties by which we were surrounded, and it would have been gained could one determined and united blow have been delivered by our whole line. As it was, victory trembled in the balance for three days, and the battle resulted in the infliction of as great an amount of injury as was received and in frustrating the Federal campaign for the season."³²¹

On September 25, 1863, following the Battle of Chickamauga (September 19-20), Lee sent the following dispatch to Confederate General James Longstreet:
☞ "My whole heart and soul have been with you and your brave corps in your late battle. It was natural to hear of [our officers] Longstreet and [Daniel Harvey] Hill charging side by side, and pleasing to find the armies of the east and west vying with each other in valour and devotion to their country. . . . Finish the work before you, my dear General, and return to me. I want you badly, and you cannot get back too soon."³²²

In October 1863, at one point during the Battle of Mine Run, Lee decided to withdrew his troops for the following reasons:
☞ "Nothing prevented my continuing in his front but the destitute condition of the men, thousands of whom are barefooted, a greater number partially shod, and nearly all without overcoats, blankets or warm clothing. I think the sublimest sight of the war was the cheerfulness and alacrity exhibited by this army in the pursuit of the enemy under all the trials and privations to which it was exposed."³²³

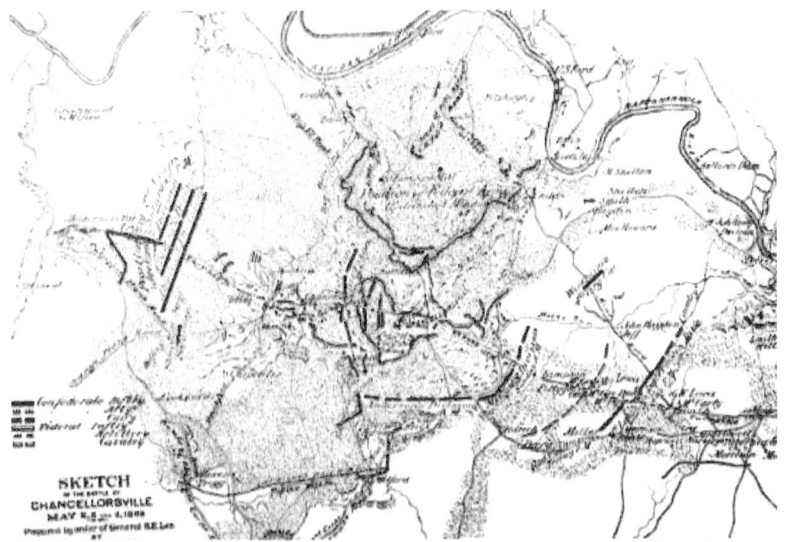

A map of the Battle of Chancellorsville, April 30-May 6, 1863, at which Lee scored another win for the South.

From Camp Rappahannock, Lee wrote the following to his wife on October 25, 1863. The General touches on Lincoln and Grant's cruel, short-sighted, and mutually destructive halt to the prisoner exchange program:

☞ ". . . I moved yesterday into a nice pine thicket, and Perry [the General's body-servant] is to-day engaged in constructing a chimney in front of my tent, which will make it warm and comfortable. I have no idea when [our imprisoned son] Fitzhugh will be exchanged. The Federal authorities still resist all exchanges, because they think it is to our interest to make them. Any desire expressed on our part for the exchange of any individual magnifies the difficulty, as they at once think some great benefit is to result to us from it. His detention is very grievous to me, and, besides, I want his services.

"I am glad you have some socks for the army. Send them to me. They will come safely. Tell the girls [the Lee's daughters] to send all they can. I wish they could make some shoes, too. We have thousands of barefooted men. There is no news. [Union] General [George Gordon] Meade, I believe, is repairing the railroad, and I presume will come on again. If I could only get some shoes and clothes for the men, I would save him the trouble. . . ."[324]

In November 1863, Lee's son Fitzhugh was still incarcerated in a Yankee prison,

prompting this statement to his wife Mary on the 21st:
☛ "... I see by the papers that our son has been sent to Fort Lafayette. Any place would be better than Fort Monroe, with [Union General Benjamin F.] Butler in command. His long confinement is very grievous to me, yet it may all turn out for the best...."[325]

On November 26, 1863, Lee issued his stirring General Orders No. 102:
☛ "The enemy is again advancing upon our capital, and the country once more looks to this army for protection. Under the blessings of God, your valor has repelled every previous attempt, and, invoking the continuance of his favor, we cheerfully commit to Him the issue of the coming conflict.

"A cruel enemy seeks to reduce our fathers and our mothers, our wives and our children, to abject slavery; to strip them of their property, and drive them from their homes. Upon you these helpless ones rely to avert these terrible calamities, and secure them the blessing of liberty and safety. Your past history gives them the assurance that their trust will not be in vain. Let every man remember that all he holds dear depends upon the faithful discharge of his duty, and resolve to fight, and, if need be, to die, in defense of a cause so sacred, and worthy the name won by this army on so many bloody fields."[326]

For much of Lincoln's War Lee's men marched and fought in various states of severe deprivation, as the following January letter, from the General to the Confederacy's quartermaster during the particularly harsh Winter of 1864, reveals:
☛ "General: The want of shoes and blankets in this army continues to cause much suffering and to impair its efficiency. In one regiment I am informed that there are only fifty men with serviceable shoes, and a brigade that recently went on picket was compelled to leave several hundred men in camp, who were unable to bear the exposure of duty, being destitute of shoes and blankets....

"The supply, by running the blockade, has become so precarious that I think we should turn our attention chiefly to our own resources, and I should like to be informed how far the latter can be counted upon. ... I trust that no efforts will be spared to develop our own resources of supply, as a further dependence upon those from abroad can result in nothing but increase of suffering and want. I am, with great respect, your obedient servant, R. E. Lee, General."[327]

On January 24, 1864, Lee wrote the following to his wife:
☞ "I have had to disperse the cavalry as much as possible, to obtain forage for their horses, and it is that which causes trouble. Provisions for the men, too, are very scarce, and, with very light diet and light clothing, I fear they suffer, but still they are cheerful and uncomplaining. I received a report from one division the other day in which it stated that over four hundred men were barefooted and over a thousand without blankets."[328]

If the Confederate soldier had one fault it was his innate individuality, his nonconformity, his distaste for rules and restrictions, and his love of personal freedom, all which, by definition, were in conflict with the regimented military life. As General Lee points out in the following statement, while the Rebel troops certainly possessed bravery, dash, and daring in abundance, their independent streak could sometimes hamper effectiveness on the battlefield and even put their own safety at risk:

Another view of Lee's antebellum home Arlington House, this one from the Summer of 1860. The Lee's could not have known it then, but within one year it would be taken over by Union troops, after which it would be despoiled, plundered, its inhabitants thrown out into the street, and detested Yankee soldiers buried in the yards.

☞ "The spirit which animates our soldiers and the natural courage with which they are so liberally endowed have led to a reliance on these good qualities to the neglect of measures that would increase their efficiency and contribute to their safety."329

From a January 1864 letter, this one to his son Robert. Jr.:
☞ ". . . Tell Fitz [General Lee's nephew] I grieve over the hardships and sufferings of his men in their late expedition. I would have preferred his waiting for more favourable weather. He accomplished much under the circumstances, but would have done more in better weather. I am afraid he was anxious to get back to the ball. This is a bad time for such things. We have too grave subjects on hand to engage in such trivial amusements. I would rather his officers should entertain themselves in fattening their horses, healing their men, and recruiting their regiments. There are too many Lees on the committee. I like them all to be present at battles, but can excuse them at balls. But the saying is, 'Children will be children.' I think he had better move his camp farther from Charlottesville, and perhaps he will get more work and less play. He and I are too old for such assemblies. I want him to write me how his men are, [and] his horses, and what I can do to fill up his ranks."330

From a February 6, 1864, letter to his wife:
☞ ". . . It is so long since we have had the foreign bean [coffee] that we no longer desire it. We have a domestic article which we procure by the bushel, that answers very well. . . . We have had to reduce our allowance of meat one-half, and some days we have none. . . . The soldiers are much in need. We have received some shoes lately, and the socks will be a great addition. Tell [our daughter] 'Life' [Mildred] I think I hear her needles rattle as they fly through the meshes."331

From a March 18, 1864, letter to his family:
☞ "There were sixty-seven pairs of socks in the bag I brought up instead of sixty-four, as you supposed, and I found here three dozen pairs of beautiful white-yarn socks, sent over by our kind cousin Julia and sweet little Carrie, making one hundred and three pairs, all of which I sent to the Stonewall brigade. One dozen of the Stuart socks had double heels. Can you not teach Mildred that stitch. They sent me also some hams,

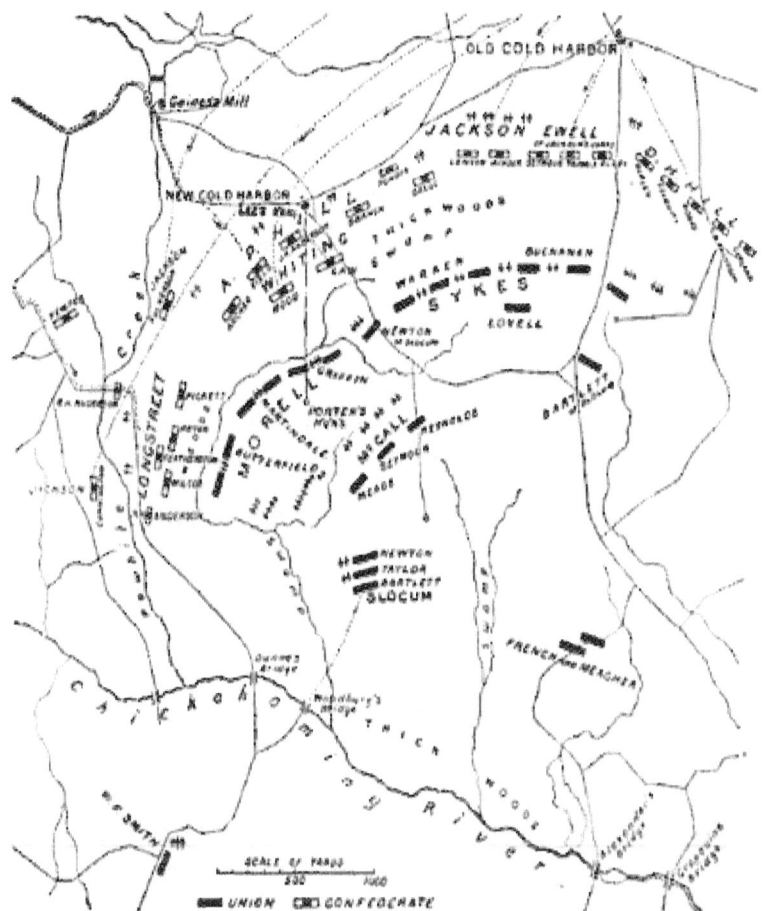

A map of the Battle of Cold Harbor II. Fought May 31-June 12, 1864, Lee won again, this time against General Ulysses S. Grant, with twice the number of men.

which I had rather they had eaten. I pray that you may be preserved and relieved from all your troubles, and that we may all be again united here on earth and forever in heaven."³³²

Another family letter, this one dated April 2, 1864:
☞ "Your note with the socks arrived last evening. I have sent them to the Stonewall brigade; the number all right—thirty pairs. Including this last parcel of thirty pairs, I have sent to that brigade two hundred and sixty-three pairs. Still, there are about one hundred and forty whose

homes are within the enemy's lines and who are without socks. I shall continue to furnish them till all are supplied. Tell the young women to work hard [knitting] for the brave Stonewallers."[333]

The hardships continued throughout the Spring of 1864, as Lee indicates in this April 12 letter to Confederate President Jefferson Davis:
☞ "Mr. President: My anxiety on the subject of provisions for the army is so great that I cannot refrain from expressing it to Your Excellency. I cannot see how we can operate with our present supplies. Any derangement in their arrival or disaster to the railroad would render it impossible for me to keep the army together, and might force a retreat into North Carolina. There is nothing to be had in this section for men or animals. We have rations for the troops to-day and to-morrow. I hope a new supply arrived last night, but I have not yet had a report. Every exertion should be made to supply the depots at Richmond and at other points. All pleasure travel should cease, and everything be devoted to necessary wants. I am, with great respect, your obedient servant, R. E. Lee, General."[334]

On May 20, 1864, after the untimely death of Confederate General James Ewell Brown "Jeb" Stuart on May 12, Lee issued this announcement:
☞ "The commanding general announces to the army with heartfelt sorrow the death of Maj. Gen. J. E. B. Stuart, late commander of the Cavalry Corps of the Army of Northern Virginia. Among the gallant soldiers who have fallen in this war, General Stuart was second to none in valour, in zeal, and in unflinching devotion to his country. His achievements form a conspicuous part of the history of this army, with which his name and services will be forever associated.

"To military capacity of a high order, and to the nobler virtues of the soldier, he added the brighter graces of a pure life, guided and sustained by the Christian's faith and hope. The mysterious hand of an all-wise God has removed him from the scene of his usefulness and fame. His grateful countrymen will mourn his loss and cherish his memory. To his comrades in arms he has left the proud recollections of his deeds and the inspiring influence of his example."[335]

In an August 14, 1864, letter to his wife, Lee sums up his typically Christian attitude toward Lincoln's War:

☞ "We must suffer patiently to the end, when all things will be made right."³³⁶

During Lincoln's War, when Lee's wife Mary pleaded with him to take better care of his health and safety, the General replied this way:

☞ ". . . But what care can a man give to himself in the time of war? It is from no desire for exposure or hazard that I live in a tent, but from necessity. I must be where I can, speedily, at all times, attend to the duties of my position, and be near or accessible to the officers with whom I have to act. I have been offered rooms in the houses of our citizens, but I could not turn the dwellings of my kind hosts into a barrack where officers, couriers, distressed women, etc., would be entering day and night. . . ."³³⁷

On February 6, 1865, Lee was made commander-in-chief of all the military forces in the Confederate States. In accepting the command he said:

☞ ". . . Deeply impressed with the difficulties and responsibilities of the position, and humbly invoking the guidance of Almighty God, I rely for

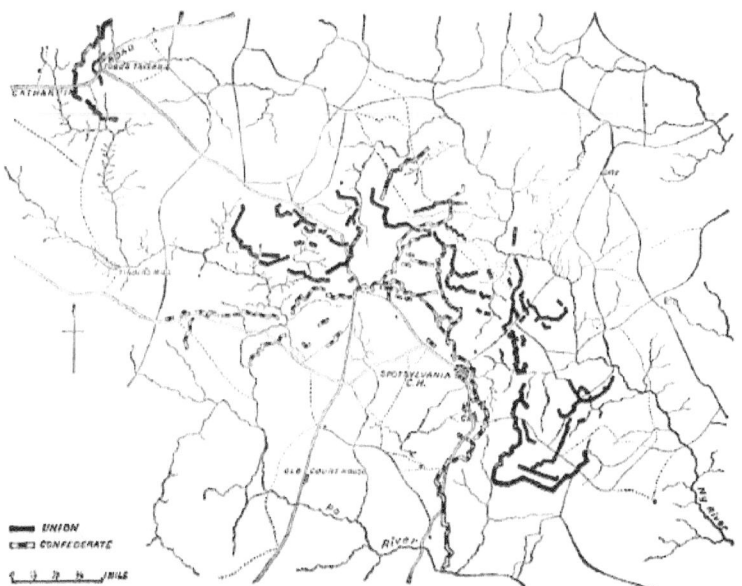

A map of the Battle of Spotsylvania Court House, May 8-21, 1864, in which Lee went up against Grant.

success upon the courage and fortitude of the army, sustained by the patriotism and firmness of the people, confident that their united efforts under the blessing of Heaven will secure peace and independence."[338]

On February 14, 1865, Lee issued his second order as commander-in-chief, this one to those Confederate soldiers who had chosen to desert:

☞ "In entering upon the campaign about to open, the general-in-chief feels assured that the soldiers who have so long and so nobly borne the hardships and dangers of the war require no exhortation to respond to the calls of honor and duty.

"With the liberty transmitted by their forefathers they have inherited the spirit to defend it.

"The choice between war and abject submission is before them.

"To such a proposal brave men, with arms in their hands, can have but one answer.

"They cannot barter manhood for peace nor the right of self government for life or property.

"But justice to them requires a sterner admonition to those who have abandoned their comrades in the hour of peril.

"A last opportunity is afforded them to wipe out the disgrace and escape the punishment of their crimes.

"By authority of the President of the Confederate States, a pardon is announced to such deserters and men improperly absent as shall return to the commands to which they belong within the shortest possible time, not exceeding twenty days from the publication of this order, at the headquarters of the department in which they may be.

"Those who may be prevented by interruption of communications, may report within the time specified to the nearest enrolling officer or other officer on duty, to be forwarded as soon as practicable, and, upon presenting a certificate from such officer showing compliance with the requirement, will receive the pardon hereby offered. Those who have deserted to the service of the enemy, or who have deserted after having been once pardoned for the same offense, and those who shall desert or absent themselves without authority after the publication of this order, are excluded from its benefits. Nor does the offer of pardon extend to other offenses than desertion and absence without permission.

THE QUOTABLE ROBERT E. LEE ❧ 169

Richmond, Virginia, as it looked to General Lee and his family *before* Lincoln's War.

"By the same authority it is also declared that no general amnesty will again be granted, and those who refuse to accept the pardon now offered, or who shall hereafter desert or absent themselves without leave, shall suffer such punishment as the courts may impose, and no application for clemency will be entertained.

"Taking new resolution from the fate which our enemies intend for us, let every man devote all his energies to the common defense.

"Our resources, wisely and vigorously employed, are ample, and with a brave army, sustained by a determined and united people, success with Gods assistance cannot be doubtful. The advantages of the enemy will have but little value if we do not permit them to impair our resolution. Let us then oppose constancy to adversity, fortitude to suffering, and courage to danger, with the firm assurance that He who gave freedom to our fathers will bless the efforts of their children to preserve it. R. E. Lee, General."[339]

As noted earlier, on February 18, 1865, Lee wrote the following concerning enlisting blacks in the Confederate military:

☞ "I think the measure not only expedient but necessary. The enemy will certainly use them against us if he can get possession of them. . . . I do not think that our white population can supply the necessities of a long war without overtaxing its capacity, and imposing great suffering upon our people; and I believe we should provide resources for a protracted struggle—not merely for a battle or campaign. . . . In my opinion, the negroes, under proper circumstances, will make efficient soldiers. . . . I think those who are employed should be freed. It would be neither just nor wise, in my opinion, to require them to serve as slaves."[340]

From a February 21, 1865, letter to his wife:
☛ ". . . I think General Grant will move against us soon—within a week, if nothing prevents—and no man can tell what may be the result; but trusting to a merciful God, who does not always give the battle to the strong, I pray we may not be overwhelmed. I shall, however, endeavour to do my duty and fight to the last."[341]

On February 24, 1865, Lee sent the following letter to the author's cousin, North

Richmond, Virginia, as it looked to General Lee and his family *after* Lincoln's War.

Carolina Governor Zebulon Baird Vance:

☞ "The state of despondency that now prevails among our people is producing a bad effect upon the troops. Desertions are becoming very frequent, and there is good reason to believe that they are occasioned to a considerable extent by letters written to the soldiers by their friends at home.

"In the last two weeks several hundred have deserted from Hill's corps, and as the divisions from which the greatest number of desertions have taken place are composed chiefly of troops from North Carolina, they furnish a corresponding proportion of deserters. I think some good can be accomplished by the efforts of influential citizens to change public sentiment, and cheer the spirits of the people.

"It has been discovered that despondent persons represent to their friends in the army that our cause is hopeless, and that they had better provide for themselves. They state that the number of deserters is so large in the several counties that there is no danger to be apprehended from the home-guard. The deserters generally take their arms with them.

"The greater number are from regiments from the western part of the State. So far as the despondency of the people occasions this sad condition of affairs, I know of no other means of removing it than by the counsel and exhortation of prominent citizens. If they would explain to the people that the cause is not hopeless, that the situation of affairs, though critical, is so to the enemy as well as ourselves, that he has drawn his troops from every other quarter to accomplish his designs against Richmond, and that his defeat now would result in leaving nearly our whole territory open to us; that this great result can be accomplished if all will work diligently, and that his successes are far less valuable in fact than in appearance,—I think our sorely tried people would be induced to make one more effort to bear their sufferings a little longer, and regain some of the spirit that marked the first two years of the war."[342]

In March 1865 Lee wrote to his son Custis:

☞ "I have been up to see the Congress and they do not seem to be able to do anything except to eat peanuts and chew tobacco, while my army is starving."[343]

The Great Seal of the Confederate States, with Lee family relation President George Washington in the center. The Latin phrase *Deo Vindice* means "God Will Vindicate Us." And He will.

On April 7, 1865, Lee said to Confederate General William Nelson Pendleton:

☞ "I have never believed we could, against the gigantic combination for our subjugation, make good in the long run our independence unless foreign powers should, directly or indirectly, assist us. . . . But such considerations really made with me no difference. We had, I was satisfied, sacred principles to maintain and rights to defend, for which we were in duty bound to do our best, even if we perished in the endeavour."³⁴⁴

On April 8, 1865, Lee and Yankee General Ulysses S. Grant began communicating concerning the termination of hostilities and the surrender of the Confederate armies. What follows is one of Lee's missives to Grant, revealing his great reluctance to give up the fight:

☞ "General: I received at a late hour your note of to-day. In mine of yesterday I did not intend to propose the surrender of the Army of Northern Virginia, but to ask the terms of your proposition. To be frank, I do not think the emergency has arisen to call for the surrender of this army, but as the restoration of peace should be the sole object of all, I desired to know whether your proposals would lead to that end. I cannot therefore meet you with a view to surrender the Army of Northern Virginia, but as far as your proposal may affect the Confederate States forces under my command and tend to the restoration of peace, I should be pleased to meet you at ten A.M. to-morrow on the old stage-road to Richmond, between the picket-lines of the two armies. R. E. Lee, General."³⁴⁵

The next day, April 9, 1865, Lee was forced to concede that Grant's well fed, well clothed, well equipped forces were five times the size of his own feisty but bedraggled, barefoot, starving army. The end had come—though not the one he would have preferred (that is, the soldier's noble death on the battlefield), as he penned forlornly that day:

☞ "There is nothing left but to go to General Grant, and I would rather die a thousand deaths. . . . How easily I could get rid of this, and be at rest. I have only to ride along the line and all will be over. But it is our duty to live. What will become of the women and children of the South, if we are not here to protect them."[346]

On the morning of April 9, 1865, just prior to Lee's "surrender," Confederate General Edward Porter Alexander found Lee sitting on a tree stump before a dying campfire. Depressed and exhausted, both knew that the end was near. However, Alexander said that their soldiers still had some ammunition left and were ready to continue the fight. To this Lee replied:

☞ "No, General Alexander, that will not do. You must remember we are a Christian people. We have fought this fight as long and as well as we know how. For us as a Christian people there is now but one course to pursue. We must accept the situation; these men must go home and plant a crop, and we must proceed to build up our country on a new basis. We cannot have recourse to the methods you suggest."[347]

Later that day, April 9, 1865, as his soldiers gathered around him on his way back from signing the "surrender" agreement at Appomattox Court House, Lee said to them:

☞ "Men, we have fought through the war together. I have done the best I could for you. My heart is too full to say more."[348]

After his "surrender," Lee wished to avoid arousing further bitterness between the South and the North. To this end he set a Christian example to other Southerners by immediately saying:
☞ "General Grant has acted with magnanimity."[349]

The next day, April 10, 1865, Lee issued his sad farewell to his troops:
☞ "After four years of arduous service, marked by unsurpassed courage and fortitude, the Army of Northern Virginia has been compelled to yield to overwhelming numbers and resources. I need not tell the brave

survivors of so many hard-fought battles, who have remained steadfast to the last, that I have consented to the result from no distrust of them. But, feeling that valor and devotion could accomplish nothing that could compensate for the loss that must have attended the continuance of the contest, I determined to avoid the useless sacrifice of those whose past services have endeared them to their countrymen. By the terms of the agreement officers and men can return to their homes and remain until exchanged. You will take with you the satisfaction that proceeds from the consciousness of duty faithfully performed; and I earnestly pray that a merciful God will extend to you his blessing and protection. With an increasing admiration of your constancy and devotion to your country, and a grateful remembrance of your kind and generous considerations for myself, I bid you all an affectionate farewell. R. E. Lee, General."[350]

Two days later, on April 12, 1865, Lee wrote to the Confederacy's leader, President Jefferson Davis, breaking the bad news:
☞ "Mr. President: It is with pain that I announce to Your Excellency the surrender of the Army of Northern Virginia. . . . Upon arriving at Amelia Court-house on the morning of the 4th with the advance of the army, . . . and not finding the supplies ordered to be placed there, nearly twenty-four hours were lost in endeavoring to collect in the country

Lee was not at the Battle of Thoroughfare Gap, August 28, 1862, but troops from the Army of Northern Virginia were present, with Confederate General James Longstreet in command.

subsistence for men and horses. This delay was fatal and could not be retrieved. The troops, wearied by continual fighting and marching for several days and nights, obtained neither rest nor refreshment; . . .

"Learning the condition of affairs on the lines, where I had gone under the expectation of meeting General Grant to learn definitely the terms he proposed in a communication received from him on the 8th, in

Another view of Richmond, in 1865, after Lincoln and his soldiers got through with it. Southerners are still asking the obvious question: why would the president of the United States willingly, knowingly, and actively bomb Southern cities into rubble and wantonly kill their citizens merely for legally and peacefully leaving the Union? The North has yet to answer.

the event of the surrender of the army, I requested a suspension of hostilities until these terms could be arranged. In the interview which occurred with General Grant in compliance with my request, terms having been agreed on, I surrendered that portion of the Army of Northern Virginia which was on the field, with its arms, artillery, and wagon trains, the officers and men to be paroled, retaining their sidearms and private effects. I deemed this course the best under all the circumstances by which we were surrounded.

"On the morning of the 9th . . . [the] enemy were more than five times our numbers. If we could have forced our way one day longer it would have been at a great sacrifice of life, and at its end I did not see how a surrender could have been avoided. We had no subsistence for man or horse, and it could not be gathered in the country. The supplies ordered to Pamplin's Station from Lynchburg could not reach us, and the men, deprived of food and sleep for many days, were worn out and exhausted. With great respect, your obedient servant, R. E. Lee, General."[351]

Lee's August 24, 1865, letter declining Washington College's offer to make him president (see pages 60-61). The school disregarded Lee, and the rest is history.

13

UNION

WAR CRIMES

There were so many war crimes committed by the United States during the "Civil War" that they will never all be known or counted. As a fish rots from the head down, we can be sure that most of the Yankee soldiers who perpetuated these crimes got their inspiration from the head of their own government, Abraham Lincoln.

President Lincoln's personal crimes are legion and I have written about them extensively in my other books. Nonetheless, in an effort to provide some context to General's Lee's life story, we will touch on a few here. Many of Lincoln's illegalities were crimes because they were unconstitutional; some were unethical and immoral; most were simply against the law.

Abraham Lincoln, war criminal.

BETWEEN 1860 AND 1865 LINCOLN:
Rigged both the 1860 and the 1864 elections, using horse-trading, bribery, lying, patronage, and cheating, and by stationing his soldiers at the polls to intimidate voters.
Tortured and imprisoned Northern antiwar advocates.
Repeatedly subverted the Constitution.

Overturned the original confederate republic of the Founding Fathers and transformed it into a socialistic democracy that bordered on a wholesale dictatorship.

Instituted personal income tax and what would become the IRS.

Declared war and spent millions, both without congressional approval.

Called up troops without congressional approval.

Seized rail and telegraph lines leading to the capital.

Issued paper money (imaginary tender, or what Jefferson called "fictitious capital").

Used profits from the Northern slave industry to fund his war.

Defied the Supreme Court.

Intimidated Congress.

Purposefully delayed calling Congress into session for four months (to hide his crimes), despite the "extraordinary occasion" of the war.

Checked (i.e., arrested) clergymen who had "become dangerous to the public interest" (i.e., who contradicted Lincoln).

Declared all medicines contraband of war while refusing to exchange prisoners with the C.S.A. (both resulted in thousands of needless deaths, including Yankee prisoners held at Andersonville prison *and* Southern noncombatants as well).

Forced foreigners (i.e., citizens of the Confederate States of America) to take an oath of allegiance to the United States of America, or face arrest and imprisonment.

Arrested members of Northern state legislatures.

Created heretofore unknown offices, such as "military governor," in conquered Southern states.

Instituted the first military draft in U.S. history.

Imposed so-called "Reconstruction" governments in Southern states.

Completely removed every inhabitant living in certain counties, "*en masse*," as Lincoln put it, in the Southern states.

Nationalized the railroads.

Forced all federal employees to contribute 5 percent of their annual income to his reelection campaign.

Censored telegraph communications.

Declared and executed Reconstruction policies (the Constitution gives the president no such power).

Countermanded the emancipation of slaves by his cabinet members and military officers, such as Simon Cameron, John W. Phelps, John C. Frémont, Jim Lane, and David Hunter (which proves once and for all, if nothing else does, that Lincoln did not wage war against the South over slavery).
Issued a naval blockade across the South, which upset world commerce and caused massive deprivations in places like England.
Confiscated private property (a violation of the Second Amendment).
Destroyed private property.
Encouraged slave revolts.
Disrupted commerce with the Southern states.
Established martial law and provisional courts in vanquished Southern states (since Southern civilian courts were still open, this was unconstitutional).
Proclaimed Confederate privateersmen "insurgents" and "pirates," subject to the death penalty.
Suspended *habeas corpus* in both the South and the North (according to the Constitution only Congress has this power).

IN THE NORTHERN STATES SPECIFICALLY LINCOLN:
Prevented governmental debate over secession.
Nullified the acts of numerous state legislatures.
Imprisoned volunteer soldiers.
Closed down over 300 newspapers, destroyed their presses, and jailed their owners, all for printing anti-war or anti-Lincoln articles.
Arrested, imprisoned, tortured, and murdered peaceful unarmed citizens.
Invaded Northern states, without permission or authority, for the express purpose of subverting their governments and overthrowing the sovereignty of the people.
Expelled state authorities.
Used state conventions to assume unlawful powers.
Elected and introduced persons to offices still occupied.
Abandoned the protection of the unalienable rights of the Northern people.
Declared martial law throughout the North (and later the South) without authority.

Emancipated Northern slaves in violation of local, state, and constitutional law.[352]

This is just a partial list!

Naturally, the always polite, diplomatic, and religious Lee—who refused to make derogatory remarks about others, even his Northern enemies—said very little about the crimes committed by Lincoln and his troops. However, he did leave us with a few statements pertaining to this topic, as this chapter amply illustrates.

On July 21, 1862, General Lee wrote the following to Union General George B. McClellan. From it we can derive a partial idea of the tremendous outrages that were being perpetuated against the Southern people by Lincoln's illicit invaders. In this case it was the illegal arrest, imprisonment, and abuse (torture) of Southerners who refused to take Lincoln's unlawful Oath of Allegiance to the United States of America:

☞ "General: It has come to my knowledge that many of our citizens, engaged in peaceful avocations, have been arrested and imprisoned because they refused to take the oath of allegiance to the United States, while others, by hard and harsh treatment, have been compelled to take an oath not to bear arms against that Government.

"I have learned that about one hundred of the latter class have recently been released from Fortress Monroe. This [Confederate]

The fight at Burnside's Bridge, during the Battle of Gettysburg, July 1863.

Government refuses to admit the right of the Authorities of the United States to arrest our citizens and extort from them their parole not to render military service to their country, under the penalty of incurring punishment in case they fall into the hands of your forces. I am directed by the Secretary of War to inform you that such oaths will not be regarded as obligatory, and persons who take them will be required to render military service. Should your Government treat the rendition of such service by these persons as a breach of parole, and punish it accordingly, this Government will resort to retaliatory measures, as the only means of compelling the observance of the rules of civilized warfare.

"I have the honor to be, very respectfully, your obedient servant, R. E. Lee, General Commanding."[353]

General Lee, normally calm under pressure and magnanimous to a fault, boiled over with anger and frustration at the manner in which Lincoln and his military officers were conducting their war on the South. What follows is an August 2, 1862, letter Lee sent to the then general-in-chief of the U.S. army, Henry W. Halleck, concerning Lincoln's soldiers, who had been ordered, under Yankee General John Pope, to assault, rob, hold hostage, and murder Southern noncombatants, innocents such as farmers and their families:

☞ "General: In obedience to the order of His Excellency, the President of the Confederate States [Jefferson Davis], I have the honor to make to you the following communication:

"On the 22d July last, a cartel for a general exchange of prisoners of war was signed between [Confederate] Major-General Daniel Harvey Hill, in behalf of the Confederate States, and [Union] Major-General John A. Dix, in behalf of the United States.

"By the terms of the cartel it is stipulated that all prisoners of war hereafter taken shall be discharged on parole till exchanged.

"Scarcely had that cartel been signed when the military authorities of the United States commenced a practice changing the whole character of the war, from such as becomes civilized nations into a campaign of indiscriminate robbery and murder.

"The general order issued by the Secretary of War of the United States, in the city of Washington, on the very day the cartel was signed in Virginia, directs the military commanders of the United States to take

The second day of the Battle of Gettysburg, July 2, 1863.

the private property of our people for the convenience and use of their armies, without compensation.

"The general order issued by [Union] Major-General [John] Pope, on the 23d day of July, the day after signing of the cartel, directs the murder of our peaceful inhabitants as spies, if found quietly tilling the farms in his rear, even outside of his lines, and one of his Brigadier-Generals, [Adolph von] Steinwehr, has seized upon innocent and peaceful inhabitants to be held as hostages, to the end that they may be murdered in cold blood if any of his soldiers are killed by some unknown persons whom he designates as 'Bushwhackers.'

"We find ourselves driven by our enemies by steady progress towards a practice which we abhor, and which we are vainly struggling to avoid. Under these circumstances, this Government has issued the accompanying general order, which I am directed by the President to transmit to you, recognizing Major-General Pope and his commissioned officers to be in the position which they have chosen for themselves,—that of robbers and murderers, and not that of public enemies, entitled, if captured, to be treated as prisoners of war.

"The President also instructs me to inform you that we renounce our right of retaliation on the innocent, and will continue to treat the private enlisted soldiers of General Pope's army as prisoners of war; but if, after notice to your Government that we confine repressive measures to the punishment of commissioned officers, who are willing participants in those crimes, the savage practice threatened in the order alluded to be persisted in, we shall be reluctantly forced to the last resort of accepting the war on the terms chosen by our enemies, until the voice of an outraged humanity shall compel a respect for the recognized usages of war.

"While the President considers that the facts referred to would justify a refusal on our part to execute the cartel by which we have agreed to liberate an excess of prisoners of war in our hands, a sacred regard for plighted faith which shrinks from the semblance of breaking a promise, precludes a resort to such an extremity; nor is it his desire to extend to any other forces of the United States the punishment merited by General Pope, and such commissioned officers as choose to participate in the execution of his infamous order.

"I have the honor to be very respectfully your obedient servant, R. E. Lee, General Commanding."[354]

Edwin M. Stanton, Lincoln's second secretary of war, condoned many of Lincoln's war crimes and so must be considered an accessory.

This is from a November 24, 1862, letter to his daughter Mary regarding the unmanly habit of U.S. troops warring against innocent and harmless women, girls, and children:

☞ ". . . [Union] General [Ambrose E.] Burnside's whole army is apparently opposite Fredericksburg, and stretches from the Rappahannock to the Potomac. What his intentions are he has not yet disclosed. I am sorry he is in position to oppress our friends and citizens of the Northern Neck. He threatens to bombard Fredericksburg, and the noble spirit displayed by its citizens, particularly the women and children, has elicited my highest admiration. They have been abandoning their homes, night and day, during all this inclement weather, cheerfully and uncomplainingly, with only such assistance as our wagons and ambulances could afford, women, girls, children, trudging through the mud and bivouacking in the open fields."[355]

On December 11, 1862, at the start of the Battle of Fredericksburg, Lee wrote the following to his wife concerning illegal Yankee activities, in this case the bombing of civilian towns and the torching and demolition of civilian homes:

☞ "... The enemy, after bombarding the town of Fredericksburg, setting fire to many houses and knocking down nearly all those along the river, crossed over a large force about dark, and now occupies the town. We hold the hills commanding it, and hope we shall be able to damage him yet. His position and heavy guns command the town entirely."[356]

Referring to the Yanks as "our barbarous enemy," in the Summer of 1863 Lee expressed his wrath over the outrages committed by Lincoln's soldiers across the South:

☞ "I grieve over the desolation of the country and the distress to innocent women and children, occasioned by spiteful excursions of the enemy, unworthy of a civilised nation."[357]

Union General George B. McClellan's headquarters at Yorktown, Virginia.

In the Fall of 1863 a loyal Confederate "soldier's wife" from Abbeville, South Carolina, visited General Lee in the field at Camp Rappahannock. In a November 1, 1863, letter to his wife Lee refers to one of Lincoln's many crimes as mentioned by his female visitor that day:

☞ "She said she was willing to give up everything she had in the world to attain our independence, and the only complaint she made of the conduct of our enemies was their arming our servants against us."[358]

What is the crime she is referring to? It was Lincoln's practice to coerce Southern black servants into "joining" the Union army at gunpoint and take up arms against their former white owners. According to eyewitnesses, those blacks who refused were beaten or shot on the spot.[359] It is little wonder that "Honest Abe" eventually got nearly 200,000 Southern African-Americans to "enlist" in the U.S. army.

14
LINCOLN'S WAR ON THE NORTH

A Union soldier. While most fought according to the rules of war, many thousands committed unspeakable crimes against the Southern populace, including the elderly, women, girls, and even infants—both white *and* black. Lincoln used these same soldiers to wage a campaign of terror across the North as well.

It is not generally known because pro-North historians have suppressed the facts, but from the day of Lincoln's first election a number of Northern states and cities sided firmly with the South. One of these was New York City, whose mayor, Fernando Wood, advocated that the city secede along with the Southern states and join the Confederacy.[360] Why? Because like most cities along the Northeastern seacoast, it was deeply tied to slavery.

Right up until the start of the "Civil War," New York City was the literal epicenter of the American slave trade, with Yankee owned and operated slave ships departing and arriving everyday from Africa and the Caribbean, their holds packed with black human cargo.[361]

What was Lincoln's response to New York's desire to link arms with the South? He sent in his troops, locked the state down under martial law, closed down the state legislature, had hundreds of influential New Yorkers arrested and thrown in prison, overturned the state's constitution, and suspended *habeas corpus*. Along with these he committed dozens of other crimes too numerous to mention, including the torture and even murder of unarmed and innocent citizens. According to Confederate President Jefferson Davis, "every State government of the Northern States was in like manner subverted."[362]

No one was safe from Lincoln's megalomaniacal wrath, not even his own Northern constituents. Tens of thousands of Yankees were illegally arrested and imprisoned—and many were tortured and even murdered—by the president's much feared vigilante gangs for nothing more than espousing pro-peace sentiment or expressing anti-Lincoln opinions. One never reads about these outrages and crimes in pro-North books. But we mention them here so that the truth will finally be known.

One of these "Northern States" was Maryland, many of whose citizens openly clamored to become a member of the Confederacy. Lincoln's response to Maryland was the same as in New York: he immediately placed the Old Line State under martial law, then began systematically threatening, terrorizing, beating, torturing, arresting, and imprisoning not only everyday citizens, but also her newspaper editors and police officers. Lincoln even illegally disbanded, then arrested and jailed, Maryland's entire governmental legislature.[363]

God only knows what became of these individuals after they were illegally shut away in the depths of Lincoln's damp, dark, lawless jails, such as Fort Lafayette, his "U.S. government gulag," a squalid, hellacious prison where untold numbers of innocent Yankees died due to abuse and unsanitary conditions.[364]

By the Autumn of 1862 the situation in Maryland had become so severe that a sympathetic General Lee decided to intervene. On September 8, after seizing the roads and railroads leading to Baltimore, he issued the following generous letter "To the People of Maryland" from his headquarters in northern Virginia:

☞ "To The People Of Maryland: It is right that you should know the purpose that has brought the army under my command within the limits of your State, so far as that purpose concerns yourselves.

"The people of the Confederate States have long watched with the deepest sympathy the wrongs and outrages that have been inflicted upon the citizens of a Commonwealth allied to the States of the South by the strongest social, political, and commercial ties. They have seen with profound indignation their sister State deprived of every right and reduced to the condition of a conquered province.

"Under the pretence of supporting the Constitution, but in violation of its most valuable provisions, your citizens have been arrested and imprisoned upon no charge and contrary to all forms of law; the faithful and manly protest against this outrage made by the venerable and illustrious Marylander to whom in better days no citizen appealed for right in vain was treated with scorn and contempt; the government of your chief city has been usurped by armed strangers; your legislature has been dissolved by the unlawful arrest of its members; freedom of the press and of speech has been suppressed; words have been declared offences by an arbitrary decree of the Federal executive, and citizens ordered to be tried by a military commission for what they may dare to speak.

The demonic John Brown, who, for reasons still not fully understood, killed countless innocent people in the name of "abolition." Captured by General Lee in October 1859 in the state where the American abolition movement began, "America's first domestic terrorist" later swung on the gallows for his many crimes. Still hailed in the liberal North as a Christ-like figure, in the conservative South Brown is rightly considered a lowly criminal and an enemy of Christianity, Dixie, the Constitution, and common sense.

"Believing that the people of Maryland possessed a spirit too lofty to submit to such a government, the people of the South have long wished to aid you in throwing off this foreign yoke, to enable you again to enjoy the inalienable rights of freemen and restore independence and sovereignty to your State.

"In obedience to this wish our army has come among you, and is prepared to assist you with the power of its arms in regaining the rights of which you have been despoiled. This, citizens of Maryland, is our mission, so far as you are concerned.

"No constraint upon your free will is intended ; no intimidation will be allowed. Within the limits of this army at least, Marylanders shall once more enjoy their ancient freedom of thought and speech. We know no enemies among you, and will protect all, of every opinion. It is for you to decide your destiny freely and without constraint. This army will respect your choice, whatever it may be; and, while the Southern people will rejoice to welcome you to your natural position among them, they will only welcome you when you come of your own free will. R. E. Lee, General commanding."[365]

As his army marched into Maryland, Lee issued the following to his men:
☞ "Soldiers, press onward! Let each man feel the responsibility now resting on him to pursue vigorously the success vouchsafed to us by Heaven. Let the armies of the East and the West vie with each other in discipline, bravery and activity, and our brethren of our sister States will soon be released from tyranny, and our independence be established upon a sure and abiding basis."[366]

Sadly, Lee had been forced to enter a part of Maryland where there was little support for the Confederacy, and so he could not induce any men from that area to join his ranks. This, coupled with the fact that Maryland did not want her soil to become part of Lincoln's destructive and bloody battleground, doomed Lee's brave attempt to liberate Maryland to failure. After the Battle of Sharpsburg (Antietam to Yanks), September 16-18, 1862, Lee headed back south, abandoning Maryland to the Union and her fate.

A Union fort.

15

POSTBELLUM

For General Lee, life after the War was certainly quieter, and safer. He returned home a hero, rejoined his family, and took up the job of president of Washington College (now Washington and Lee University).

Despite his blissful homecoming, all was not well. Not only were the Lees now homeless (their beautiful estate, Arlington House, had been stolen and ransacked by the U.S. government), but shortly after the War ended the General was indicted, along with President Davis, for "treason" by a U.S. grand jury in Norfolk, Virginia.

Lee as he looked while president of Washington College.

Since Lee was never officially "pardoned," and because so-called "Reconstruction" did not end until 1877, tragically, Lee's death in 1870 means that he was considered a "prisoner on parole" for the remainder of his days.

Still, despite the North's attempt to humiliate and ruin Lee after the War, his final five years were among the happiest of his life.

One of Lee's aides, Colonel Walter Herron Taylor, wrote to General Lee to inform him of the sobering fact of his indictment, and to let him know that his former soldiers could not find work. Here is Lee's June 17, 1865, response:

☞ "My Dear Colonel: I am very much obliged to you for your letter of the 13th. I had heard of the indictment by the grand-jury at Norfolk, and made up my mind to let the authorities take their course. I have no wish to avoid any trial the Government may order, and cannot flee. I hope others may be unmolested, and that you at least may be undisturbed.

"I am sorry to hear that our returned soldiers cannot obtain employment. Tell them they must all set to work, and, if they cannot do what they prefer, do what they can. Virginia wants all their aid, all their support, and the presence of all her sons to sustain and recuperate her. They must therefore put themselves in a position to take part in her government, and not be deterred by obstacles in their way. There is much to be done which they only can do. . . . Very truly yours, R. E. Lee."[367]

After Lincoln's War came to an end, many Southerners, not wanting to live under Yankee tyranny, left the United States for such countries as England (which Lee considered his "second home")[368] and Mexico. The General was against such emigrations, as can be seen in this August 28, 1865, letter he wrote to Virginia Governor John Letcher:

☞ "The questions which for years were in dispute between the State and General Government, and which unhappily were not decided by the dictates of reason, but referred to the decision of war, having been decided against us, it is the part of wisdom to acquiesce in the result, and of candour to recognise the fact.

"The interests of the State are, therefore, the same as those of the United States. Its prosperity will rise or fall with the welfare of the country. The duty of its citizens, then, appears to me too plain to admit of doubt. All should unite in honest efforts to obliterate the effects of war, and to restore the blessings of peace. They should remain, if possible, in the country; promote harmony and good feeling; qualify themselves to vote, and elect to the State and General Legislatures wise and patriotic men who will devote their abilities to the interests of the country, and the healing of all dissensions. I have invariably recommended this course since the cessation of hostilities, and have endeavoured to practise it myself. I am much obliged to you for the interest you have expressed in my acceptance of the presidency of Washington College. . . ."[369]

Lee made a similar statement after the emperor of Mexico began encouraging

former Confederates to emigrate to his country:
☞ "I do not know how far their emigration to another land will conduce to their prosperity. Although prospects may not now be cheering, I have entertained the opinion that, unless prevented by circumstances or necessity, it would be better for them and the country if they remained at their homes and shared the fate of their respective States."370

During and after the War, Lee was repeatedly assailed by uneducated Yankees for having committed "treason" against the United States of America (indeed, these absurd attacks on the General continue to this day). Lee was, of course, correct in siding with the Confederate States of America, for he considered his home state of Virginia "his country." As a Virginian, when she legally seceded under the auspices of the Constitution (Ninth and Tenth Amendments), his strong sense of duty and loyalty left him no choice but to follow her out of the Union, a choice he vigorously defended in a postbellum letter to Confederate General Pierre Gustave Toutant Beauregard:
☞ "I need not tell you that true patriotism sometimes requires men to act exactly contrary at one period to that which it does at another, and the motive which impels them—the desire to do right—is precisely the same. History is full of illustrations of this. Washington himself is an example. He fought at one time against the French under Braddock, in the service of the king of Great Britain; at another, he fought with the French at Yorktown, under the orders of the Continental Congress, against him. He has not been branded by the world with reproach for this; but his course has been applauded."371

In a June 1869 letter to Confederate General Wade Hampton, Lee said much the same thing:
☞ "I could have taken no other course save in dishonor, and if it were all to be gone over again, I should act in precisely the same way."372

During the early months following the South's "surrender," Lee promoted reconciliation and peace with the North. In a letter to Captain Josiah Tatnall of the Confederate States Navy, the General wrote:
☞ "I believe it to be the duty of every one to unite in the restoration of the country and the reestablishment of peace and harmony. These

considerations governed me in the counsels I gave to others, and induced me on the 13th of June to make application to be included in the terms of the amnesty proclamation."[373]

Lee practiced what he preached, as the following story reveals:
☞ "[After a friend of Lee's one day saw him] talking at his gate with a stranger to whom, as he ended, he gave some money, he inquired who the stranger was. 'One of our old soldiers,' said the general. 'To whose command did he belong?' 'Oh, he was one of those who fought against us,' said General Lee. 'But we are all one now, and must make no difference in our treatment of them.'"[374]

After the War a woman whose husband had died in the conflict came to see Lee. She expressed a deep and abiding hatred for the North, and sought the General's advice. Calmly and tenderly he replied:
☞ "Madam, do not train up your children in hostility to the Government of the United States. Remember that we are one country now. Dismiss from your mind all sectional feeling, and bring them up to be Americans."[375]

In April 1865, when Lee was told that he had been indicted by the U.S. government on the charge of "treason," he remarked:
☞ "We must forgive our enemies. I can truly say that not a day has passed since the war began that I have not prayed for them."[376]

Lee, of course, was not the only Rebel to be indicted for "treason." In fact, all Confederate officers were formally charged with "subversiveness" by the U.S. government. Despite this brutal and unnecessary treatment, the General sought to work with the U.S. government instead of against it. On June 13, 1865, he penned the following letter to Yankee General Ulysses S. Grant:
☞ "Upon reading the President's [Andrew Johnson] proclamation of the 29th ult., I came to Richmond to ascertain what was proper or required of me to do, when I learned that, with others, I was to be indicted for treason by the grand jury at Norfolk. I had supposed that the officers and men of the Army of Northern Virginia were, by the terms of their surrender, protected by the United States Government from molestation so long as they conformed to its conditions. I am ready to meet any

The Confederates' nighttime retreat from Gettysburg across the Potomac River on a precarious pontoon bridge.

charges that may be preferred against me, and do not wish to avoid trial; but, if I am correct as to the protection granted by my parole, and am not to be prosecuted, I desire to comply with the provisions of the President's proclamation, and, therefore, inclose the required application, which I request, in that event, may be acted on. I am, with great respect, your obedient servant, R. E. Lee."[377]

A July 31, 1865, letter to his former aide, Colonel Walter Herron Taylor, reveals that Lee was now thinking seriously about preserving the true history of the Southern Confederacy, with an eye toward writing his autobiography:

☞ "I am desirous that the bravery and devotion of the Army of Northern Virginia be correctly transmitted to posterity. This is the only tribute that can be paid to the worth of its noble officers and soldiers. And I am anxious to collect the necessary information for the history of its campaigns, including the operations in the Valley of Western Virginia, from its organisation to its final surrender. I am particularly anxious that its actual strength in the different battles it has fought be correctly stated."[378]

In late Summer 1865 Lee was asked to help manage a magazine. He refused with this September 4 reply:

☞ "It should be the object of all to avoid controversy, to allay passion, [and] give full scope to reason and every kindly feeling. By doing this, and encouraging our citizens to engage in the duties of life with all their heart and mind, with a determination not to be turned aside by thoughts of the past and fears of the future, our country will not only be restored in material prosperity, but will be advanced in science, in virtue, and in religion."[379]

Also on September 4, 1865, Lee sent the following response to the well-known eccentric actor "Count Joannes" [George Jones] in New York City. We will note here that Lee is either unaware of the fact, or politely hiding the fact, that there was massive celebrating across the South at the news of Lincoln's death—the anti-South president who Southerners still hold directly responsible for the deaths of up to 2 million inhabitants of the Confederacy:[380]

☞ "In your letter to me you do the people of the South but simple justice in believing that they heartily concur with you in opinion in regard to the assassination of the late President Lincoln. It is a crime previously unknown to this country, and one that must be deprecated by every American."[381]

On September 7, 1865, Lee wrote the following regarding the South and President Jefferson Davis (who had been arrested for "treason" and was awaiting trial in prison):

☞ ". . . I believe it to be the duty of everyone to unite in the restoration of the country, and the re-establishment of peace and harmony. . . . It appears to me that the allayment of passion, the dissipation of prejudice, and the restoration of reason, will alone enable the people of the country to acquire a true knowledge and form a correct judgment of the events of the past four years. It will, I think, be admitted that Mr. Davis has done nothing more than all the citizens of the Southern States, and should not be held accountable for acts performed by them in the exercise of what had been considered by them unquestionable right."[382]

On September 8, 1865, Lee wrote to Matthew F. Maury regarding the emigration of former Confederates to Mexico:

☞ ". . . As long as virtue was dominant in the republic, so long was the happiness of the people secure. I cannot, however, despair of it yet. I look forward to better days, and trust that time and experience, the great teachers of men, under the guidance of an evermerciful God, may save us from destruction, and restore to us the bright hopes and prospects of the past. The thought of abandoning the country and all that must be left in it is abhorrent to my feelings, and I prefer to struggle for its restoration and share its fate, rather than to give up all as lost. I have a great admiration for Mexico; the salubrity of its climate, the fertility of its soil, and the magnificence of its scenery possess for me great charms; but I still look with delight upon the mountains of my native State. . . ."383

On October 3, 1865, Lee penned this letter to Confederate General Pierre Gustave Toutant Beauregard:
☞ "I hope both you and [Confederate General Joseph Eggleston] Johnston will write the history of your campaigns. Everyone should do all in his power to collect and disseminate the truth, in the hope that it may find a place in history, and descend to posterity. I am glad to see no indication in your letter of an intention to leave the country. I think the South requires the aid of her sons now more than at any period of her history. As you ask my purpose, I will state that I have no thought of abandoning her unless compelled to do so. . . ."384

On October 30, 1865, Lee wrote the following to one of his sons:
☞ ". . . I accepted the presidency of the [Washington] College in the hope that I might be of some service to the country and the rising generation, and not from any preference of my own. I should have selected a more quiet life, and a more retired abode than Lexington, and should have preferred a small farm where I could have earned my daily bread. If I find I can accomplish no good here, I will then endeavour to pursue the course to which my inclinations point."385

In December 1865 Lee made this accurate prediction to Confederate General Cadmus Marcellus Wilcox:
☞ "I fear the South has yet to suffer many evils [under "Reconstruction"], and it will require time, patience, and fortitude to heal her afflictions."386

After the War, when asked about the alleged "cruelty" toward Yankee prisoners in Southern prisons, Lee replied:

☞ "I never knew that any cruelty was practised, and I have no reason to believe that it was practised. I can believe, and have reason to believe, that privations may have been experienced by the prisoners, because I know that provisions and shelter could not be provided for them [due, in great part, to Lincoln's illegal naval blockade]."[387]

In the mid 1860s Lord Garnet J. Wolseley, commanding general of the British armies, met with Lee at Washington College at Lexington, Virginia, where he was then serving as president. The English officer asked Lee: "Who do you think was the greatest military genius developed by the war?", to which Lee replied:
☞ "General Nathan Bedford Forrest, of Tennessee, whom I have never met. He accomplished more with fewer troops than any other officer on either side."[388]

On January 5, 1866, Lee wrote of the North's alleged "Reconstruction" of the South:
☞ "All that the South has ever desired was that the Union, as established by our forefathers should be preserved; and that the Government, as originally organised, should be administered in purity and truth. If such is the desire of the North, there can be no contention between the two sections; and all true patriots will unite in advocating that policy which will soonest restore the country to tranquility and order, and serve to perpetuate true republicanism."[389]

On numerous occasions it was suggested to the General that the South would support him if he ran for governor of Virginia, or even president of the United States. On January 23, 1866, Lee gave his usual reply to such propositions:
☞ "I am not in a position to make it proper for me to take a public part in the affairs of the country. I have done and continue to do, in my private capacity, all in my power to encourage our people to set manfully to work to restore the country, to rebuild their homes and churches, to educate their children, and to remain with their States, their friends, and countrymen. But, as a prisoner on parole, I cannot with propriety do more."[390]

On January 27, 1866, Lee wrote to Reverdy Johnson regarding the imposition of the U.S. Oath of Allegiance on former Confederates, and also his attempts to settle

his wife's father's will:
☛ ". . . I have hoped that Congress would have thought proper to have repealed the acts imposing it and all similar tests. To pursue a policy which will continue the prostration of one-half the country, alienate the affections of its inhabitants from the Government, and which must eventually result in injury to the country and the American people, appears to me so manifestly injudicious that I do not see how those responsible can tolerate it.

"I sincerely thank you for the repetition of your kind offer to aid me in any way in your power. I have been awaiting the action of President Johnson upon my application to be embraced in his proclamation of May 29, and for my restoration to civil rights, before attempting to close the estate of [my wife's father] Mr. George Washington Parke Custis, of which I am sole administrator. His servants were all liberated [in 1862], agreeably to the terms of his will; but I have been unable to place his grandchildren in possession of the property bequeathed them.

"A portion of his landed property has been sold by the [U.S.] Government, in the belief, I presume, that it belonged to me; whereas I owned no part of it, nor had any other charge than as administrator. His will, in his own handwriting, is on file in the court of Alexandria county. Arlington, and the tract on 'Four-Mile Run,' given him by General Washington, he left to his only child, Mrs. Lee, during her life, and at her death, to his eldest grandson. Both of these tracts have been sold by [the U.S.] Government. It has also sold Smith's Island (off Cape Charles), which Mr. Custis directed to be sold to aid in paying certain legacies to his granddaughters. . . ."[391]

When, after the War, Lee was asked whether his former Confederate soldiers still hated the U.S. government or not, the General said simply:
☛ "They looked upon the war as a necessary evil and went through it. I have seen them relieve the wants of Federal soldiers on the field. The orders always were that the whole field should be treated alike. Parties were sent out to take the Federal wounded as well as the Confederate, and the surgeons were told to treat the one as they did the other. These orders, given by me, were respected on every field."[392]

In March 1866 Lee was hauled before the so-called "Reconstruction Committee" of Congress and grilled by a panel of hostile Yankees who were bent on catching the General in a lie or a treasonous phrase. Lee, considered a U.S. "prisoner on parole" at the time,[393] bore the absurd and insulting interrogation in his typically dignified way, despite the impertinence, guilefulness, and stupidity of many of the questions. What follows are a few excerpts. Lee's responses are marked with "A" (for "Answer"):

Q. How do the people of Virginia, secessionists more particularly, feel toward the freedmen [that is, freed slaves]?

A. Every one with whom I associate expresses the kindest feelings toward the freedmen. They wish to see them get on in the world, and particularly to take up some occupation for a living, and to turn their hands to some work. I know that efforts have been made among the farmers near where I live to induce them to engage for the year at regular wages.

Q. Do you think there is a willingness on the part of their old masters to give them fair living wages for their labor?

A. I believe it is so; the farmers generally prefer those servants who have been living with them before; I have heard them express their preferences for the men whom they knew, who had lived with them before, and their wish to get them to return to work.

Q. Are you aware of the existence of any combination among the "whites" to keep down the wages of the "blacks?"

A. I am not; I have heard that in several counties the land-owners have met in order to establish a uniform rate of wages, but I never heard, nor do I know of any combination to keep down wages or establish any rule which they did not think fair; the means of paying wages in Virginia are very limited now, and there is a difference of opinion as to how much each person is able to pay.

Q. How do they feel in regard to the education of the blacks? Is there a general willingness to have them educated?

A. Where I am, and have been, the people have exhibited a willingness that the blacks should be educated, and they express an opinion that it would be better for the blacks and better for the whites. . . .

Q. Do they [Southern blacks] show a capacity to obtain knowledge of mathematics and the exact sciences?

A. I have no knowledge on that subject; I am merely acquainted with those who have learned the common rudiments of education.

Q. General, are you aware of the existence among the blacks of Virginia, anywhere within the limits of the State, of combinations, having in view the disturbance of the peace, or any improper or unlawful acts?

A. I am not; I have seen no evidence of it, and have heard of none; wherever I have been they have been quiet and orderly; not disposed to work; or, rather, not disposed to any continuous engagement to work, but just very short jobs to provide them with the immediate means of subsistence.

Q. Has the colored race generally as great love of money and property as the white race possesses?

A. I do not think it has; the blacks with whom I am acquainted look more to the present time than to the future.

Q. Does that absence of a lust of money and property arise more from the nature of the negro than from his former servile condition?

A. Well, it may be in some measure attributed to his former condition; they are an amiable, social race; they like their ease and comfort, and I think look more to their present than to their future condition. . . .

Q. The question I am about to put to you, you may answer or not, as you choose. Did you take an oath of fidelity, or allegiance, to the Confederate Government?

A. I do not recollect having done so, but it is possible that when I was

On April 9, 1865, at Lee's final conflict, the Battle of Appomattox Court House, Confederate General Edward P. Alexander positions his troops for the last time.

commissioned [after graduating from West Point in 1829] I did; I do not recollect whether it was required; if it was required, I took it, or if it had been required I would have taken it; but I do not recollect whether it was or not. . . .

Q. Is there any difference in their [Southern whites] relations to the colored people? Is their prejudice increased or diminished?

A. I have noticed no change; so far as I do know the feelings of all the people of Virginia, they are kind to the colored people; I have never heard any blame attributed to them as to the present condition of things, or any responsibility.

Q. There are very few colored laborers employed, I suppose?

A. Those who own farms have employed, more or less, one or two colored laborers; some are so poor that they have to work themselves.

Q. Can capitalists and workingmen from the North go into any portion of Virginia with which you are familiar and go to work among the people?

A. I do not know of any thing to prevent them. Their peace and pleasure there would depend very much on their conduct. If they confined themselves to their own business and did not interfere to provoke controversies with their neighbors, I do not believe they would be molested.

Q. There is no desire to keep out [Northern] capital?

A. Not that I know of. On the contrary, they are very anxious to get capital [of any kind] into the State.

Q. You see nothing of a disposition to prevent such a thing?

A. I have seen nothing, and do not know of any thing, as I said before; the manner in which they would be received would depend entirely upon the individuals themselves; they might make themselves obnoxious, as you can understand.

Q. Is there not a general dislike of Northern men among secessionists?

A. I suppose they would prefer not to associate with them; I do not know that they would select them as associates.

Q. Do they [Virginians] avoid and ostracize them socially?

A. They might avoid them; they would not select them as associates unless there was some reason; I do not know that they would associate with them unless they became acquainted; I think it probable they would not admit them into their social circles. . . .

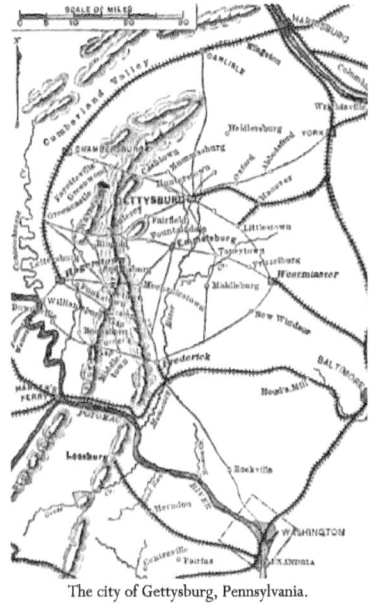
The city of Gettysburg, Pennsylvania.

Q. What is your opinion in regard to the material interests of Virginia; do you think they will be equal to what they were before the rebellion under the changed aspect of affairs?
A. It will take a long time for them to reach their former standard; I think that after some years they will reach it, and I hope exceed it; but it cannot be immediately, in my opinion.
Q. It will take a number of years?
A. It will take a number of years, I think.
Q. On the whole, the condition of things in Virginia is hopeful both in regard to its material interests and the future peace of the country?
A. I have heard great hopes expressed, and there is great cheerfulness and willingness to labor.
Q. Suppose this policy of President [Andrew] Johnson should be all you anticipate, and that you should also realize all that you expect in the improvement of the material interests, do you think that the result of that will be the gradual restoration of the old feeling?
A. That will be the natural result, I think; and I see no other way in which that result can be brought about.
Q. There is a fear in the public mind that the friends of the policy in the South adopt it because they see in it the means of repairing the political position which they lost in the recent contest. Do you think that that is the main idea with them, or that they merely look to it, as you say, as the best means of restoring civil government and the peace and prosperity of their respective States?
A. As to the first point you make, I do not know that I ever heard any person speak upon it; I never heard the points separated; I have heard them speak generally as to the effect of the policy of President Johnson; the feeling is, so far as I know now, that there is not that equality extended to the Southern States which is enjoyed by the North.

Q. You do not feel down there that, while you accept the result, we are as generous as we ought to be under the circumstances?
A. They think that the North can afford to be generous.
Q. That is the feeling down there?
A. Yes; and they think it is the best policy; those who reflect upon the subject and are able to judge.
Q. I understand it to be your opinion that generosity and liberality toward the entire South would be the surest means of regaining their good opinion?
A. Yes, and the speediest.
Q. I understand you to say generally that you had no apprehension of any combination among the leading secessionists to renew the war, or any thing of the kind?
A. I have no reason in the world to think so.
Q. Have you heard that subject talked over among any of the politicians?
A. No, sir; I have not; I have not heard that matter even suggested.
Q. Let me put another hypothetical state of things. Suppose the executive government of the United States should be held by a President who, like Mr. [James] Buchanan, rejected the right of coercion [to force states that wished to secede to remain in the Union], so called, and suppose a Congress should exist here entertaining the same political opinions, thus presenting to the once rebel States the opportunity to again secede from the Union, would they, or not, in your opinion, avail themselves of that opportunity [to secede], or some of them?
A. I suppose it would depend upon the circumstances existing at the time; if their feelings should remain embittered, and their affections alienated from the rest of the States, I think it very probable they might do so, provided they thought it was to their interests.
Q. Do you not think that at the present time there is a deep-seated feeling of dislike toward the Government of the United States on the part of the secessionists?
A. I do not know that there is any deep-seated dislike; I think it is probable there may be some animosity still existing among the people of the South.
Q. Is there not a deep-seated feeling of disappointment and chagrin at the result of the war?
A. I think that at the time they were disappointed at the result of the

war.

Q. Do you mean to be understood as saying that there is not a condition of discontent against the Government of the United States among the secessionists generally?

A. I know none.

Q. Are you prepared to say that they respect the Government of the United States, and the loyal people of the United States, so much at the present time as to perform their duties as citizens of the United States, and of the States, faithfully and well?

A. I believe that they will perform all the duties that they are required to perform; I think that is the general feeling so far as I know.

Q. Do you think it would be practicable to convict a man in Virginia of treason for having taken part in this rebellion against the Government by a Virginian jury without packing it with direct reference to a verdict of guilty?

A. On that point I have no knowledge, and I do not know what they would consider treason against the United States—if you refer to past acts.

Q. Yes, sir.

A. I have no knowledge what their views on that subject in the past are.

Q. You understand my question. Suppose a jury was impanelled in your own neighborhood, taken by lot, would it be possible to convict, for instance, Jefferson Davis, for having levied war upon the United States, and thus having committed the crime of treason?

A. I think it is very probable that they would not consider he had committed treason.

Q. Suppose the jury should be clearly and plainly instructed by the Court that such an act of war upon the part of Mr. Davis or any other leading man constituted the crime of treason under the Constitution of the United States, would the jury be likely to heed that instruction, and, if the facts were plainly in proof before them, convict the offender?

A. I do not know, sir, what they would do on that question.

Q. They do not generally suppose that it was treason against the United States, do they?

A. I do not think that they so consider it.

Q. In what light would they view it? What would be their excuse or justification? How would they escape, in their own mind? I refer to the past—I am referring to the past and the feelings they would have.

A. So far as I know, they look upon the action of the State in withdrawing itself from the Government of the United States as carrying the individuals of the State along with it; that the State was responsible for the act, not the individuals, and that the ordinance of secession, so called, or those acts of the State which recognized a condition of war between the State and the General Government stood as their justification for their bearing arms against the Government of the United States; yes, sir, I think they would consider the act of the State as legitimate; that they were merely using the reserved rights, which they had a right to do.

Q. State, if you please—and if you are disinclined to answer the question you need not do so—what your own personal views on that question are.

A. That was my view; that the act of Virginia in withdrawing herself from the United States carried me along as a citizen of Virginia, and that her laws and her acts were binding on me.

Q. And that you felt to be your justification in taking the course you did?

A. Yes, sir.

Q. I have been told, general, that you have remarked to one of your friends, in conversation, that you were rather wheedled or cheated into that course by [Southern] politicians.

A. I do not recollect ever making any such remark; I do not think I ever made it.

Q. If there be any other matter about which you wish to speak on this occasion, do so, freely.

A. Only in reference to that last question you put to me. I may have said and may have believed that the positions of the two sections which they held to each other was brought about by the politicians of the country; that the great masses of the people, if they understood the real question, would have avoided it; but not that I had been individually wheedled by the politicians.

Q. That is probably the origin of the whole thing.

A. I may have said that, but I do not even recollect that; but I did believe at the time that it was an unnecessary condition of affairs, and might have been avoided if forbearance and wisdom had been practised on both sides.

Q. You say that you do not recollect having sworn allegiance and fidelity to the Confederate Government?
A. I do not recollect it, nor do I know it was ever required. I was regularly commissioned in the army of the Confederate States, but I do not really recollect that that oath was required. If it was required, I have no doubt I took it; or, if it had been required, I would have taken it.
Q. Is there any other matter which you desire to state to the committee?
A. No, sir; I am ready to answer any question which you think proper to put to me. . . .
Q. Are you acquainted with the proposed amendment now pending in the Senate of the United States [to allow blacks to vote]?
A. No, sir, I am not; I scarcely ever read a paper. So far as I can see, I do not think that the State of Virginia would object to it.
Q. Would she consent, under any circumstances, to allow the black people to vote, even if she were to gain a large number of representatives in Congress?
A. That would depend upon her interests; if she had the right of determining that, I do not see why she would object; if it were to her interest to admit these people to vote, that might overrule any other objection that she had to it.
Q. What, in your opinion, would be the practical result? Do you think that Virginia would consent to allow the negro to vote?
A. I think that at present she would accept the smaller representation; I do not know what the future may develop; if it should be plain to her that these persons will vote properly and understandingly, she might admit them to vote.
Q. Do you not think it would turn a good deal, in the cotton States, upon the value of the labor of the black people; upon the amount which they produce?
A. In a good many States in the South, and in a good many counties in Virginia, if the [illiterate among the] black people were allowed to vote, it would, I think, exclude proper representation—that is, proper, intelligent people would not be elected, and, rather than suffer that injury, they would not let them vote at all.
Q. Do you not think that the question as to whether any Southern State would allow the colored people the right of suffrage in order to increase representation would depend a good deal on the amount which the

colored people might contribute to the wealth of the State, in order to secure two things—first, the larger representation, and, second, the influence desired from those persons voting?

A. I think they would determine the question more in reference to their opinion as to the manner in which those votes would be exercised, whether they consider those people qualified to vote; my own opinion is, that at this time they cannot vote intelligently, and that giving them the right of suffrage would open the door to a good deal of demagogism, and lead to embarrassments in various ways; what the future may prove, how intelligent they may become, with what eyes they may look upon the interests of the State in which they may reside, I cannot say more than you can.[394]

A letter to Confederate General Jubal A. Early, dated March 16, 1866, illustrates Lee's Christian response to his critics:

☞ "My Dear General: I am very much obliged to you for the copies of my letters, forwarded with yours of January 25th. I hope you will be able to send me reports of the operations of your commands in the campaign, from the Wilderness to Richmond, at Lynchburg, in the Valley, Maryland, etc.; all statistics as regards numbers, destruction of private property by the Federal troops, etc., I should like to have, as I wish my memory strengthened on these points. It will be difficult to get the world to understand the odds against which we fought, and the destruction or loss of all returns of the army embarrass me very much.

"I read your letter from Havana to the New York *Times*, and was pleased with the temper in which it was written. I have since received the paper containing it, published in the City of Mexico, and also your letter in reference to Mr. [Jefferson] Davis. I understand and appreciate the motives which prompted both letters, and think they will be of service in the way you intended. I have been much pained to see the attempts made to cast odium upon Mr. Davis, but do not think they will be successful with the reflecting or informed portion of the country.

"The accusations against myself I have not thought proper to notice, or even to correct misrepresentations of my words and acts. We shall have to be patient and suffer for awhile at least; and all controversy, I think, will only serve to prolong angry and bitter feeling, and postpone the period when reason and charity may resume their sway. *At present, the public mind is not prepared to receive the truth* [emphasis added].

"The feelings which influenced you to leave the country were natural, and, I presume, were uppermost in the breasts of many. It was a matter which each one had to decide for himself, as he only could know the reasons which governed him. I was particularly anxious on your account, as I had the same apprehensions to which you refer. I am truly glad that you are beyond the reach of annoyance, and hope you may be able to employ yourself profitably and usefully. . . .

"I hope, in time, peace will be restored to the country, and that the South may enjoy some measure of prosperity. I fear, however, much suffering is still in store for her, and that her people must be prepared to exercise fortitude and forbearance. I must beg you to present my kind regards to the gentlemen with you, and, with my best wishes for yourself and undiminished esteem, I am, most truly yours, R. E. Lee."[395]

During Jefferson Davis' imprisonment (1865 to 1867), Lee wrote this February 23, 1866, letter to the Confederate president's wife Varina (Howell) Davis:
☞ "My Dear Mrs. Davis: Your letter of the 12th inst. reached Lexington during my absence at Washington. I have never seen [U.S. Representative] Mr. [Schuyler] Colfax's speech, and am, therefore,

General Lee at the Battle of Gettysburg in the Summer of 1863.

ignorant of the statements it contained. Had it, however, come under my notice, I doubt whether I should have thought it proper to reply. I have thought, from the time of the cessation of hostilities, that silence and patience on the part of the South was the true course; and I think so still. Controversy of all kinds will, in my opinion, only serve to continue excitement and passion, and will prevent the public mind from the acknowledgment and acceptance of the truth. These considerations have kept me from replying to accusations made against myself, and induced me to recommend the same to others.

"As regards the treatment of the Andersonville prisoners, to which you allude, I know nothing and can say nothing of my own knowledge. I never had anything to do with any prisoners, except to send those taken on the fields, where I was engaged, to the Provost Marshal General at Richmond.

"I have felt most keenly the sufferings and imprisonment of your husband, and have earnestly consulted with friends as to any possible mode of affording him relief and consolation. He enjoys the sympathy and respect of all good men; and if, as you state, his trial is now near, the exhibition of the whole truth in his case will, I trust, prove his defense and justification. With sincere prayers for his health and speedy restoration to liberty, and earnest supplications to God that He may take you and yours under His guidance and protection, I am, with great respect, your obedient servant, R. E. Lee."[396]

On April 13, 1866, Lee penned a similar reply to an individual at Baltimore, Maryland, regarding what seems to have been a Yankee newspaper article criticizing the General for committing "treason" against the United States:

☞ "My Dear Sir: Your letter of the 5th inst., inclosing a slip from the Baltimore *American*, has been received. The same statement has been published at the North for several years. The statement is not true; but I have not thought proper to publish a contradiction, being unwilling to be drawn into a newspaper discussion, believing that those who know me would not credit it and those who do not would care nothing about it. I cannot now depart from the rule I have followed. It is so easy to make accusations against the people at the South upon similar testimony, that those so disposed, should one be refuted, will immediately create another; and thus you would be led into endless controversy. I think it

The home of Wilmer McLean. Strangely, Lincoln's War began and ended with Mr. McLean: the first shots of the first major land battle, the Battle of First Manassas, occurred on McLean's farm, Yorkshire Plantation, at Manassas, Virginia, on July 21, 1861. In 1863, in order to protect his family from further disturbances caused by the War, McLean moved some 100 miles to the south, settling in Appomattox, Virginia. But he could not escape. After the final conflict, the Battle of Appomattox Court House on April 9, 1865, a place was needed to formalize the Confederacy's surrender. The most convenient location was McLean's second home (above), where Lee ended up meeting with Grant and signing the papers of capitulation. Later McLean commented: "The war started in my front yard and ended in my front parlor."

better to leave their correction to the return of reason and good feeling.

"Thanking you for your interest in my behalf, and begging you to consider my letter as intended only for yourself, I am, most respectfully your obedient servant, R. E. Lee."[397]

On April 17, 1866, Lee wrote of the ill-fated wartime prisoner exchange program that had been agreed to by the Yanks:

☞ ". . . Sufficient information has been officially published, I think, to show that whatever sufferings the Federal prisoners at the South underwent, were incident to their position as prisoners and produced by the destitute condition of the country, arising from the operations of war. . . . It was the desire of the Confederate authorities to effect a continuous and speedy exchange of prisoners of war. . . . [Judge Robert Ould] offered, when all hopes of effecting the exchange had ceased, to deliver all the Federal sick and wounded, to the amount of fifteen thousand, without an equivalent, provided transportation was furnished.

Previously to this, I think, I offered to General Grant to send into his lines all the prisoners within my department . . . provided he would return me man for man; and when I informed the Confederate authorities of my proposition, I was told that, if it was accepted, they would place all the prisoners at the South at my disposal. . . . But my proposition was not accepted."³⁹⁸

Concerning the enormous ill will leftover from Lincoln's War, Lee made his feelings plain as to how he meant to deal with them in an August 22, 1866, letter to Englishman Herbert C. Saunders:
☞ ". . . I prefer remaining silent to doing anything that might excite angry discussion at this time, when strong efforts are being made by conservative men, North and South, to sustain President [Andrew] Johnson in his policy, which, I think, offers the only means of healing the lamentable divisions of the country . . ."³⁹⁹

On October 6, 1866, Lee wrote the following to Charles W. Law of London, England:
☞ "Allow me to thank you for your kind letter of the 17ᵗʰ ult., inclosing an article from the London *Standard*. The complimentary remarks of the letter I understand as referring to the cause in which I was engaged, and not to myself. The good opinion of the English people as to the justice of that cause, *constitutional government*, is highly appreciated by the people of the South; and my thanks are due to you for the sympathy and support you gave it [emphasis added]."⁴⁰⁰

Once, while the General and his family were taking their health retreat at White Sulphur Springs, they attended an evening "promenade," a Victorian party with food and live music. While there the General came across a group of young Southern women who were expressing feelings of bitterness, hatred, and revenge toward the North. He did not approve of this attitude and said so, to which one of the teenage girls asked him: "But, General Lee, did you never feel resentment towards the North?" To this he replied:
☞ "I believe I may say, looking into my own heart, and speaking as in the presence of God, that I have never known one moment of bitterness or resentment. When you go home, I want you to take a message to your young friends. Tell them from me that it is unworthy of them as

women, and especially as Christian women, to cherish feelings of resentment against the North. Tell them that it grieves me inexpressibly to know that such a state of things exists, and that I implore them to do their part to heal our country's wounds."[401]

In the Winter of 1867 Lee had occasion to pass through Petersburg, Virginia, the site of the Battle of Petersburg II (June 15-18, 1864). Though it had been a Confederate victory, it had been at a high cost and the scene brought back many conflicting memories. In a December 21, 1867, letter to his son Fitzhugh, Lee writes:

☛ "My visit to Petersburg was extremely pleasant. Besides the pleasure of seeing my daughter and being with you, which was very great, I was gratified in seeing many friends. In addition, when our armies were in front of Petersburg I suffered so much in body and mind on account of the good townspeople, especially on that gloomy night when I was forced to abandon them, that I have always reverted to them in sadness and sorrow. My old feelings returned to me, as I passed well-remembered spots and recalled the ravages of the hostile shells. But when I saw the cheerfulness with which the people were working to restore their condition, and witnessed the comforts with which they were surrounded, a load of sorrow which had been pressing upon me for years was lifted from my heart."[402]

On February 4, 1867, Lee declined an offer to run for the governor of Virginia in a letter to Judge Robert Ould:

☛ ". . . You will agree with me, I am sure, in the opinion that this is no time for the indulgence of personal or political considerations in selecting a person to fill that office; nor should it be regarded as a means of rewarding individuals for supposed former services. The welfare of the State, and the interests of her citizens should be the only principle of selection. Believing that there are many men in the State more capable than I am to fill the position, and who could do more to promote the interests of the people, I most respectfully decline to be considered a candidate for the office.

". . . If my disfranchisement and privation of civil rights would secure to the citizens of the State the enjoyment of civil liberty and equal rights under the Constitution, I would willingly accept them in their stead...."⁴⁰³

On *May 23, 1867, Lee wrote the following to the author's cousin Confederate General Dabney Herndon Maury concerning "Reconstruction":*
👉 "... I look upon the Southern people as acting under compulsion, not of their free choice, and that it is their duty to consult the best interests of their States as far as it may be in their power to do so.... Every man must now look to his own affairs and depend upon his good sense and judgment to push them onward. We have but little to do with general politics. We cannot control them; but by united efforts, harmony, prudence and wisdom, we may shape and regulate our domestic policy."⁴⁰⁴

On *March 12, 1869, Lee wrote to Captain James May concerning his family's numerous attempts to have Arlington House, and its invaluable contents and family heirlooms, returned to the Lees. Arrogantly and incredibly, the U.S. Congress had recently called the Lees' request "an insult to the loyal people of the United States":*
👉 "I am sorry to learn from your letters, the trouble you have incurred by your kind endeavours to have restored to Mrs. Lee certain articles taken from Arlington, and I particularly regret the inconvenience occasioned to yourself and Mr. Browning in having been summoned before the investigating committee of Congress. I had not supposed that the subject would have been considered of such importance, and had I conceived the view taken of it by Congress, I should have dissuaded Mrs. Lee from making the application. But I thought that there would not only have been no objection to restoring to her family relics bequeathed her by her father, now that the occasion for their seizure had passed, but that the government would thus be relieved of their disposition. As Congress has, however, forbidden their restoration, she must submit, and I beg that you will give yourself no further concern about the matter.

"... I do not see what my character had to do with their restoration, for whatever fault may be attributed to me, Mrs. Lee is in no way to blame for it; and if by your indorsation of me, you meant that I am not antagonistic to the government, or hostile to the Union, you were certainly correct."⁴⁰⁵

Lee followed up with this March 22, 1869, letter to George W. Jones:
☞ "In reference to certain articles which were taken from Arlington [House], Mrs. Lee is indebted to our old friend, Capt. James May for the order from the late administration for their restoration to her. Congress, however, passed a resolution forbidding their return. They were valuable to her as having belonged to her great-grandmother [Mrs. George Washington] and having been bequeathed to her by her father. But as the country desires them she must give them up. I hope their presence at the Capital will keep in the remembrance of all Americans the principles and virtues of Washington."[406]

In the Summer of 1870, just a few months before Lee passed away, he had occasion to meet up with the former of governor of Texas, Fletcher Stockdale, to whom he said privately:
☞ "Governor, if I had foreseen the use those people [Lee's standard term for Yankees] designed to make of their victory, there would have been no surrender at Appomattox Courthouse; no, sir, not by me. Had I foreseen these results of subjugation, I would have preferred to die at Appomattox with my brave men, my sword in this right hand."[407]

In September 1870 Lee wrote the following to Lieutenant Colonel Charles Marshall:
☞ "My experience of men has neither disposed me to think worse of them, nor indisposed me to serve them; nor in spite of failures, which I lament; of errors, which I now see and acknowledge, or of the present aspect of affairs, do I despair of the future. The truth is this: the march of Providence is so slow and our desires so impatient, the work of progress is so immense and our means of aiding it so feeble, the life of humanity is so long and that of the individual so brief, that we often see only the ebb of the advancing wave, and are thus discouraged. It is history that teaches us to hope."[408]

Another Confederate victory.

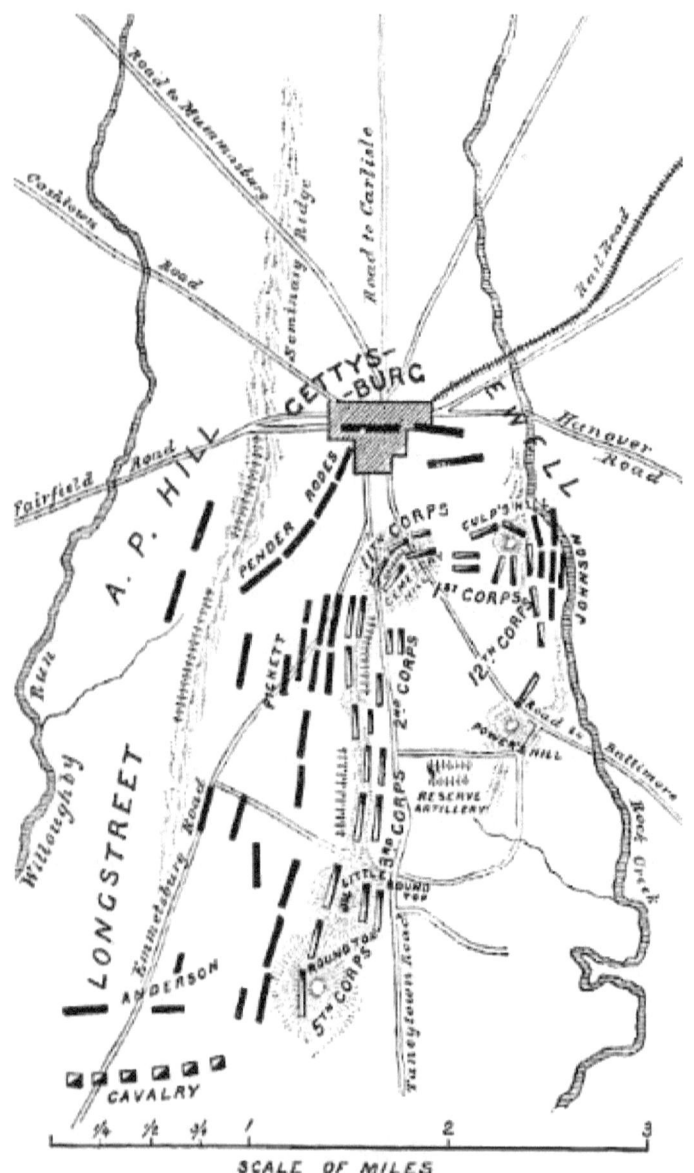

GETTYSBURG

THE POSITIONS ON THE THIRD OF JULY

UNION   CONFEDERATE

This map shows the positions of the Rebels and the Yanks on the last day of the Battle of Gettysburg.

16

IN DEFENSE
OF THE SOUTH

Despite Lee's Christ-like, almost passive response to his postwar Northern foes and critics, he did in fact hold strong views regarding the Southern Confederacy, the cause for which she fought (self-determination and constitutional government), and the rights of the Southern people, as the following quotes show.

In an October 25, 1865, letter, just six months after the end of Lincoln's War, Lee replied to a publisher asking him if he would like to write his autobiography, with these words:

☞ "I cannot now undertake the work you propose, nor can I enter into an engagement which I may never be able to accomplish. *It will be some time before the truth can be known*, and I do not think that time has yet arrived [emphasis added]."[409]

What is "the truth" Lee is speaking of, and why did he believe it was too early to reveal it? "The truth" concerns the "true history of the war," as Lee phrased it in an 1866 letter,[410] and it was premature to unveil it because the public, still in mourning over Lincoln's bloody and unconstitutional assault on the South, was not yet ready to hear it. Sadly, though Lee began assembling documents in order to "transmit the truth to posterity,"[411] he passed away before writing his autobiography. But he did leave us with a hint as to why he felt the truth about the War needed to someday be told. It comes from a letter he wrote to one of his

Lee's final resting place: The Lee Memorial Chapel (now known simply as Lee Chapel), Washington and Lee University, Lexington, Virginia.

relatives, Cassius F. Lee, Jr. Dated June 6, 1870, from Lexington, Virginia, it reads:

☞ "My Dear Cassius: I am very much obliged to you for your letter of the 1st and the interest you evince in the character of the people of the South and their defence of the rights which they believed were guaranteed by the Constitution. The reputation of individuals is of minor importance to the opinion which posterity may form of *the motives which governed the South in their late struggle for the maintenance of the principles of the Constitution. I hope, therefore, a true history will be written and justice be done them.* . . . I am, very truly, your cousin, R. E. Lee [emphasis added]."[412]

On July 9, 1866, Lee wrote the following to Captain James May of Illinois:
☞ ". . . I must give you my special thanks for doing me the justice to believe that my conduct during the last five eventful years has been governed by my sense of duty. I had no other guide, *nor had I any other object than the defence of those principles of American liberty upon which the constitutions of the several States were originally founded; and unless they are strictly observed, I fear there will be an end to Republican government in this*

country. . . . [emphasis added]"⁴¹³

On December 15, 1866, Lee wrote this powerful letter to Britain's First Lord Acton (Sir John Dalberg Acton), then in Rome, Italy:

☞ ". . . while I have considered the preservation of the constitutional power of the General Government to be the foundation of our peace and safety at home and abroad, *I yet believe that the maintenance of the rights and authority reserved to the States, and to the people, not only essential to the adjustment and balance of the general system, but the safeguard of the continuance of a free government. I consider it as the chief source of stability to our political system; whereas the consolidation of the States into one vast republic, sure to be aggressive abroad and despotic at home, will be the certain precursor of that ruin which has overwhelmed all those that have preceded it.* I need not refer one so well acquainted as you are with American history, to the State papers of [George] Washington and [Thomas] Jefferson, the representatives of the federal and democratic parties, *denouncing consolidation and centralisation of power, as tending to the subversion of State Governments, and to despotism.*

"The New England states, whose citizens are the fiercest opponents of the Southern states, did not always avow the opinions they now advocate. Upon the purchase of Louisiana by Mr. Jefferson, they virtually asserted the right of secession through their prominent men; and in the convention which assembled at [the] Hartford [Convention] in 1814, they threatened the disruption of the Union unless the war should be discontinued. The assertion of this right has been repeatedly made by their politicians when their party was weak, and *Massachusetts, the leading state in hostility to the South*, declares in the preamble to her constitution, that the people of that commonwealth 'have the sole and exclusive right of governing themselves as a free sovereign and independent state, and do, and forever hereafter shall, exercise and enjoy every power, jurisdiction, and right which is not, or may hereafter be by them expressly delegated to the United States of America in congress assembled.' Such has been in substance the language of other State governments, and such the doctrine advocated by the leading men of the country for the last seventy years.

"Judge [Salmon P.] Chase, the present Chief Justice of the U.S., as late as 1850, is reported to have stated in the Senate, of which he was a member, that he 'knew of no remedy in case of the refusal of a state to perform its stipulations,' thereby acknowledging the sovereignty and independence of state action.

"But I will not weary you with this unprofitable discussion. Unprofitable because the judgment of reason has been displaced by the arbitrament of war, waged for the purpose as avowed of maintaining the union of the states. If, therefore, the result of the war is to be considered as having decided that the union of the states is inviolable and perpetual under the constitution, it naturally follows that it is as incompetent for the general government to impair its integrity by the exclusion of a state, as for the states to do so by secession; and that the existence and rights of a state by the constitution are as indestructible as the union itself. *The legitimate consequence then must be the perfect equality of rights of all the states; the exclusive right of each to regulate its internal affairs under rules established by the Constitution, and the right of each state to prescribe for itself the qualifications of suffrage. The South has contended only for the supremacy of the Constitution and the just administration of the laws made in pursuance of it. . . . Although the South would have preferred any honourable compromise to the fratricidal war which has taken place, she now accepts in good*

An interior view of the Lee Memorial Chapel, with Lee's recumbent statue and the Lee family mausoleum beneath it in the back center.

faith its constitutional results, and agrees without reserve to the amendment which has already been made to the Constitution for the extinction of slavery. That is an event which has been long sought, though in a different way, and by none has it been more earnestly desired than by citizens of Virginia [emphasis added]."⁴¹⁴

While pro-North scholars, authors, and historians have spent the past 150 years denigrating the South in an attempt to hide the truth about Lincoln's War, General Lee and thousands of other Southerners made it one of their lifelong goals to expose it. Why? Because they knew that the Northern victor and her many anti-South supporters would one day rewrite Civil War history in order to justify it. Why, in the eyes of pro-North supporters, does the Civil War need justifying? They are afraid that the truth will come out, and that truth is that liberal Lincoln fought the conservative South to stamp out states' rights so that he could establish big government in Washington, D.C. In a February 8, 1867, letter to his son Fitzhugh, the General once again mentions this "truth":

☞ "We have now nothing to do but to attend to our material interests which collectively will advance the interests of the State, and to await events. The dominant party [that is, the liberal Yankee Republicans] cannot reign forever, and truth and justice will at last prevail."⁴¹⁵

On January 5, 1866, Lee included these words in a letter to Mr. C. Chauncey Burr:

☞ "All that the South has ever desired was that the Union, as established by our forefathers, should be preserved, and that the government as originally organised should be administered in purity and truth. If such is the desire of the North, there can be no contention between the two sections, and all true patriots will unite in advocating that policy which will soonest restore the country to tranquillity and order, and serve to perpetuate true republicanism [emphasis added]."⁴¹⁶

In this June 8, 1867, letter to Fitzhugh the General touches on the "dark," "evil," "angry cloud" of "Reconstruction" that loomed over the South at the time:

☞ "My Dear Son: Your letter written on your birthday has been welcomed by the whole family, and I assure you that we reciprocate your regrets at the distance which separates us. Although the future is still dark, and the prospects gloomy, I am confident that, if we all unite in doing our duty, and earnestly work to extract what good we can out of

A closeup of Lee's recumbent statue, Lee Memorial Chapel, Washington and Lee University, Lexington, Virginia.

the evil that now hangs over our dear land, the time is not distant when the angry cloud will be lifted from our horizon and the sun in his pristine brightness again shine forth. I, therefore, can anticipate for you many years of happiness and prosperity, and in my daily prayers to the God of mercy and truth I invoke His choicest blessings upon you.

"May He gather you under the shadow of His almighty wing, direct you in all your ways, and give you peace and everlasting life. It would be most pleasant to my feelings could I again, as you propose, gather you all around me, but I fear that will not be in this world. Let us all so live that we may be united in that world where there is no more separation, and where sorrow and pain never come."[417]

The following excerpt is from an October 29, 1867, letter to the author's cousin Confederate General James Longstreet during "Reconstruction." Here, the conservative Lee clearly states that he does not support the policies or actions of the ruling Republican (then the liberal) party:

☞ ". . . I have avoided all discussion of political questions since the cessation of hostilities, and have, in my own conduct, and in my recommendations to others, endeavoured to conform to existing circumstances. I consider this the part of wisdom, as well as of duty;

but, while I think we should act under the law and according to the law imposed upon us, *I cannot think the course pursued by the dominant political party the best for the interests of the country, and therefore cannot say so or give it my approval....*

"I am of the opinion that all who can should vote for the most intelligent, honest, and conscientious men eligible to office, irrespective of former party opinions, who will endeavour to make the new constitutions and the laws passed under them as beneficial as possible to the true interests, prosperity, and liberty of all classes and conditions of the people [emphasis added]."[418]

While former Confederate President Jefferson Davis had his critics, General Lee was not one of them, saying:
☞ "If my opinion is worth anything, you can always say that few people could have done better than Mr. Davis. I knew of none that could have done as well."[419]

A Confederate sentinel.

Though after the War, Lee's "material, social, and political interests" were, as he put it, "naturally with the whites," he was not against blacks, as he noted in this March 12, 1868, letter to his son Robert, Jr.:
☞ "... I wish them no evil in the world—on the contrary, will do them every good in my power, and know that they are misled by those to whom they have given their confidence [that is, the Radicals, or abolitionists, and the Northern Republicans, the liberals of that day]."[420]

On August 28, 1868, Lee wrote to Union General William Starke Rosecrans concerning his views on the situation then current across the United States:
☞ "... Whatever opinions may have prevailed in the past with regard to African slavery or the right of a State to secede from the Union, we believe we express the almost unanimous judgment of the Southern people when we declare that they consider that these questions were decided by the war, and that it is their intention, in good faith, to abide by that decision.

"At the close of the war, the Southern people laid down their arms and sought to resume their former relations to the government of the United States. Through their State conventions they abolished slavery and annulled their ordinances of secession; and they returned to their peaceful pursuits with a sincere purpose to fulfill all their duties under the Constitution of the United States which they had sworn to support. If their action in these particulars had been met in a spirit of frankness and cordiality, we believe that, ere this, old irritations would have passed away, and the wounds inflicted by the war would have been, in a great measure, healed.

"As far as we are advised, the people of the South entertain no unfriendly feeling towards the government of the United States, but they complain that their rights under the Constitution are withheld from them in the administration thereof. *The idea that the Southern people are hostile to the negroes, and would oppress them, if it were in their power to do so, is entirely unfounded. They have grown up in our midst, and we have been accustomed from childhood to look upon them with kindness. The change in the relations of the two races has wrought no change in our feelings towards them.*

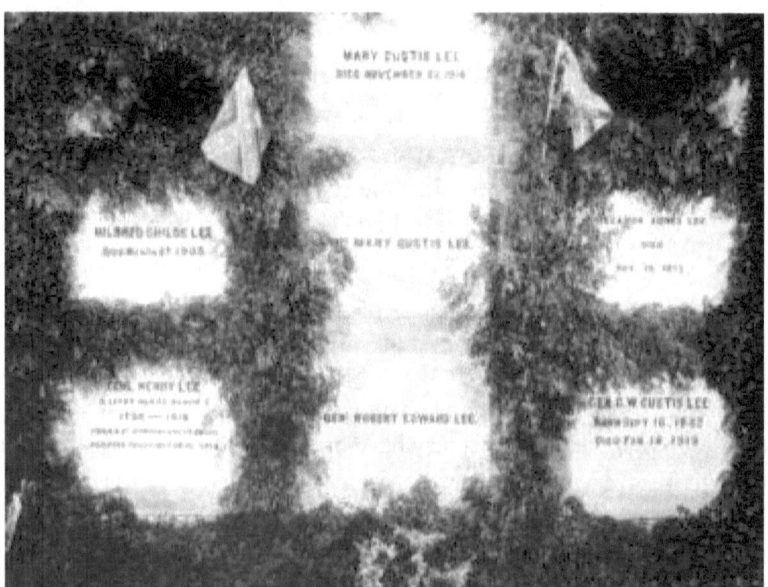

The mausoleum located beneath Lee's recumbent statue, showing the burial sites of the General, his wife, and other family members.

They still constitute an important part of our labouring population. Without their labour, the lands of the South would be comparatively unproductive; without the employment which Southern agriculture affords, they would be destitute of the means of subsistence, and become paupers dependent upon public bounty. Self-interest, if there were no higher motive, would therefore prompt the whites of the South to extend to the negroes care and protection.

Confederate troops repelling Lincoln's illegal invaders in Virginia.

"The important fact that the two races are, under existing circumstances, necessary to each other, is gradually becoming apparent to both, and we believe that but for influences exerted to stir up the passions of the negroes, the relations of the two races would soon adjust themselves on a basis of mutual kindness and advantage.

"It is true that the people of the South, in common with a large majority of the people of the North and West, are, for obvious reasons, inflexibly opposed to any system of laws which would place the political power of the country in the hands of the negro race. But this opposition springs from no feeling of enmity, but from a deep-seated conviction that, at present, the negroes have neither the intelligence nor the other qualifications which are necessary to make them safe depositories of political power. They would inevitably become the victims of demagogues who, for selfish purposes, would mislead them to the serious injury of the public.

"The great want of the South is peace. The people earnestly desire tranquillity and a restoration of the Union. They deprecate disorder and excitement as the most serious obstacle to their prosperity. They ask a restoration of their rights under the Constitution. They desire relief from oppressive misrule. Above all, they would appeal to their countrymen for the re-establishment, in the Southern States, of that which has justly been regarded as the birthright of every

American, the right of self-government. Establish these on a firm basis, and we can safely promise, on behalf of the Southern people, that they will faithfully obey the Constitution and laws of the United States, treat the negro population with kindness and humanity, and fulfil every duty incumbent on peaceful citizens, loyal to the Constitution of their country [emphasis added]."[421]

In his March 22, 1869, letter to George W. Jones, Lee wrote:
☞ "I was not in favour of secession and was opposed to war. In fact I was for the Constitution and the Union established by our forefathers. No one now is more in favour of that Union and that Constitution, and as far as I know, it is that for which the South has all along contended; and if restored, as I trust they will be, I am sure there will be no truer supporters of that Union and that Constitution than the Southern people. . . . Present my kindest regards to your brave sons who aided in our struggle for State rights and Constitutional government. *We failed, but in the good providence of God, apparent failure often proves a blessing. I trust it may eventuate so in this instance* [emphasis added]."[422]

On October 12, 1870, as the General lay in bed nearly unconscious, in his mind he returned to the battlefield of Lincoln's War. At 8:30 AM that morning he uttered his last words: "Strike the tent. Tell Hill he must come up!"[423] *Around 9:00 AM he slipped quietly away into the Great Beyond, or what he himself called the "bliss in the land of the blessed." May he rest in eternal peace.*

APPENDIX A

LEE'S PLAN TO EMANCIPATE & ENLIST SOUTHERN SLAVES

"To the Hon. Andrew Hunter, January 11, 1865—Dear Sir: I have received your letter of the 7th instant, and without confining myself to the order of your interrogatories, will endeavor to answer them by a statement of my views on the subject. I shall be most happy if I can contribute to the solution of a question in which I feel an interest commensurate with my desire for the welfare and happiness of our people.

"Considering the relation of master and slave, controlled by humane laws and influenced by Christianity and an enlightened public sentiment, as the best that can exist between the white and black races while intermingled as at present in this country, I would deprecate any sudden disturbance of that relation unless it be necessary to avert a greater calamity to both. I should therefore prefer to rely upon our white population to preserve the ratio between our forces and those of the enemy, which experience has shown to be safe. But in view of the preparations of our enemies, it is our duty to provide for continued war and not for a battle or a campaign, and I fear that we cannot accomplish this without overtaxing the capacity of our white population.

"Should the war continue under existing circumstances, the enemy may in course of time penetrate our country and get access to a large part of our negro population. It is his avowed policy to convert the able-bodied men among them into soldiers, and to emancipate all. The success of the Federal aims in the South was followed by a proclamation of President Lincoln for 280,000 men, the effect of which will be to stimulate the Northern States to procure as substitutes for their own people the negroes thus brought within their reach. Many have already been obtained in Virginia, and should the fortune of war expose more of her territory, the enemy would gain a large accession to his strength. His progress will thus add to his numbers, and at the same time destroy slavery in a manner most pernicious to the welfare of our people. Their negroes will be used to hold them in subjection, leaving the remaining force of the enemy free to extend his conquest. Whatever may be the effect of our employing negro troops, it cannot be as mischievous as this. If it end in subverting slavery it will be accomplished by ourselves, and we can devise the means of alleviating the evil consequences to both races. I think, therefore, we must decide whether slavery shall be extinguished by our enemies and the slaves be used against us, or use them ourselves at the risk of the effects which may be produced upon our social institutions. My own opinion is that we should employ them without delay. I believe that with proper regulations they can be made efficient soldiers. They possess the physical qualifications in an eminent degree. Long habits of obedience and subordination, coupled with the moral influence which in our country the white man possesses over the black, furnish an excellent foundation for that discipline which is the best guaranty of military efficiency. Our chief aim should be to secure their fidelity.

"There have been formidable armies composed of men having no interest in the cause for which they fought beyond their pay or the hope of plunder. But it is certain that the surest foundation upon which the fidelity of an army can rest, especially in a service which imposes peculiar hardships and privations, is the personal interest of the soldier in the issue of the contest. Such an interest we can give our negroes by giving immediate freedom to all who enlist, and freedom at the end of the war to the families of those who discharge their duties faithfully (whether they survive or not), together with the privilege of residing at the South. To this might be added a bounty for faithful service.

"We should not expect slaves to fight for prospective freedom when they can secure it at once by going to the enemy, in whose service they will incur no greater risk than in ours. The reasons that induce me to recommend the employment of negro troops at all render the effect of the measures I have suggested upon slavery immaterial, and in my opinion the best means of securing the efficiency and fidelity of this auxiliary force would be to accompany the measure with a well-digested plan of gradual and general emancipation. As that will be the result of the continuance of the war, and will certainly occur if the enemy succeed, it seems to me most advisable to adopt it at once, and thereby obtain all the benefits that will accrue to our cause.

"The employment of negro troops under regulations similar in principle to those above indicated would, in my opinion, greatly increase our military strength and enable us to relieve our white population to some extent. I think we could dispense with the reserve forces except in cases of necessity.

"It would disappoint the hopes which our enemies base upon our exhaustion, deprive them in a great measure of the aid they now derive from black troops, and thus throw the burden of the war upon their own people. In addition to the great political advantages that would result to our cause from the adoption of a system of emancipation, it would exercise a salutary influence upon our whole negro population, by rendering more secure the fidelity of those who become soldiers, and diminishing the inducements to the rest to abscond.

"I can only say in conclusion that whatever measures are to be adopted should be adopted at once. Every day's delay increases the difficulty. Much time will be required to organize and discipline the men, and action may be deferred until it is too late. Very respectfully, your obedient servant, Robert E. Lee, General."[424]

APPENDIX B

ROBERT E. LEE'S DESCENDANTS
Three Generations - From the Author's Personal Family Tree
Copyright © 2011 Lochlainn Seabrook

NOTES
- The General's name and those belonging to his direct line are bolded.
- Spouses are listed below their husband or wife and are marked with a cross (+).
- Children are listed below their parents.
- All of the General's descendants descend from European royalty, through both his father and his mother.
- I have limited the tree to three generations to protect the privacy of living relations.
- Warning: while I believe most of this information is accurate, not all of it has been genealogically validated.

---

1 **ROBERT EDWARD LEE, SR.**, b: 19 Jan 1807, Stratford Hall, Stratford, Westmoreland Co., VA; d: 12 Oct 1870, Lexington, VA; Number of children: 7; Gender: Male; Burial: Lee Chapel, Lexington, VA
..+MARY ANNE RANDOLPH CUSTIS, b: 01 Oct 1808, Arlington Co., VA; m: 30 Jun 1831 at Arlington House, VA; d: 05 Nov 1873, Stratford Hall, Westmoreland Co., VA; Number of children: 7; Father: George Washington Parke Custis; Mother: Mary Ann Randolph Fitzhugh; Gender: Female; Burial: Lee Chapel, Lexington, VA (Mary and Robert were cousins)

....2 **GEORGE WASHINGTON CUSTIS "BOO" LEE**, b: 16 Sep 1832, Arlington House, Arlington, VA; d: 18 Feb 1913, Ravensworth, Fairfax, VA; Gender: Male; Burial: Lee Chapel, Lexington, VA (he never married)
....2 **MARY CUSTIS LEE**, b: 12 Jul 1835, Arlington House, Arlington, VA; d: 22 Nov 1918 in VA; Gender: Female; Burial: Lee Chapel, Lexington, VA (she never married)
....2 **WILLIAM HENRY "ROONEY" FITZHUGH LEE**, b: 31 May 1837, Arlington House, Arlington , VA; d: 15 Oct 1891 in VA; Total number of children: 7; Gender: Male; Burial: Lee Chapel, Lexington, VA
.......+CHARLOTTE GEORGIANA WICKHAM (1st wife of William Henry Fitzhugh Lee), b: 1841, Fairfax Co., VA; m: 23 Mar 1859 at Shirley Plantation, Richmond, VA; d: 26 Dec 1863; Number of children: 2; Father: George Wickham; Mother: Charlotte Carter; Gender: Female; Burial: Shockoe Hill Cemetery, Richmond, VA

........3 **ROBERT EDWARD LEE, III** (a), b: 09 Mar 1860, New Kent Co., VA; d: 30 June 1862, Richmond, VA; Burial: Shockoe Hill Cemetery, Richmond, VA
........3 **CHARLOTTE CARTER LEE**, b: 19 Oct 1862, VA; d: 06 Dec 1862, VA; Burial: Shockoe Hill Cemetery, Richmond, VA

.......+MARY TABB BOLLING (2nd wife of William Henry Fitzhugh Lee), b: 27 Aug 1846, Petersburg, VA; m: 28 Nov 1867, VA; d: 05 May 1924; Number of children: 5; Father: George Washington Bolling; Mother: Martha Smith Nichols; Gender: Female; Burial: Lee Chapel, Lexington, VA

........3 **ANNE AGNES LEE**, b: unknown; d: 1874; Gender: Female; Burial: Lee Chapel, Lexington, VA (died young)
........3 **WILLIAM HENRY FITZHUGH LEE, JR.**, b: unknown; d: 1875; Gender: Male; Burial: Lee Chapel, Lexington, VA (died young)
........3 **MARY TABB LEE**, b: unknown, Petersburg, VA; d: 1871; Gender: Female; Burial: Lee Chapel, Lexington, VA (died young)
........3 **ROBERT EDWARD LEE, III** (b), b: 11 Feb 1869, Petersburg, VA; d: 07 Sep 1922, Petersburg, VA; Gender: Male; Burial: Magnolia Cemetery, Charleston, SC
...........+MARY WILKERSON MIDDLETON, b: 14 Aug 1874, Charleston, SC; d: 19 May 1959, Asheville, NC; Father: Ralph Izard Middleton; Mother: Sarah Virginia Memminger; Gender: Female; Burial: Magnolia Cemetery, Charleston, SC
........3 **GEORGE BOLLING LEE**, b: 31 Aug 1872, Fairfax Co., VA; d: 13 Jul 1948, New York, NY; Gender: Male; Burial: Lee Chapel, Lexington, VA
...........+HELEN KEENEY, b: 26 Sep 1895, San Francisco, CA; d: 08 Jul 1968; Father: Charles C. Keeney; Mother: Adele Maria Jones; Gender: Female; Burial: Lee Chapel, Lexington, VA

....2 **ANNE CARTER "ANNIE" LEE**, b: 18 Jun 1839, Arlington House, Arlington, VA; d: 20 Oct 1862, Warrenton, NC; Gender: Female; Burial: Lee Chapel, Lexington, VA (she never married)
....2 **ELEANOR AGNES "WIGS" LEE**, b: 27 Feb 1841, Arlington House, Arlington, VA; d: 1873, Lexington, VA; Gender: Female; Burial: Lee Chapel, Lexington, VA (she never married)

....2 **ROBERT EDWARD LEE, JR.**, b: 27 Oct 1843, Arlington House, Arlington, VA; d: 19 Oct 1914, Richmond, VA; Number of children: 2; Gender: Male; Burial: Lee Chapel, Lexington, VA

........+CHARLOTTE TAYLOR HAXALL (1st wife of Robert E. Lee, Jr.), b: 23 Oct 1848, Orange Co., VA; m: 16 Nov 1871; d: 22 Sep 1872, West Point, King William Co., VA; Father: Richard Barton Haxall; Mother: Octavia Robinson; Number of children: none known; Gender: Female; Burial: Hollywood Cemetery, Richmond, VA

........+JULIET CARTER (2nd wife of Robert E. Lee, Jr.), b: 06 Apr 1860; m: abt. 1896; d: 17 Nov 1915; Number of children: 2; Father: Thomas Hill Carter; Mother: Susan Elizabeth Roy; Gender: Female; Burial: Lee Chapel, Lexington, VA

........3 **ANNE CARTER LEE**, b: 21 Jul 1897; d: 08 Nov 1978, Upperville, Fauquier Co., VA; Number of children: 2; Gender: Female; Burial: Ivy Hill Cemetery, Upperville, Fauquier Co., VA

............+HANSON EDWARD ELY, JR., b: 31 Mar 1896, MT; d: 29 Sep 1938, NJ; Number of children: 2; Father: Hanson Edward Ely, Sr.; Mother: Mary Barber; Gender: Male: Burial: Arlington National Cemetery, Arlington, VA

........3 **MARY CUSTIS LEE**, b: 23 Dec 1900, Richmond, VA; d: 26 Dec 1994, VA; Number of children: 3; Gender: Female

............+WILLIAM HUNTER DE BUTTS, b: 23 Oct 1899, VA; m: 01 Oct 1925; d: 23 Nov 1987; Number of children: 3; Father: Dulaney Forrest De Butts; Mother: Emma Ashby; Gender: Male; Burial: Ivy Hill Cemetery, Upperville, Fauquier Co., VA

....2 **MILDRED CHILDE "PRECIOUS LIFE" LEE**, b: 10 Feb 1846, Arlington House, Arlington, VA; d: March 27, 1905, New Orleans, LA; Gender: Female; Burial: Lee Chapel, Lexington, VA (she never married)

APPENDIX C

Interesting & Unusual Facts About the Lee Family
By Lochlainn Seabrook

🔫 Robert E. Lee is universally thought of as a Confederate officer. Yet he served with the United States army for thirty-two years, far longer than the four years he served with the Confederate army.

🔫 One of the great contradictions about Lee is that while he is known to this day primarily as a great military figure, an aggressive soldier, and an international war hero, he was actually a gentle, kind, considerate, loving Christ-like figure, who some actually called, in a complimentary way, "effeminate" and "motherly."

🔫 Lee was the archetypal family man and homebody. Ironically, due to his demanding military career, he spent the majority of his time away from both.

🔫 During Lincoln's War it was the custom of both Southern and Northern generals to occupy civilian homes for use as their headquarters. Lee being the kind of man he was, rejected this tradition and slept on the cold hard ground with his men. Sometimes he "treated" himself to the comfort of a tent.

🔫 Lee attained the highest ranks in the Confederate army, that of a full four-star general and commander-in-chief of all military forces. Being of a modest nature, however, throughout the War he continued to wear his colonel's uniform with three stars on the collar. This at times caused some confusion, such as when a courier would arrive at camp with papers for the commander, asking for "General Lee." He would them be escorted to a small ragged tent with a "colonel" sitting inside of it!

🔫 Throughout his postwar years General Lee turned down millions of dollars in gifts, homes, positions, and business opportunities that were offered to him, preferring to earn his own way, live humbly, and be with his family.

🔫 Lee had originally dreamed of becoming a gentleman farmer, but ended up following the military path of his famous father, American Revolutionary war hero Major General Henry Light Horse Lee, forever changing the course of American history.

🔫 Unlike most military historians then as today, Lee chalked up the Confederacy's loss to "God's will," not to Yankee military superiority or the so-called "righteousness" of the Union Cause.

🔫 Later in life Lee's mother Anna and his wife Mary became invalids. He cared for both of them, personally and tenderly, into old age.

🔫 Of Lee's seven children only two married: his second and third sons, William and Robert, Jr. His four daughters, Mary, Anne, Eleanor, and Mildred, and his oldest son, George, remained single throughout their lives.

🔫 Both William and Robert, Jr.'s first wives were named Charlotte.

🔫 Both Charlottes died within a few years of marriage.

🔫 William's two children, Robert, III, and Charlotte, died as infants shortly before their mother Charlotte herself passed away, leaving William widowed and childless. Like his brother Robert, Jr., he remarried.

🔫 Lee was a typical old-fashioned, disciplined, reserved, calm, hard-working Capricorn.

🔫 Traveller, General Lee's warhorse, passed away in 1871 shortly after his master's death in the Fall of 1870. The illustrious steed was buried just outside Lee Chapel so the two could be near one another in death.

🔫 Lincoln stripped Lee's U.S. citizenship from him in 1861. Exactly 114 years later, in 1975, the General's U.S. citizenship was posthumously restored to him by an act of the U.S. Congress under the direction of President Gerald Ford.

🔫 Lee is often held up as an emblem of the ultimate pro-South Southerner, the embodiment of the unreconstructed Confederacy, and the immortal enemy of the North. In fact, the General was extremely lenient and unbiased when it came to the Union, and detested the type of demagogic sectional divisiveness employed by Lincoln and many others at the time. While often thoroughly disgusted with the manner in which the United States conducted itself during Lincoln's War, afterward Lee eschewed any sense of bitterness and refused to allow his fellow Southerners to denigrate Yankees. "We, both South and North," he was fond of reminding everyone, "are all Americans."

🔫 After years of legal wrangling by the Lees and a lawsuit in the 1870s, their stolen home Arlington House was finally returned to them by the U.S. government. However, it was now part of Arlington National Cemetery and could not be lived in. Lee's eldest son George then sold it back to the U.S. government for $150,000, the modern equivalent of about $4 million. It remains the architectural centerpiece of the cemetery to this day.

🔫 Robert E. Lee is related to the following mainly English royals: King Edward I "Longshanks," King Edward II, King Edward III, King Charles I, King Charles II, King Charles III, King George V, King George VI, King Henry V, King Henry VI, King Henry VII, King Henry VIII, King James II, King James III, King Richard II, King Richard III, King William III, King William IV, Alfred the Great, Queen Victoria, Queen Mary I "Bloody Mary," the current Queen Elizabeth, Prince Charles, the late Princess Diana, Princes William and Harry, Kate Middleton, and Duchess Sarah "Fergie" Ferguson. Lee's other famous relations include: George Washington, Thomas Jefferson, Meriwether Lewis, Charlemagne, Alexander Hamilton, Nathan Bedford Forrest, John Quincy Adams, and Zachary Taylor and his two children Sarah Knox Taylor (the first wife of Jefferson Davis) and Confederate General Richard Taylor. (This is a partial list from my personal family tree.)

From left to right: General George Washington Custis Lee (the General's eldest son), General Robert E. Lee, and Colonel Walter Herron Taylor (one of Lee's aides). Date of photo unknown.

NOTES

1. Seabrook, EYWTACWW, pp. 44, 192.
2. Seabrook, AL, p. 430.
3. Seabrook, AL, pp. 521-523. Scandals under President Grant included: Black Friday, the New York Custom House Ring, the Star Route Postal Ring, the Salary Grab, the Sanborn Contract, the Delano Affair, the Pratt and Boyd Affair, the Whiskey Ring, the Trading Post Ring, the Cattell and Company Affair, and the Safe Burglary Conspiracy. See Seabrook, TMCP, pp. 367-368; Seabrook, AL, pp. 521-523.
4. Pollard, LC, p. 699.
5. Long and Wright, p. 485.
6. Page, p. 676.
7. Long and Wright, p. 485.
8. Riley, p. 18.
9. R. E. Lee, Jr., p. 205.
10. Long and Wright, p. 485.
11. R. E. Lee, Jr., p. 333.
12. Riley, p. 25.
13. R. E. Lee, Jr., p. 277.
14. Childe, p. 37.
15. R. E. Lee, Jr., p. 366.
16. Long and Wright, p. 486.
17. Long and Wright, p. 486.
18. Trent, p. 41.
19. Long and Wright, p. 486.
20. McGuire, p. 23.
21. R. E. Lee, Jr., p. 396.
22. R. E. Lee, Jr., p. 305.
23. R. E. Lee, Jr., p. 305.
24. R. E. Lee, Jr., p. 358.
25. R. E. Lee, Jr., p. 303.
26. R. E. Lee, Jr., p. 395.
27. R. E. Lee, Jr., p. 247.
28. Long and Wright, p. 486.
29. Gilman, p. 19.
30. Speer, p. 58.
31. Riley, p. 153.
32. Riley, pp. 32-33.
33. Long and Wright, p. 34.
34. Butler, pp. 305-306.
35. R. E. Lee, Jr., p. 96.
36. R. E. Lee, Jr., p. 91.
37. Riley, p. 155.
38. Page, p. 637.
39. R. E. Lee, Jr., p. 278.
40. W. H. Taylor, p. 77.
41. G. Bradford, p. 226.
42. Long and Wright, p. 494.
43. Riley, p. 92.
44. R. E. Lee, Jr., p. 55.
45. Childe, p. 35.
46. See Riley, pp. 159-160.
47. Riley, p. 158.
48. R. E. Lee, Jr., p. 55.

49. Riley, p. 161.
50. White, p. 447.
51. White, p. 447.
52. White, p. 448.
53. Riley, p. 25.
54. White, p. 454.
55. Cooke, p. 66.
56. R. E. Lee, Jr., p. 142.
57. R. E. Lee, Jr., p. 46.
58. Page, p. 680.
59. Long and Wright, p. 434.
60. R. E. Lee, Jr., p. 205.
61. Jones, PR, p. 174.
62. Long and Wright, p. 440.
63. White, p. 454.
64. Jones, PR, p. 166.
65. Long and Wright, pp. 484-485.
66. Riley, p. 92.
67. R. E. Lee, Jr., pp. 119-120.
68. R. E. Lee, Jr., pp. 120-121.
69. R. E. Lee, Jr., p. 134.
70. R. E. Lee, Jr., p. 376.
71. R. E. Lee, Jr., p. 103.
72. McGuire, pp. 28-30.
73. R. E. Lee, Jr., p. 17.
74. Jones, LL, p. 35.
75. Jones, PR, pp. 371, 373.
76. White, p. 38.
77. White, p. 38.
78. White, p. 46.
79. Page, p. 27.
80. Long and Wright, p. 62.
81. F. Lee, pp. 49-50.
82. R. E. Lee, Jr., p. 5.
83. R. E. Lee, Jr., p. 6.
84. R. E. Lee, Jr., p. 265.
85. Riley, p. 93.
86. R. E. Lee, Jr., p. 16.
87. R. E. Lee, Jr., p. 16.
88. R. E. Lee, Jr., pp. 14-15.
89. R. E. Lee, Jr., pp. 18-19.
90. Long and Wright, p. 74.
91. Long and Wright, p. 464.
92. Long and Wright, p. 465. Note: some dispute the authenticity of this letter.
93. White, p. 49.
94. Long and Wright, p. 79.
95. R. E. Lee, Jr., pp. 22-23.
96. For more on how Lincoln nefariously tricked the South into firing the opening shot of the "Civil War," see Seabrook, EYWTACWW, pp. 35-39; Seabrook, ARB, pp. 265-270. See also Tilley, pp. 38-39.
97. R. E. Lee, Jr., pp. 25-26.
96. R. E. Lee, Jr., p. 29.
97. R. E. Lee, Jr., p. 29.
98. Williamson, pp. 42-43.
99. R. E. Lee, Jr., pp. 29-30.

THE QUOTABLE ROBERT E. LEE ❧ 235

100. R. E. Lee, Jr., p. 30.
101. R. E. Lee, Jr., p. 30.
102. Liberals (and uninformed conservatives) continue to foment the falsehood that because Lincoln was a Republican, he could not have been a socialist, or even socialistic. The confusion surrounding this issue is unraveled in the "Notes to the Reader" section of this book. For more on Lincoln's socialistic tendencies and Marxist agendas, see Seabrook, AL, pp. 487-492. See also Seabrook, TUAL, pp. 8, 11, 23-24, 35, 91; Seabrook, TMCP, p. 958; Seabrook, L, p. 156.
103. R. E. Lee, Jr., pp. 32-33.
104. R. E. Lee, Jr., p. 35.
105. R. E. Lee, Jr., p. 36.
106. R. E. Lee, Jr., p. 37.
107. R. E. Lee, Jr., p. 59.
108. R. E. Lee, Jr., pp. 65, 66.
109. R. E. Lee, Jr., pp. 66-67.
110. Seabrook, AL, p. 417.
111. White, pp. 173-174.
112. White, p. 178.
113. White, p. 226.
114. R. E. Lee, Jr., pp. 79-80.
115. White, p. 239.
116. Alexander, pp. 253-254.
117. Long and Wright, pp. 242-243.
118. Long and Wright, p. 243.
119. Long and Wright, pp. 243-244.
120. Long and Wright, pp. 244-245.
121. Long and Wright, pp. 496-497.
122. R. E. Lee, Jr., pp. 109-110.
123. R. E. Lee, Jr., p. 114.
124. Long and Wright, pp. 350-351.
125. Long and Wright, p. 389.
126. Long and Wright, pp. 397-399.
127. R. E. Lee, Jr., pp. 142-143.
128. R. E. Lee, Jr., p. 20.
129. R. E. Lee, Jr., pp. 181-182.
130. R. E. Lee, Jr., pp. 20-21.
131. R. E. Lee, Jr., p. 235.
132. R. E. Lee, Jr., p. 210.
133. R. E. Lee, Jr., p. 238.
134. R. E. Lee, Jr., pp. 246-247.
135. R. E. Lee, Jr., p. 243.
136. R. E. Lee, Jr., pp. 252-253.
137. R. E. Lee, Jr., p. 255.
138. R. E. Lee, Jr., p. 268.
139. Speer, p. 51.
140. Lee nicknamed both of his daughters, Mary and Mildred, "Life." R. E. Lee, Jr., p. 41.
141. Long and Wright, pp. 465-466.
142. Jones, LL, pp. 460-461.
143. R. E. Lee, Jr., pp. 297-298.
144. R. E. Lee, Jr., p. 324.
145. White, p. 455.
146. R. E. Lee, Jr., p. 329.
147. R. E. Lee, Jr., p. 334.
148. Childe, p. 333.
149. R. E. Lee, Jr., pp. 337-338.

150. R. E. Lee, Jr., p. 343.
151. R. E. Lee, Jr., pp. 365-366.
152. R. E. Lee, Jr., pp. 373-374.
153. White, p. 455.
154. R. E. Lee, Jr., p. 397.
155. R. E. Lee, Jr., pp. 401-403.
156. R. E. Lee, Jr., pp. 412-413.
157. R. E. Lee, Jr., p. 430.
158. R. E. Lee, Jr., pp. 431-432.
159. R. E. Lee, Jr., pp. 432-433.
160. "Lee's Centennial," *Washington and Lee University, October 1916 Bulletin*, Vol. 15, No. 5, Address of Charles Francis Adams, January 19, 1907, p. 19.
161. R. E. Lee, Jr., p. 39.
162. R. E. Lee, Jr., p. 42.
163. R. E. Lee, Jr., p. 65.
164. Riley, p. 88.
165. Riley, p. 88.
166. Riley, p. 28.
167. R. E. Lee, Jr., p. 58.
168. R. E. Lee, Jr., p. 58.
169. R. E. Lee, Jr., p. 64.
170. R. E. Lee, Jr., pp. 65-66.
171. R. E. Lee, Jr., p. 68.
172. R. E. Lee, Jr., p. 75.
173. White, pp. 250-251.
174. R. E. Lee, Jr., pp. 88-89.
175. White, p. 256.
176. Jones, LL, p. 242.
177. White, p. 282.
178. I descend from the Bollings/Bowlings, and am close cousins with Mary and her family.
179. Jones, LL, pp. 245-246.
180. R. E. Lee, Jr., p. 101.
181. R. E. Lee, Jr., pp. 101-102.
182. R. E. Lee, Jr., p. 108.
183. R. E. Lee, Jr., p. 100.
184. Jones, PR, pp. 421-422.
185. R. E. Lee, Jr., p. 116.
186. White, pp. 337-338.
187. R. E. Lee, Jr., pp. 117-118.
188. R. E. Lee, Jr., p. 123.
189. R. E. Lee, Jr., p. 133.
190. Page, p. 636.
191. Riley, pp. 177-178.
192. Jones, LL, p. 471.
193. Page, p. 624.
194. Riley, p. 178.
195. Cooke, p. 495.
196. White, pp. 448-449.
197. White, p. 455.
198. Riley, p. 191.
199. R. E. Lee, Jr., p. 260.
200. R. E. Lee, Jr., p. 362.
201. R. E. Lee, Jr., p. 386.

202. White, p. 456. Lee's father Henry was later re-interred at Lee Chapel, Washington and Lee University, Lexington, Virginia.
203. See Long and Wright, p. 92.
204. Childe, pp. 29-30.
205. Long and Wright, p. 88.
206. Trent, pp. 37-38.
207. Long and Wright, p. 88.
208. Long and Wright, p. 88.
209. Page, p. 54.
210. Long and Wright, p. 89.
211. R. E. Lee, Jr., pp. 27-28.
212. Long and Wright, p. 94.
213. Childe, p. 32.
214. Trent, p. 47.
215. Seabrook, TUAL, pp. 40, 42.
216. Seabrook, TQJD, p. 56.
217. R. E. Lee, Jr., p. 270.
218. Long and Wright, pp. 82-83.
219. Long and Wright, p. 86.
220. At the start of Lincoln's War, like Lee, Floyd resigned from the U.S. army and sided with the Confederacy. General Floyd is often noted for his surrender at the Battle of Fort Donelson (February 11-16, 1862) against the advice of his subordinate, famed Rebel cavalry commander Nathan Bedford Forrest. See Seabrook, ARB, pp. 285-299.
221. R. E. Lee, Jr., pp. 21-22.
222. R. E. Lee, Jr., p. 214.
223. Page, p. 656.
224. Seabrook, AL, p. 197.
225. Seabrook, AL, p. 191.
226. Seabrook, TUAL, pp. 54-55.
227. Seabrook, EYWTACWW, pp. 77-80.
228. Seabrook, TMCP, pp. 178-179.
229. Seabrook, L, pp. 80, 81, 332, 599, 601.
230. Seabrook, EYWTACWW, p. 82.
231. Seabrook, TMCP, pp. 75-78,
232. Seabrook, AL, pp. 447-451.
233. For a full and truthful accounting of American slavery, see Seabrook, EYWTACWW, pp. 71-99; Seabrook, TMCP, pp. 65-231; Seabrook, L, pp. 353-562; Seabrook, AL, pp. 137-260; Seabrook, ARB, pp. 89-165; Seabrook, NBF, pp. 33-60.
234. Seabrook, TMCP, pp. 198-201.
235. White, pp. 50-51.
236. Brock and Lewis, p. 259.
237. R. E. Lee, Jr., pp. 222-223.
238. Seabrook, TQJD, p. 68.
239. Seabrook, EYWTACWW, pp. 100-102.
240. Seabrook, TMCP, pp. 185-218.
241. Long and Wright, pp. 83-84.
242. Munford, p. 156.
243. F. Lee, p. 235.
244. F. Lee, p. 237.
245. Page, pp. 619-620.
246. Page, p. 620.
247. Page, p. 620.
248. Seabrook, EYWTACWW, pp. 82-85.
249. Page, pp. 589-590.

250. Page, p. 652.
251. Wood, p. 78.
252. Long and Wright, p. 102.
253. R. E. Lee, Jr., p. 124.
254. Long and Wright, p. 125.
255. Long and Wright, pp. 125-127.
256. ORA, Ser. 1, Vol. 10, Pt. 2, p. 483.
257. ORA, Ser. 1, Vol. 12, Pt. 3, p. 779.
258. ORA, Ser. 1, Vol. 12, Pt. 3, p. 910.
259. We in the South define a "private soldier" as Union General August Valentine Kautz did in 1864: "In the fullest sense, any man in the military service who receives pay, whether sworn in or not, is a soldier, because he is subject to military law. Under this general head, laborers, teamsters, sutlers, chaplains, etc., are soldiers." Seabrook, AL, p. 340.
260. Pro-North historians like to play down or, more often, completely deny the reality of black Confederate soldiers; this despite the fact that we in the South have carefully calculated that as many as 1 million African-Americans served in *integrated* units in the Confederate army and navy in one capacity or another—not only as teamsters, nurses, construction workers, and cooks, but often as fully trained and armed soldiers, spies, and sharpshooters. Meanwhile, on the Northern side, early in the War Lincoln would not allow his measly 190,000 *segregated* black troops to serve as soldiers, but instead assigned them slave-like grunt work that white soldiers refused to do. One of the more disingenuous tricks used by anti-South writers is to count all of these particular black workers as "soldiers" while refusing to acknowledge black Confederate workers as "soldiers." In truth, I have determined that 80 percent more blacks fought for the Confederacy than for the Union. For more on this topic see Seabrook, EYWTACWW, pp. 157-176; Seabrook, AL, pp. 333-376; Seabrook, L, pp. 915-917; Seabrook, TMCP, pp. 106-115.
261. ORA, Ser. 1, Vol. 18, p. 1070.
262. ORA, Ser. 1, Vol. 27, Pt. 2, p. 295.
263. ORA, Ser. 1, Vol. 27, Pt. 2, p. 299.
264. ORA, Ser. 1, Vol. 27, Pt. 2, pp. 299-300.
265. ORA, Ser. 1, Vol. 29, Pt. 2, p. 648.
266. ORA, Ser. 1, Vol. 32, Pt. 2, pp. 566-567.
267. ORA, Ser. 1, Vol. 37, Pt. 2, p. 604.
268. ORA, Ser. 1, Vol. 46, Pt. 3, p. 666.
269. ORA, Ser. 1, Vol. 46, Pt. 3, p. 667. To this document was appended the following arrogant statement by Union Assistant Provost-Marshal-General George H. Sharpe: "The within named officers will not be disturbed by the United States authorities so long as they observe their parole and the laws in force where they may reside."
270. White, p. 239.
271. White, p. 336.
272. Childe, p. 27.
273. For a full treatment of Lincoln's agenda, crimes, and plans for the U.S., see Seabrook, AL, passim; Seabrook, L, passim; Seabrook, TUAL, passim; Seabrook, EYWTACWW, passim.
274. Jones, PR, p. 483.
275. R. E. Lee, Jr., pp. 69-70.
276. White, p. 110.
277. R. E. Lee, Jr., p. 37.
278. R. E. Lee, Jr., p. 43.
279. Alexander, pp. 261-262.
280. R. E. Lee, Jr., p. 44.
281. R. E. Lee, Jr., p. 49.
282. White, p. 121.
283. White, p. 124.
284. R. E. Lee, Jr., pp. 55-56.
285. White, pp. 128-129.
286. White, p. 129.

287. White, p. 129.
288. Hopkins, pp. 261-262.
289. Long and Wright, p. 233. Lee is speaking here of Union General George B. McClellan, a longtime foe of President Lincoln—whom McClellan referred to as a "well meaning baboon" and "the original gorilla." Seabrook, TUAL, p. 129.
290. R. E. Lee, Jr., p. 64.
291. White, p. 135.
292. White, p. 142.
293. White, p. 142.
294. Childe, pp. 97-98.
295. White, p. 169.
296. White, p. 198.
297. White, p. 233.
298. Long and Wright, pp. 225-226.
299. White, p. 228.
300. White, p. 234.
301. White, p. 239.
302. White, p. 248.
303. White, p. 252.
304. White, p. 254.
305. White, p. 254.
306. White, p. 255.
307. Pollard, p. 122.
308. R. E. Lee, Jr., pp. 93-94. When Jackson read this he is said to have responded: "Better that ten Jacksons should fall than one Lee." R. E. Lee, Jr., p. 94.
309. R. E. Lee, Jr., p. 94.
310. ORA, Ser. 1, Vol. 25, Pt. 2, p. 793.
311. Jones, LL, p. 247.
312. White, p. 276.
313. Bruce, p. 349.
314. White, p. 283.
315. ORA, Ser. 1, Vol. 27, Pt. 3, pp. 942-943. Lee's soldiers strictly adhered to their commander's order, as is illustrated by a comment made by British officer Sir Arthur J. L. Fremantle: "I saw no straggling into the houses, nor were any of the inhabitants disturbed or annoyed by the soldiers. . . . I went into Chambersburg again, and witnessed the singular good behavior of the troops toward the citizens. . . . To any one who has seen as I have the ravages of the Northern troops in Southern towns, this forbearance seems most commendable and surprising." Fremantle, pp. 238, 245-246.
316. White, pp. 142-143.
317. White, p. 300.
318. Long and Wright, p. 296.
319. Long and Wright, p. 296.
320. White, p. 322.
321. R. E. Lee, Jr., p. 102.
322. White, p. 326.
323. White, p. 327.
324. R. E. Lee, Jr., p. 111.
325. R. E. Lee, Jr., p. 117.
326. Jones, PR, pp. 422-423.
327. R. E. Lee, Jr., pp. 104-105.
328. White, p. 336.
329. Bruce, p. 346.
330. White, p. 339.
331. Alexander, p. 259.
332. White, pp. 336-337.

333. Alexander, p. 258.
334. ORA, Ser. 1, Vol. 33, p. 1275.
335. ORA, Ser. 1, Vol. 36, Pt. 3, p. 800.
336. R. E. Lee, Jr., p. 137.
337. R. E. Lee, Jr., p. 140.
338. ORA, Ser. 1, Vol. 46, Pt. 2, p. 1226.
339. ORA, Ser. 1, Vol. 46, Pt. 2, pp. 1229-1230.
340. White, pp. 416-417.
341. R. E. Lee, Jr., p. 146.
342. White, pp. 417-418.
343. *South Atlantic Quarterly*, July 1927, Durham, NC.
344. R. E. Lee. Jr., p. 151.
345. ORA, Ser. 1, Vol. 34, Pt. 1, p. 55.
346. *Current Literature*, Vol. 22, July-December 1897, New York, p. 533.
347. *Confederate Veteran*, Vol. 25, No. 5, May 1917, p. 207.
348. Page, p. 639.
349. Page, p. 640.
350. ORA, Ser. 1, Vol. 46, Pt. 1, p. 1267.
351. ORA, Ser. 1, Vol. 46, Pt. 1, pp. 1265-1267.
352. For a complete discussion of Lincoln's crimes, see Seabrook, L, pp. 758-860.
353. McCabe, pp. 639-640.
354. McCabe, pp. 643-645. To truly appreciate what the Confederacy was up against, Halleck's reply to Lee is worth recording here: "Headquarters of The U.S. Army, Washington, Aug. 9, 1862. General Lee: Your two communications of the 2d instant, with enclosures, are received. As these papers are couched in language exceedingly insulting to the Government of the United States, I must respectfully decline to receive them. They are returned herewith. Very respectfully, your obedient servant, H. W. Halleck, General-in-Chief U. S. Army." McCabe, p. 645.
355. F. Lee, p. 234.
356. R. E. Lee, Jr., p. 86.
357. White, p. 283.
358. R. E. Lee, Jr., p. 113.
359. Seabrook, AL, pp. 353-357.
360. Seabrook, AL, p. 169.
361. Seabrook, EYWTACWW, pp. 79-80.
362. Seabrook, L, pp. 728-749.
363. Seabrook, L, pp. 719-728.
364. Seabrook, L, p. 719.
365. Childe, pp. 142-143.
366. White, p. 200.
367. W. H. Taylor, p. 155.
368. R. E. Lee, Jr., p. 231.
369. White, p. 431.
370. R. E. Lee, Jr., p. 163.
371. Page, pp. 63-64.
372. Page, p. 64.
373. R. E. Lee, Jr., p. 163.
374. Page, p. 671.
375. Cooke, pp. 488-489.
376. Cooke, p. 490.
377. R. E. Lee, Jr., p. 164.
378. W. H. Taylor, p. 156.
379. White, p. 431.
380. Seabrook, AL, p. 299.
381. Jones, PR, p. 204.

382. White, p. 432.
383. Jones, PR, p. 206.
384. Jones, PR, p. 207.
385. White, p. 438.
386. White, p. 439.
387. Page, p. 657.
388. Seabrook, ARB, p. 8; Riley, pp. 71-72.
389. Jones, PR, p. 210.
390. White, p. 442.
391. Jones, PR, pp. 210-211.
392. Page, p. 659.
393. After the War the U.S. refused to reinstate Lee's U.S. citizenship. Thus, thanks to Lincoln and his followers, the General died "a man without a country." Phillips, FWNE, s.v. "Robert Edward Lee."
394. Cooke, pp. 474-485.
395. R. E. Lee, Jr., pp. 220-221.
396. Jones, PR, p. 212.
397. Jones, PR, p. 217.
398. White, p. 444.
399. R. E. Lee, Jr., p. 230.
400. Jones, PR, p. 220.
401. Bond, pp. 33-34.
402. R. E. Lee, Jr., p. 293.
403. White, p. 447.
404. White, p. 449.
405. White, pp. 452-453.
406. Hill, p. 290.
407. T. C. Johnson, pp. 499-500. Note: the authenticity of this quote is disputed by some.
408. *Southern Historical Society Papers*, Vol. 17, p. 352, Richmond, VA, 1889.
409. Long and Wright, p. 3.
410. R. E. Lee, Jr., p. 219.
411. R. E. Lee, Jr., p. 219.
412. Long and Wright, p. 4.
413. White, p. 446.
414. Figgis and Laurence, pp. 303-305.
415. R. E. Lee, Jr., p. 258.
416. R. E. Lee, Jr., p. 225.
417. R. E. Lee, Jr., pp. 259-260.
418. Jones, LL, p. 394.
419. R. E. Lee, Jr., p. 287.
420. R. E. Lee, Jr., p. 306.
421. White, pp. 450-452.
422. White, p. 453.
423. Some dispute the validity of the claim that these were Lee's last words.
424. ORA, Ser. 4. Vol. 3, pp. 1012-1013.

General Robert E. Lee's monument at Richmond, Virginia.

BIBLIOGRAPHY

Alexander, Frederick Warren. *Stratford Hall and the Lees Connected With its History: Biographical, Genealogical and Historical*. Oak Grove, VA: Historical Society of Virginia, 1912.

Bond, Christiana. *Memories of General Robert E. Lee*. Baltimore, MD: Norman, Remington Co., 1926.

Bradford, Gamaliel, Jr. *Lee the American*. Boston, MA: Houghton Mifflin Co., 1912.

Bradford, James C. (ed.). *Atlas of American Military History*. New York, NY: Oxford University Press, 2003.

Brock, Robert Alonzo, and Virgil Anson Lewis. *Virginia and Virginians* (Vol. 1). Richmond, VA: H. H. Hardesty, 1888.

Bruce, Philip Alexander. *Robert E. Lee*. Philadelphia, PA: George W. Jacobs and Co., 1907.

Butler, Pierce. *Judah P. Benjamin*. Philadelphia, PA: George W. Jacobs and Co., 1906.

Childe, Edward Lee. *The Life and Campaigns of General Lee*. London, UK: Chatto and Windus, 1875.

Cooke, John Esten. *A Life of Gen. Robert E. Lee*. New York, NY: D. Appleton and Co., 1883.

Encyclopedia Britannica: A New Survey of Universal Knowledge. 1768. Chicago, IL/London, UK: Encyclopedia Britannica, 1955 ed.

Figgis, John Neville, and Reginald Vere Laurence (eds.). *Selections From the Correspondence of the First Lord Acton* (Vol. 1). London, UK: Longmans, Green and Co., 1917.

Foote, Henry Stuart. *Casket of Reminiscences*. Washington, D.C.: Chronicle Publishing Co., 1874.

Fremantle, Arthur James Lyon. *Three Months in the Southern States: April-June, 1863*. Edinburgh, UK: William Blackwood and Sons, 1863.

Gilman, Bradley. *Robert E. Lee*. New York, NY: The Macmillan Co., 1915.

Hill, Frederick Trevor. *On the Trail of Grant and Lee*. New York, NY: D. Appleton and Co., 1911.

Hopkins, Luther W. *From Bull Run to Appomattox: A Boy's View*. Baltimore, MD: Fleet-McGinley Co., 1914.

Johnson, Thomas Carey. *The Life and Letters of Robert Lewis Dabney* (Vol. 3). Richmond, VA: The Presbyterian Committee of Publication, 1903.

Jones, John William. *Personal Reminiscences, Anecdotes, and Letters of Gen. Robert E. Lee.* New York, NY: D. Appleton and Co., 1874.

———. *Life and Letters of Robert Edward Lee: Soldier and Man.* New York, NY: Neale Publishing Co., 1906.

Lee, Fitzhugh. *General Lee.* New York, NY: The University Society, 1905.

Lee, Robert E. Lee, Jr. *Recollections and Letters of General Robert E. Lee.* New York, NY: Doubleday, Page, and Co., 1904.

Long, Armistead Lindsay, and Marcus J. Wright. *Memoirs of Robert E. Lee: His Military and Personal History.* New York, NY: J. M. Stoddart and Co., 1887.

Longstreet, James. *From Manassas to Appomattox: Memoirs of the Civil War in America.* Philadelphia, PA: J. B. Lippincott Co., 1908.

McCabe, James Dabney. *Life and Campaigns of General Robert E. Lee.* Atlanta, GA: National Publishing Co., 1866.

McGuire, Judith White. *General Robert E. Lee, the Christian Soldier.* Philadelphia, PA: Claxton, Remsen and Haffelfinger, 1873.

Munford, Beverly Bland. *Virginia's Attitude Toward Slavery and Secession.* New York, NY: Longmans, Green, and Co., 1909.

ORA (full title: *The War of the Rebellion: A Compilation of the Official Records of the Union and Confederate Armies*). Multiple volumes. Washington, D.C.: Government Printing Office, 1880.

Page, Thomas Nelson. *Robert E. Lee: Man and Soldier.* New York, NY: Charles Scribner's Sons, 1911.

Phillips, Robert S. (ed.). *Funk and Wagnalls New Encyclopedia.* 1971. New York, NY: Funk and Wagnalls, Inc., 1979 ed.

Pollard, Edward Alfred. *Lee and His Lieutenants: Comprising the Early Life, Public Services, and Campaigns of General Robert E. Lee and His Companions in Arms.* New York, NY: E. B. Treat, 1867.

Riley, Franklin Lafayette (ed.). *General Robert E. Lee After Appomattox.* New York, NY: The Macmillan Co., 1922.

Seabrook, Lochlainn. *Nathan Bedford Forrest: Southern Hero, American Patriot: Honoring a Confederate Hero and the Old South.* 2007. Franklin, TN: Sea Raven Press, 2010 ed.

———. *Abraham Lincoln: The Southern View - Demythologizing America's Sixteenth President.* 2007. Franklin, TN: Sea Raven Press, 2010 ed.

———. *The McGavocks of Carnton Plantation: A Southern History - Celebrating One of Dixie's Most Noble Confederate Families and Their Tennessee Home.* 2008. Franklin, TN: Sea Raven Press, 2011 ed.

———. *A Rebel Born: A Defense of Nathan Bedford Forrest - Confederate General,*

American Legend. Franklin, TN: Sea Raven Press, 2010.

——. *Everything You Were Taught About the Civil War is Wrong, Ask a Southerner! - Correcting the Errors of Yankee "History."* Franklin, TN: Sea Raven Press, 2010.

——. *Lincolnology: The Real Abraham Lincoln Revealed in His Own Words - A Study of Lincoln's Suppressed, Misinterpreted, and Forgotten Writings and Speeches*. Franklin, TN: Sea Raven Press, 2011.

——. *The Quotable Jefferson Davis: Selections From the Writings and Speeches of the Confederacy's First President*. Franklin, TN: Sea Raven Press, 2011.

——. *The Unquotable Abraham Lincoln: The President's Quotes They Don't Want You to Know!* Franklin, TN: Sea Raven Press, 2011.

——. *The Old Rebel: Robert E. Lee As He Was Seen By His Contemporaries*. Franklin, TN: Sea Raven Press, 2011.

Speer, Emory. *Lincoln, Lee, Grant, and Other Biographical Addresses*. New York, NY: Neale Publishing Co., 1909.

Stiles, Robert. *Four Years Under Marse Robert*. New York, NY: Neal Publishing Co., 1910.

Taylor, Walter Herron. *Four Years With General Lee*. 1877. New York, NY: D. Appleton and Co., 1878 ed.

Tilley, John S. *Facts the Historians Leave Out: A Confederate Primer*. 1951. Nashville, TN: Bill Coats Ltd., 1999 ed.

Trent, William Peterfield. *Robert E. Lee*. London, UK: Kegan Paul, Trench, Trübner and Co., 1899.

Walker, Evelyn Harriet (ed.). *Leaders of the 19th Century With Some Noted Characters of Earlier Times*. Chicago, IL: A. B. Kuhlman Co., 1900.

Warner, Ezra J. *Generals in Gray: Lives of the Confederate Commanders*. 1959. Baton Rouge, LA: Louisiana State University Press, 1989 ed.

——. *Generals in Blue: Lives of the Union Commanders*. 1964. Baton Rouge, LA: Louisiana State University Press, 2006 ed.

White, Henry Alexander. *Robert E. Lee and the Southern Confederacy, 1807-1870*. 1897. New York, NY: G. P. Putnam's Sons, 1900 ed.

Williamson, Mary Lynn. *Life of Robert E. Lee*. 1895. Richmond, VA: Johnson Publishing Co., 1918 ed.

Wood, Norman Barton. *The White Side of a Black Subject*. Chicago, IL: American Publishing House, 1897.

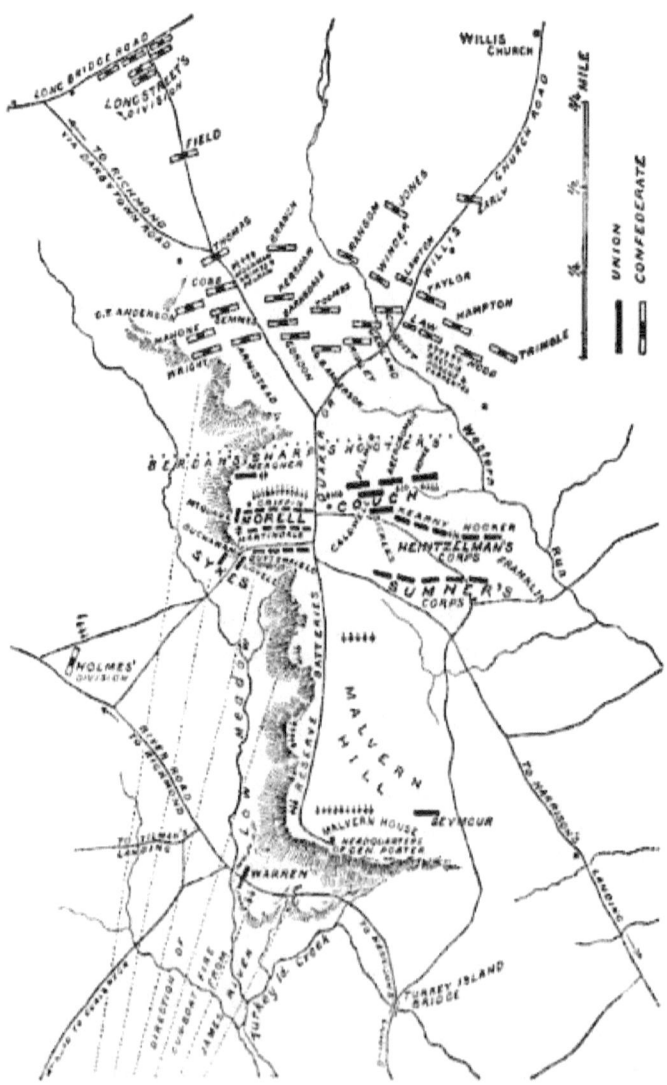

A map of the Battle of Malvern Hill, July 1, 1862, at which Lee lost to Union General George B. McClellan.

MEET THE AUTHOR

LOCHLAINN SEABROOK, the 2011 winner of the Jefferson Davis Historical Gold Medal for his "masterpiece," *A Rebel Born: A Defense of Nathan Bedford Forrest*, is an unreconstructed Southern historian, Tennessee author, and traditional Southern Agrarian of Scottish, English, Irish, Welsh, German, and Italian extraction. An encyclopedist, lexicographer, musician, artist, graphic designer, genealogist, and photographer, as well as an award-winning poet, songwriter, and screenwriter, he has a thirty year background in historical nonfiction.

Due to similarities in their writing styles, ideas, and literary works, Seabrook is referred to as the "American ROBERT GRAVES," after his cousin, the prolific English writer, historian, mythographer, poet, and author of the classic tomes *The White Goddess* and *The Greek Myths*.

The grandson of an Appalachian coal-mining family, Seabrook is a seventh-generation Kentuckian, co-chair of the Jent/Gent Family Committee (Kentucky), founder and director of the Blakeney Family Tree Project, and a board member of the Friends of Colonel Benjamin E. Caudill. Seabrook's literary works have been endorsed by leading authorities, museum curators, award-winning historians, bestselling authors, celebrities, noted scientists, well respected educators, renown military artists, esteemed Southern organizations, and distinguished academicians from around the world.

(Illustration © Tracy Latham)

As a professional writer Seabrook has authored some thirty popular adult books specializing in the following topics: the American Civil War, pro-South studies, Confederate biography and history, the anthropology of religion, genealogical monographs, Goddess-worship (thealogy), ghost stories, the paranormal, family histories, military encyclopedias, etymological dictionaries, ufology, social issues, comparative analysis of the origins of Christmas, and cross-cultural studies of the family and marriage.

Seabrook's seven children's books include a dictionary of religion and myth, a rewriting of the King Arthur legend (which reinstates the original pre-Christian motifs), two bedtime stories for preschoolers, a naturalist's guidebook to owls, a worldwide look at the family, and an examination of the Near-Death Experience.

Of blue-blooded Southern stock through his Kentucky, Tennessee, Virginia, West Virginia, and North Carolina ancestors, he is a direct descendant of European royalty via his 6th great-grandfather, the EARL OF OXFORD, after which London's famous Harley Street is named. Among his celebrated male Celtic ancestors is ROBERT THE BRUCE, King of Scotland, Seabrook's 22nd great-grandfather. The 21st great-grandson of EDWARD I "LONGSHANKS" PLANTAGENET), King of England, Seabrook is a thirteenth-generation Southerner through his descent from the colonists of Jamestown, Virginia (1607).

The 2nd, 3rd, and 4th great-grandson of dozens of Confederate soldiers, one of his closest connections to the War for Southern Independence is through his 3rd great-grandfather, ELIAS JENT, SR., who fought for the Confederacy in the Thirteenth Cavalry Kentucky under Seabrook's 2nd cousin, Colonel BENJAMIN E. CAUDILL. The Thirteenth, also known as "Caudill's Army," fought in numerous conflicts, including the Battles of Saltville, Gladsville, Mill Cliff, Poor Fork, Whitesburg, and Leatherwood.

Seabrook is also related to the following Confederates and other 19th-Century luminaries: ROBERT E. LEE, STEPHEN DILL LEE, JOHN SINGLETON MOSBY, STONEWALL JACKSON, NATHAN BEDFORD FORREST, JAMES LONGSTREET, JOHN HUNT MORGAN, JEB STUART, P. G. T. BEAUREGARD (designed the Confederate Battle Flag), JOHN BELL HOOD, ALEXANDER PETER STEWART, ARTHUR M. MANIGAULT, JOSEPH MANIGAULT, CHARLES SCOTT VENABLE, THORNTON A. WASHINGTON, JOHN A. WASHINGTON, JOHN H. WINDER, GIDEON J. PILLOW, STATES RIGHTS GIST, EDMUND WINCHESTER RUCKER, HENRY R. JACKSON, JOHN C. BRECKINRIDGE, LEONIDAS POLK, ZACHARY TAYLOR, SARAH KNOX TAYLOR (the first wife of JEFFERSON DAVIS), RICHARD TAYLOR, DAVY CROCKETT, DANIEL BOONE, MERIWETHER LEWIS (of the Lewis and Clark Expedition) ANDREW JACKSON, JAMES K. POLK, ABRAM POINDEXTER MAURY (founder of Franklin, TN), WILLIAM GILES HARDING, ZEBULON VANCE, THOMAS JEFFERSON, GEORGE WYTHE RANDOLPH (grandson of Jefferson), FELIX K. ZOLLICOFFER, FITZHUGH LEE, NATHANIEL F. CHEAIRS, JESSE JAMES, FRANK JAMES, ROBERT BRANK VANCE, CHARLES SIDNEY WINDER, JOHN W. MCGAVOCK, CARRIE (WINDER) MCGAVOCK, DAVID HARDING MCGAVOCK, LYSANDER MCGAVOCK, JAMES RANDAL MCGAVOCK, RANDAL WILLIAM MCGAVOCK, FRANCIS MCGAVOCK, EMILY MCGAVOCK, WILLIAM HENRY F. LEE, LUCIUS E. POLK, MINOR MERIWETHER (husband of noted pro-South author Elizabeth Avery Meriwether), ELLEN BOURNE TYNES (wife of Forrest's chief of artillery, Captain John W. Morton), South Carolina Senators PRESTON SMITH BROOKS and ANDREW PICKENS BUTLER, and famed South Carolina diarist MARY CHESNUT.

Seabrook's modern day cousins include: PATRICK J. BUCHANAN (conservative author), REBECCA GAYHEART (Kentucky-born actress), SHELBY LEE ADAMS (Letcher County, Kentucky, portrait photographer), BERTRAM THOMAS COMBS (Kentucky's fiftieth governor), EDITH BOLLING (wife of President Woodrow Wilson), and actors ROBERT DUVALL, REESE WITHERSPOON, LEE MARVIN, and TOM CRUISE.

Born with music in his blood, Seabrook is an award-winning, multi-genre, BMI-Nashville songwriter and lyricist who has composed some 3,000 songs (250 albums). A musician, producer, multi-instrumentalist, and renown performer—whose keyboard work has been variously compared to pianists from HARGUS ROBBINS and VINCE GUARALDI to ELTON JOHN and LEONARD BERNSTEIN—Seabrook has opened for groups such as the EARL SCRUGGS REVIEW, TED NUGENT, and BOB SEGER, and has performed privately for such public figures as President RONALD REAGAN, BURT REYNOLDS, and Senator EDWARD W. BROOKE.

Seabrook's cousins in the music business include: JOHNNY CASH, ELVIS PRESLEY, BILLY RAY and MILEY CYRUS, PATTY LOVELESS, TIM MCGRAW, LEE ANN WOMACK, DOLLY PARTON, PAT BOONE, NAOMI, WYNONNA, and ASHLEY JUDD, RICKY SKAGGS, the SUNSHINE SISTERS, MARTHA CARSON, and CHET ATKINS.

Seabrook lives with his wife and family in historic Middle Tennessee, the heart of the Confederacy, where his conservative Southern ancestors fought valiantly against liberal Lincoln and the progressive North in defense of Jeffersonianism, constitutional government, and personal liberty.

LochlainnSeabrook.com

MEET THE COVER ARTIST

CHRISTOPHER ROMMEL is an award-winning Master Caricaturist and freelance illustrator who has been drawing ever since he was old enough to hold a pencil. He is the founder and owner of Exaggerated Entertainment, through which he serves as a party caricaturist for all types of events, including holiday parties, company picnics, birthdays, anniversaries, bar/bat mitzvahs, confirmations, wedding receptions, reunions, banquets, proms, student lock-ins, graduations, open houses, grand openings, trade shows, conventions, conferences, concerts, fund raisers, and boat cruises.

A member of the International Society of Caricature Artists, Rommel won the organization's prestigious "Golden Nosey" award (the Oscar of the caricature industry) for Caricaturist of the Year in 2006. The recipient of numerous other awards for such likenesses as Donald Trump and Christopher Reeve, he is also a nationally published illustrator whose work has appeared in a variety of periodicals and publications, such as *Playboy*, *FHM*, *Flex*, *Exaggerated Features*, and Sea Raven Press.

(Illustration © Chris Rommel)

Rommel launched his career as a professional caricature artist in 1998 when he applied for a summer job at Valleyfair Amusement Park in Shakopee, Minnesota. While employed there he came under the tutelage of renowned *MAD Magazine* artist Tom Richmond. His enrollment at the Academy of Art University in San Francisco, California, as well as two Wisconsin state universities, educated him in a variety of art concentrations. He earned a Bachelor of Fine Arts degree from the University of Wisconsin-Eau Claire in 1999.

Since then, Rommel has drawn some 50,000 live caricatures of people at amusement parks, state fairs, shopping malls, corporate events and private parties. Among his better known clients are Harley-Davidson, Applebee's, Bank of America, Pillsbury, Mars Chocolate, Wells Fargo, First Bank and Trust, Hormel Foods, Petco, Absolut Vodka, Boston Scientific, Walmart and The Home Depot.

Rommel currently resides in Eau Claire, Wisconsin, where he continues to develop both his craft and his well deserved reputation as one of America's premier artists.

ChrisRommel.com

If you enjoyed Mr. Seabrook's *The Quotable Robert E. Lee* you will be interested in his excellent companion work:
THE OLD REBEL: ROBERT E. LEE AS HE WAS SEEN BY HIS CONTEMPORARIES
Available from Sea Raven Press and wherever fine books are sold.

www.ingramcontent.com/pod-product-compliance
Lightning Source LLC
Chambersburg PA
CBHW020328170426
43200CB00006B/305